STANDARD OPERATING PROCEDURE

PHILIP GOUREVITCH is the award-winning author of *We wish to inform you that tomorrow we will be killed with our families: Stories from Rwanda* and *A Cold Case*. He is the editor of the *Paris Review*, and long-time staff writer for the *New Yorker*.

ERROL MORRIS is a world-renowned filmmaker – the Academy Award-winning director of *The Fog of War* and the recipient of a MacArthur 'genius' award. His other films include *Mr. Death*, *Fast, Cheap and Out of Control*, *A Brief History of Time* and *The Thin Blue Line*. Most recently, his film *Standard Operating Procedure* won the Silver Bear, the Grand Jury Award, of the 2008 Berlin Film Festival.

'An extra[...] the soldiers
speak for[...] able'
Guardian

'In his analysis of the hooded man picture, Gourevitch lets his own voice be heard, soft and angry. But for most of *Standard Operating Procedure*, he is invisible. Like an exemplary butler, he ushers in the characters, serves up the facts, keeps everything in its proper order and then retreats to a discreet distance'   *Observer*

'Compelling . . . Gourevitch's book raises the issue of whether interrogation was intended to lead to valuable information, or whether humiliation and brutality were ends in themselves'
Scotland on Sunday

'A fascinating if disturbing look at the big picture that produced those small digital images . . . This is a train wreck of a book – horrifying yet hard to avert your eyes from. The self-appointed goodies turn out to be baddies, and women are as cruel as men'   *Sunday Herald*

'The book is a compelling meditation on a descent into cruelty. It shows how, in a prison where at least three-quarters of the inmates were innocent, the guards' self-righteousness and fear combined to create an atmosphere of toxic complacency'   *Daily Telegraph*

'This is a disturbing postscript to the dreadful story of the Iraq invasion . . . There is shame all around, but it is clear from reading this extraordinary book that the real culpability lies in Washington'
Culture, *Sunday Times*

'No other book I have read about warfare in recent times offers a more graphic account, brilliantly reported, illustrating this inner conflict and the madness integral to war. Thank you, Philip Gourevitch and Errol Morris, for an epic example of brilliant journalism'   *Tribune*

'A short but devastating account of US policy in Iraq . . . Gourevitch breathes life into the cliché with his astonishingly detailed account of the context that allowed the torture to take place. While the soldiers involved are condemned by their own words and deeds, Gourevitch also portrays them as victims of the system, and he traces the line of responsibility to the very top . . . Considered, emotive and intelligent, file it alongside George Packer's *The Assassins' Gate* as the second great work of the Iraq war'   *Time Out*

'Excellent . . . a beautifully written, clear, eloquent book. *Standard Operating Procedure* is an important, disturbing book, and its conclusions are profoundly depressing . . . It should be read by anyone interested in what is really happening in the world of politics and power today'   *Literary Review*

'A compelling and damning deconstruction of the story behind the infamous photographs that emerged in April 2004 . . . What impresses most in Gourevitch's brilliant study is the manner in which he painstakingly establishes how the Abu Ghraib photographs have a place in – but by no means are the entire story of – what transpired at the prison'   *Irish Times*

'*Standard Operating Procedure* is a devastating critique of the Bush administration. It inspires outrage at everything and everyone from the Bush Doctrine to former attorney general Alberto Gonzales to the CIA'   *Washington Post*

'This is one of the most devastating of the many books on Iraq'
                                                             New York Times

'The enormous punch of the book is such that you can hardly read it without throwing up. The book is an old-fashioned shocker that makes you want to rip that haunted prison to shreds and impeach the face cards in the Bush administration'   *New York Observer*

STANDARD OPERATING PROCEDURE

A WAR STORY

PHILIP GOUREVITCH
and **ERROL MORRIS**

PICADOR

First published 2008 by the Penguin Press, New York

First published in Great Britain 2008 by Picador

First published in paperback 2008 by Picador

This edition published 2009 by Picador
an imprint of Pan Macmillan Ltd
Pan Macmillan, 20 New Wharf Road, London N1 9RR
Basingstoke and Oxford
Associated companies throughout the world
www.panmacmillan.com

ISBN 978-0-330-45201-4

100726115ㄱ

For L.M. & J.S.

A NOTE ON AUTHORSHIP

This book is written by Philip Gourevitch. It is a collaborative work, which stems from a year and a half of continuous conversations with Errol Morris about the hundreds of hours of interviews he conducted and the thousands of documents that he collected for his motion picture of the same title, *Standard Operating Procedure.* All speech quoted in the text is drawn from those interviews and documents, and a complete description of these sources appears at the back of the book.

That which is possible is inevitable . . .
Allons! Commençons la danse.

WILLIAM CARLOS WILLIAMS

BAGHDAD

October 2002

ONE SUNDAY MORNING, the president released all the prisoners. Nobody knew why. Maybe even he didn't know. The announcement was read on the radio. It was the president's way, the announcer said, of thanking the people for reelecting him a few days earlier in a national referendum. Everyone knew the referendum was a charade—running unopposed, Saddam Hussein had claimed a hundred percent of the vote—yet the announcement of the prison amnesty ("complete, comprehensive, and final," except for Zionist and American spies) was greeted with real excitement in the streets, much honking of car horns and celebratory firing of assault rifles. All at once, all over the country, people began to mass outside prison gates, believing that they might see again someone long missing: a thief or an intellectual, a democracy advocate or a rapist.

Saddam's prisons were the engine houses of his power, factories of terror and annihilation. For stealing a chicken or a bottle of shampoo you could be locked away for years. For crimes against the state—real or imagined—there was no limit to the torture. Wednesdays and Sundays were hanging days at Abu Ghraib prison, twenty miles west of Baghdad. It was not unusual for a hundred people a week to have their necks snapped on the gallows, and when overcrowding made it hard to accommodate new prisoners, the death house worked over-

time. Abu Ghraib was the biggest of Saddam's prisons, and the most
notorious, a synonym for living hell, and it was there, where the outer
fringe of Baghdad's suburban sprawl met the flat drab waste of desert
beyond the airport, that word of the amnesty drew the largest spon-
taneous gathering that anyone could remember seeing in Iraq.

By late morning, it appeared that there were as many Iraqis mill-
ing outside the walls of Abu Ghraib as there were prisoners inside—
ten to fifteen thousand, the reports said—and thousands more kept
arriving from every direction. At midday the outside mob was esti-
mated to be fifty thousand strong, and when it surged, it tore the
despised prison gate off its hinges, and spilled inside. There, coming
toward it, was another mob of thousands: the prisoners, harrowed,
unwashed, weeping, clutching the foul bedrolls that were their only
belongings, seeking the way out. Prisoners too weak to walk emerged
draped over their cellmates' shoulders, while others, even though they
were fit, were trampled to death on the verge of release. In this pandemonium and cacophony some guards joined in the carnival mood
of liberation, ripping bricks from dungeon walls to free those inside,
and dancing happily with their former wards; and some guards, less
adaptable, kept beating prisoners until there were none left at hand.
It was said that some even took the opportunity to perform a few final
executions.

In this way, an entire penal system was disbanded, and as many
as a hundred fifty thousand convicts set loose. Nothing of the kind
had ever happened before anywhere in the world—and on that same
day, Saddam sponsored a nationwide mass wedding. Hundreds of
couples were married at once, and again the radio explained the occasion as a celebration of the president's reelection. There was more
honking of car horns, more gunfire in the streets. The state outfitted
the brides from top to toe: dress, veil, shoes, handbag, gloves. Only
the dresses had to be returned.

Prisoners, brides—such pageantry, such wild emotion. There it was, for all to see, and seeing it hardly made it comprehensible. What was Saddam up to?

The president of the United States was threatening to take over his country. The threat was personal and unrelenting. There was great impatience in Washington to get on with the war: to do Iraq—that was the phrase. After all, who would mourn Saddam, with his dungeons and torture chambers? Nobody—that was one of the arguments. So, when Saddam opened Abu Ghraib, it was reported that he was knuckling under, or at least kowtowing, trying to make nice, to appease; and that without firing a shot or landing a boot on Iraqi soil, we had made him relinquish one of the most sinister instruments of his regime. Several foreign newspapermen even compared that Sunday at Abu Ghraib to the storming of the Bastille at the outset of the French Revolution: the moment when a people asserted its sovereignty and set an absolute ruler back on his heels. The analogy was recklessly wishful. In reality, the emptying of Iraq's prisons was just one more caprice of the tyrant—not a concession, but an assertion of power.

Amid the lunatic riot of conflicting impressions that came out of Abu Ghraib—the crawling stench and hellish filth, the sudden crack of pistol shots to calm the crowd, the wailing of a mother who found her son, the wailing of a mother who learned her son had already been put to death, the crazed eyes of captives suddenly set loose—perhaps the most astonishing spectacle was that of fleeing convicts, chanting until they were hoarse: "Our blood, our souls, we'll sacrifice for you, oh Saddam."

PART 1

BEFORE

1.

TEN MONTHS LATER, in August 2003, Lane McCotter and Gary Deland, two former executive directors of the Utah Department of
Corrections, were driving around Baghdad, trying to find a metal
worker who could make bunk beds. McCotter and Deland had spent
the summer refurbishing a couple of cell blocks at Abu Ghraib. In
the old days, under Saddam, the cells were unfurnished and prisoners
slept on the floor. "There were no standards," McCotter said. "They
just crammed them in there like cordwood." He thought bunks
would be a nice touch to mark the prison's transformation. But Iraqis
didn't know what he was talking about. One bed on top of another?
"We had to draw pictures of them," he said. "We finally found someone. He made a prototype, we made changes to it, and we bought a
thousand of them as fast as he could make them to start putting in
these cells."

Deland took photographs of McCotter standing proudly beside
Iraq's first bunk beds. Deland was proud too. In July he had set up
Iraq's first ever corrections academy, and the first class of new Iraqi
prison guards was just completing its training. McCotter and Deland
decided to show off their work at Abu Ghraib with an open house and
a graduation ceremony for the corrections academy. They were getting
ready to go home—their contract with the United States Justice De-

partment ran out at the end of the month—so they invited their colleagues from the Coalition Provisional Authority and the Army and the incipient Iraqi Ministry of Justice; they told some of the soldiers at Abu Ghraib's military prison camp to come on over; they hired buses for the corrections graduates and told them to bring their families; they laid on food; they even hired an Iraqi bagpipe-and-drum band. "The worst sound I've ever heard," Deland said. "You couldn't exaggerate how hard that was on the ears."

The big day was August 25. A week before, a group of reporters had come to the prison to report on the aftermath of a mortar attack that had killed six prisoners in the Army's tented camps and wounded more than fifty, and one of them—a Reuters cameraman who was filming outside the wall with permission from the Military Police guards at the gate—was shot dead by an American soldier in the turret of a passing tank. Now the restored cell blocks were bright with new paint, a new prison kitchen was almost finished, a new prison medical center was getting there—"a first-class facility," McCotter said, "probably the best in all of Iraq"—the band was playing, and McCotter and Deland were showing their guests Abu Ghraib's new prisoner recreation yards.

"We had the speeches," McCotter said. "We did a ribbon cutting. We took a little tour to show them what these cell blocks were going to look like when the whole prison was done and how nice it was going to be. We'd set up every cell. We had bunks. We had mattresses. We had washcloths. We had towels. We had toothpaste. We had toothbrushes. We had health and comfort items—even prayer rugs on the floor for the Muslims, which we don't even do in most American prisons. We were trying to teach them what the humanitarian things are in running prisons the American way, or the Western way. To have that done in four months, to me, was miraculous. What we did I don't think has ever been done in the history of corrections before. We had a lot of help, but it was a miracle."

WHEN THE CALL HAD COME, in mid-April, asking him if he'd like to
go to Iraq, Lane McCotter thought maybe it was a joke. It was around
eight o'clock on a Saturday morning. McCotter was in Midway, Utah,
having breakfast with his wife. American forces had just taken Baghdad—on television you could watch looters there sacking the minis-
tries—and the man on the phone was telling McCotter, on behalf of
the Attorney General of the United States, that a team was being
mustered to go see what could be done about Iraq's criminal justice
system. "Your name came into the mix," the man said.

McCotter listened, and noticed his wife watching him closely.
"Being an old military wife, I guess she knows all the signals," he
said: the phone call at an unlikely hour; the one-sided conversation
(the side she couldn't hear); the sudden gravity of his attention. He
told his caller he needed to think about it, and when he hung up he
told her, "Of course, I won't go. I'm sixty-three years old." She knew
him better than that. He hadn't served overseas since Vietnam, but
he'd always felt bad about how we'd abandoned the Vietnamese in the
end, and she knew he liked the idea of getting it right for a change.
She said, "If your country asks you to go, you will go. So go on. Get
it out of your system. Get it over with. Do what they want you to do.
And come back home."

McCotter got back on the phone, and said, "If this is on the level
then I'm willing."

A week later he was in Washington for a briefing. The message
was: We've never done this before. Sure, we've helped whip a police
force into shape or trained some judges in this and that wrecked
country. But soup to nuts—cops, courts, corrections—making a
whole criminal justice system over in our image after a major hostility, this is a first. And we're doing it right, assessment before reconstruction. You—the assessment team—will have four months to get

the lay of the land, compile a comprehensive report on the conditions of every police station, courthouse, and prison in the country, and draft a blueprint for getting them operational. Then you come home. Let the next team worry about implementation.

McCotter liked the sound of that. He had spent a third of his life in corrections. He'd run three state prison systems; he had a hell of a résumé. But corrections had not been a calling for McCotter, not at the outset anyway. In the beginning it was about getting a girl—or more like about keeping her. His first true love was the military, and on his first tour in Vietnam, in 1962, he was proud to be infantry, commissioned as a second lieutenant, artillery corps, special ops, attached to the regional and popular forces: the South Vietnamese. He got overrun three times, and came home a captain, wearing the Bronze Star, the Air Medal, the Legion of Merit, and, the one that made him proudest, the Combat Infantryman Badge for closing with and destroying the enemy. Then he got married, and it occurred to him that if he wanted to stay that way he'd better learn a profession other than soldier. He switched to the Military Police, got made a major, and landed back in Vietnam right after Labor Day 1968, when the American stockade there, Long Binh Jail, was torched in a race riot. The rubble was still smoking when he arrived, and he was part of the operation to rebuild the place.

That had been McCotter's first prison job. He might not have minded if it had been his last. Only he was still looking for a way to live with his wife, so he put in for graduate school, and got sent to Sam Houston University in Huntsville, Texas, for a master's degree in criminology and corrections. When he finished in 1972, he was named warden in command of the military confinement facility at Fort Sill, Oklahoma. A decade later he was the commander of the United States Disciplinary Barracks at Fort Leavenworth, Kansas, the military's only maximum-security prison. When he left there, he left the Army—retiring out as a full-bird colonel—to sign on with the Texas Department of Corrections, which was the second-largest state prison system in America, and by pretty much every measure the worst.

McCotter called Texas his third tour of combat. In 1980, a federal court had found the state's prisons to be so comprehensively barbarous that the entire Texas system was declared unconstitutional. "It is impossible," Judge William Wayne Justice wrote, "to convey the pernicious conditions and the pain and degradation which ordinary inmates suffer within TDC prison walls." Judge Justice went on to enumerate the terrors: the rape and murder of inmates by inmates; the cruel—at times suffocating—overcrowding, on the one hand, and on the other hand, the arbitrary and abusive administration of solitary confinement; the incessant physical discomfort and psychological stress of prisoners preyed upon by prison gangs and by guards; the bitter helplessness of inmates at being prevented from seeking legal relief from these injustices. In 1985, McCotter was appointed as Texas's fourth new prison director in two years, and in both those years the state had set new national records for prison homicides. McCotter ordered a total lockdown of half the state's prisons, and the number of attacks on inmates fell by forty percent. In his second year, there were just two prison homicides in Texas. There was also a new governor, Bill Clements, the state's first Republican governor since Reconstruction, who denounced McCotter as too liberal, and welcomed his resignation.

Before a month was out, McCotter was sworn in as secretary of corrections in New Mexico, which was recovering from one of the nastiest prison riots anyone could remember anywhere in the country. Once again McCotter was brought in as a reformer, and once again he lasted two years. Then there was Utah, where he ran Corrections for five years before a twenty-nine-year-old schizophrenic named Michael Valent, who was in the state prison at Draper because he had obeyed voices in his mind that told him to kill his grandmother, pulled a pillowcase over his head and refused to take it off. Prison staff shackled Valent to a restraining chair for sixteen hours, and when they released him he collapsed and died from a blood clot blocking an artery to his heart. McCotter's defense of the restraining chair did not go over well with the public, so he resigned.

That's how it went as a prison director, McCotter said: no matter what you do, either you're too soft or you're too hard. He said, "There's somebody going to be throwing tar at you every day of your life. You live in a glass house. Somebody is always shooting at you." So he went to work as the director of marketing for America's third-largest private adult prison and jail contractor, Management & Training Corporation. He'd been there seven years when he packed his bags for Iraq. He had followed the war with keen interest, and he said, "I think we have an obligation to the world. We are the most blessed nation on the earth. And we need to help other people enjoy the freedoms that our children and grandchildren take for granted, literally every day of their lives, until they go to a country like Iraq, where freedoms are not there."

So McCotter had thought it was "kind of interesting" when his team landed in Kuwait and the weapons they'd been promised for the drive into Iraq weren't there. Already, Gary Deland's passport had been mishandled in Washington, so that he was delayed and the Justice Department's prison team consisted of just three men. The next day, when their unarmed convoy arrived at the Iraqi border before first light and the military escort that was supposed to meet them never showed up, McCotter upgraded his assessment of the situation to "very interesting." The team reached Baghdad just before midnight. A curfew was in effect, but there was gunfire everywhere.

In the morning McCotter was driven to the Green Zone, the American garrison that had been carved out of the central Baghdad neighborhoods around Saddam Hussein's former palace on the Tigris. The city appeared trashed and abandoned—not a person out walking. The word that came to McCotter's mind was "eerie." And against this desolation stood the barricades and cordons of troops and armor that marked the perimeter of the Green Zone. McCotter took note of the level of security, and in his mind the word "supposedly" appended itself to the phrase "hostilities have ceased." It was obvious that there was still a lot of trouble.

The prison team's headquarters was in the palace itself, a vast and labyrinthine extravagance that remained the seat of power, home to the Coalition Provisional Authority. There was no electricity, no running water, and, McCotter's team was told at a CPA briefing that first morning, time was running out, too. Now the message was: Forget about four months. Do your assessment in thirty days, write your plan, and by the way, in that thirty-day period, we want you to have the first prison up and running.

MCCOTTER DIDN'T OBJECT to the change in mission. He thought it was extremely interesting, and he had an idea where to begin—with the Military Police, his old service. At that time there was no independent civilian police authority, and the 18th MP Brigade was in charge of law and order in Iraq. The MPs had run POW camps during the invasion—major operations, like Camp Bucca, down by the Kuwait border, and local holding pens, dotted throughout the country— and the MPs now ran these same facilities as detention centers that had to double as Iraqi jails. They had no means to segregate military prisoners from ordinary criminal suspects, as Army doctrine and the Geneva Conventions require, so they were happy to take the prison team around to see what kind of lockups Iraq had to offer. They set out that afternoon, McCotter's first day in country, and by the end of the week they had found seven abandoned prisons—all of them gutted, as if they'd been bombed from inside.

Prison by prison, the demolition was absolute. McCotter's translators explained that after Saddam's amnesty inmates and guards had returned to ransack the prisons with an omnivorous thoroughness that made the pillage of Baghdad in the early days of the occupation look almost restrained. All the doors were gone, and not just the windows, but the window frames, too. Every floor tile, every electrical fixture, every light switch—even the wiring in the walls—had been stripped away. Anything of value had been carried off, and what was left had been set ablaze. Nothing remained but scorched walls and rubble. McCotter thought a few of these shells might be salvaged, and his team began taking bids from local contractors. But the demand for usable jails was rapidly growing. The country was fractious and effectively lawless, and much of the population had machine guns, including as many as a hundred thousand ex-convicts who had been armed after their amnesty so that they could fight the Americans. So when one of the MPs who'd been assisting the prison team told McCotter there was a great big prison he should check out on the outskirts of Baghdad, he drove there the next morning.

MCCOTTER'S first impression of Abu Ghraib was not encouraging. The gate was a fortress of stacked sandbags and barbed wire, and the grounds had been used for the past half year as the city dump. The whole place stank, and its scale was disorienting: the perimeter wall, crowned by twenty-four watchtowers, was two and a half miles long, enclosing two hundred eighty acres. It took McCotter the whole appallingly hot morning to walk the space, most of which was empty—a desolation of trash-strewn gritty desert floor. A rudimentary American base had been set up just inside the main gate, a cluster of tents and armor and a large pen made of concertina wire that was known as Camp Vigilant, where three or four hundred prisoners were kept under MP guard in primitive conditions: without running water or electricity or cooked food, and with an open trench for a toilet that afforded its users no privacy.

But what caught McCotter's eye were the deserted compounds of Saddam's old penal colony: five self-contained prison complexes, built in the mid-1960s by British engineers working from American blueprints, and laid out like a campus, with an administrative center and death house and a laundry and guard barracks. One of these prisons was reduced to rubble, a tangle of iron girders and broken masonry, and McCotter could see at once that two more were beyond repair. But while looters had also trashed the other two, one remained largely intact—a two-story, flat-roofed, concrete structure, with ten cell blocks staggered like cross-arms along a central corridor, a layout known in the business as a telephone-pole design—and as he explored it, McCotter felt almost at home. "It was just like the prisons that I ran in Texas," he said. "Even had American Folger Adam locks on the doors. That's how Americanized this prison was. It was the only place that we found that was capable of handling maximum-security criminals. Abu Ghraib prison was a prison. It was literally the first one that I had seen in all of Iraq that even looked like what you and I would call a prison, frankly. So I got kind of excited."

Back in Baghdad, McCotter told his team, "We need to get two cell blocks up and running to handle the worst of worst of the real bad guys that are being arrested. When we get that done, I will come back and we will rebuild the entire prison." He drew up a plan to overhaul the favored compound—the hard site, as everyone called it, because it was bullet-proof, unlike the soft-skinned tents the military was using in Camp Vigilant—and he got the go-ahead from the CPA finance board. He was still excited, but he wasn't satisfied. He'd come to Iraq to do things right, and he kept having his crew draw up more ambitious plans for the Abu Ghraib project. "We wanted a really first-class medical facility," he said. "We wanted a kitchen, dining areas, a bakery. We were going to make it into a model prison."

McCotter went back to his board to ask for an extra million dollars for the hard site. "This time," he said, "somebody's light came on—'Is this the Abu Ghraib prison where all the people were hung?' I said, 'Yes, it is.' 'We are not going to approve that.' I said, 'You have already approved the first two cell blocks. We are building.' 'Well, if we had known, we would have never approved that. This is too political. We can't let you do this.'"

2.

MCCOTTER HAD NOT KNOWN Abu Ghraib's history or its symbolism
when he first admired its possibilities. The buildings alone were
mute, and the flamboyant murals of Saddam that decked their walls
were no different from a thousand others he'd seen in Iraq: a stern
Saddam pointing an admonishing finger; a playboy Saddam in shades
and a Panama hat; a happy soldier Saddam in epaulets, crowned by
crossed swords and circled by fluttering white doves. But he had
since heard the harrowing stories of the prison's past: how so many
prisoners were kept in some cells that half of them had to stand while
the other half slept; how they were fed one meal a day of soup, rice
or lentils, and a piece of bread; how guards extorted protection money
from prisoners and their families; how Saddam's son Qusay, the
secret-police chief, would stop by and order a thousand executions
because he felt like it; how prisoners were bolted to the floor and
hung from the rafters, subjected to electric shocks, and beaten until
they might feel lucky to be killed. McCotter had explored the death
house—the torture chambers and cells for the condemned within
earshot of the clanging iron trapdoors of the gallows. His interpreters had read to him the last words of prayer and despair scratched
into those cell walls, and one day, while inspecting work at the
prison, he had been summoned to the gate because an American

reporter was there accompanying four Iraqis who had their own desperate plea.

"All of them were missing either their hands or their forearms," McCotter said. "Their story was that when they were incarcerated there, under the Saddam Hussein regime, their arms or their hands had been amputated for punishment. They said they knew where they were buried on the prison grounds, and they wanted to recover those bones and things for proper disposal or burial or something of that nature." McCotter explained that he could not grant them access on account of security regulations. Besides, he said, the American reporter had cameras, and he wasn't about to let anybody come into a prison site and start taking pictures.

So McCotter and his team understood the political sensitivity of Abu Ghraib. But they couldn't see any alternative to Abu Ghraib. "Of course it had a bad reputation," Gary Deland said. "Find me a place of any size in Iraq that didn't have a bad reputation. Who was running the system? Saddam Hussein and his henchmen. His sons killed for sport, for hell's sake." To build an equivalent prison from scratch would take two years. When that happened, McCotter said, good— tear the place down, do whatever—but for now, Iraq needed Abu Ghraib and Abu Ghraib was his baby. "So I'm pushing as hard as I can to get this done," he said. "I take full responsibility for that. As a correctional professional I have no regrets whatsoever." Only the harder he pushed, the more resistance he got. "This thing was run all the way up the ladder to Washington," he said. "That was above my level." At the end of June, Amnesty International reported allegations of abusive treatment of Iraqis in military custody at Abu Ghraib and at Camp Cropper, a military detention center at Baghdad airport. The report described prisoners held for weeks without charges or judicial review, without access to family members or lawyers, and in wretched conditions. On June 12, the prisoners at Abu Ghraib's Camp Vigilant held a demonstration, demanding that they be told how long they would be there. An MP captain promised them an answer the next day. But no answer came, and there was another demonstration. This time prisoners threw bricks and other projectiles at the MPs, and the MPs opened fire. One prisoner was shot dead. He was in his tent when he was hit. Seven prisoners were wounded in the fusillade, and several of them were also in their tents.

The first press reports on the reopening of Abu Ghraib appeared two weeks later. On July 13, an Associated Press dispatch said, "Apparently recognizing the public relations problem, the Americans replaced a Saddam portrait at the prison with a big sign in English and Arabic: 'America is a friend of all Iraqi people.' " The story told of Iraqis gathered in staggering heat at the prison gate, pleading with unresponsive MP guards to know whether missing family members were inside. The CPA chief, U.S. Ambassador L. Paul Bremer, was quoted, scolding Amnesty International for failing to mention that "the Iraqi people are living in freedom today." In fact, Bremer said, "the human rights of the average Iraqi are light-years better today than they were twelve weeks ago." Yet Bremer, who was on the Pentagon payroll despite his civilian diplomatic title, also said that the military detention camps in Iraq were "completely and utterly unacceptable under any international standards," and CPA officials said they were hustling to improve them.

Such reports did not help McCotter's cause, as he lobbied to make Abu Ghraib Iraq's flagship prison. He kept explaining that his project to renovate the hard site had nothing to do with military detention, and he decided that if the problem with Abu Ghraib was its symbolism he would make a symbolic gesture. He had his contractors build an extension to the prison's perimeter wall to dogleg around the old death house, sealing it off from the grounds and giving it a separate outside entrance. "Let the Iraqis turn it into a museum or an Iraqi memorial," he said. That seemed to help. In the third week of July Bremer helicoptered in to check out the prison with the special envoy of the United Nations, Sergio Vieira de Mello. "And the next thing I know," McCotter said, "the deputy secretary of defense, Paul Wolfo- witz, shows up. We spent half a day out there walking him through everything. We took him through the death house. We briefed him on why we needed what we needed. We briefed him on the other prisons. He took it very, very seriously, and less than a week later the word came down—rebuild the complex."

"HAVE YOU EVER BEEN FISHING for halibut?" Gary Deland said. "It's like hauling up a piece of plywood. It's not that the halibut fights you so much. It's not aerodynamic. It's a big, flat fish that lays on the bottom. In fact, its eyes roll around to one side so it can look up. But it's a very hard fish to land without really fighting, and the bureau- cracy was kind of like that. It was this constant weight, that no mat- ter what you wanted to do, you knew you have to go fight."

By comparison, he said, getting shot at was the easy part of being in Iraq—and frankly, part of the thrill. Deland had avoided going to Vietnam with a college deferment, and he had come to regret that he missed the action. "I figured I owed my country something. Other people had gone in harm's way for me. Why shouldn't I, now that I have the chance, do the same?" And he said, "The other thing is I tend to enjoy doing things that involve adrenaline."

Deland found plenty to enjoy in Iraq. Security was deteriorating; the civilian cell phone service could not communicate with the military network; the military was too thin on the ground to provide reliable escort service; and he loved the high-speed, stop-for-nothing driving, the "little tight pucker" he felt, hurtling into unsecured neighborhoods of Baghdad in a car full of men with guns, his pockets stuffed with tens of thousands of dollars in cash (because there were no banks) to buy photocopy machines, or a fleet of buses to serve as paddy wagons, on the local gray market (because there was no other way to get them). "Beyond exciting," he said. At one point, the prison team had three million dollars in cash stashed with their weapons in their office bathroom—a folly of marble and gold plate with no running water.

Deland loved the daredevil lunacy of this system of finance, procuring receipts in Arabic and praying they added up. He loved hitching a ride on a Black Hawk to check on a project in An Najaf one day, then tearing down the highway to Al Hillah or Abu Ghraib the next, and seeing progress. He loved getting out of the Green Zone. Beyond the blinders and sclerosis of the bureaucracy, he discovered a sense of almost dizzying possibility in Iraq's pandemonium, where the absence of government allowed him to implement sweeping institutional changes with a speed and autonomy he had never known before. For instance, when it became apparent that the Saddam-era guards the prison team had rehired in its haste to open its first prison were refusing to feed prisoners whose families didn't bribe them, Deland fired the whole corrupt lot, and established his corrections academy to train a new generation of recruits to replace them.

"The very first academy we had, a third of the class left the first day, when we said you couldn't shake down families and inmates for money," he said. "People got up and walked out—'What do you mean? How am I going to feed my family, then, on what you pay us?' They weren't going to hide the fact that they were doing this. It was the way it was always done." So there were bad days, and there was no end of setbacks. "We would create these role plays," Deland said, and he gave an example of how they would go:

"OK, we have this inmate who is saying this and doing this and you tell him to leave his cell and he won't do it. Based on the training you just had, what do you do?"

"Well, you go beat him until he moves or he dies.

"OK, that would be one way, yes. Now, let's look at some other options here."

BY EARLY JULY, two of the original members of the prison team had quit in exasperation, and at the end of the month, Lane McCotter flew home for an emergency leave because his father-in-law had died. For three weeks in August, Gary Deland said, "I was the only person in Iraq that was part of the Justice Department's team sent over to build and maintain a corrections system." He, too, would be going home soon, but nobody had yet been hired to take over his mission. Deland pressed on with his corrections academy; he looked after his prison projects; he paid the contractors at Abu Ghraib to triple their crew and work around the clock to get the new medical facility ready in a month instead of six. But at the same time, Army contractors were throwing up a huge new tented camp at Abu Ghraib—Camp Ganci, named after a New York City firefighter killed on September 11, a facility that would double or triple the military's prison capacity before Deland could open a single cell block at the hard site.

Deland felt "a terrible frustration." He had seen enough danger, racing between prison projects, that the speed and scale of Camp Ganci's construction made sense to him. The military was conducting an average of two thousand patrols a day to counter lawlessness and armed resistance. "Instead of simply going in and machine-gunning a whole bunch of people, they had more and more and more and more people to incarcerate," Deland said. The problem was that he didn't have the prisons to house them. He had analyzed the inmate populations of other countries in the region—Iran, Jordan, Kuwait, Turkey, Syria, and Saudi Arabia—crunched the statistics, and concluded that the Iraqi corrections system he was there to build would need seventy-five thousand beds. So far, his team had three prisons that were back in business or about to be, with a total of seventeen hundred beds. The hard site would add two hundred by summer's end, and as the work at Abu Ghraib continued into the fall there would be a thousand more. "It's still a drop in the ocean," he said. "Despite the strongest possible efforts to get this thing done, we were enormously undermanned."

It wasn't just the lack of manpower that discouraged Deland. What upset him more was the waste of the occupation's limited resources on keeping a growing number of people in prison without cause. "We had people that were there when I arrived, they were there when I left, and there was no reason in the world for them to be there. They were picked up in sweeps, and nobody knew what to release them for. Their only charge might be 'wrong place, wrong time,' literally written on their arrest sheet. You got some soldiers going down the street, somebody starts shooting at them, OK—close the street off, pick people up. But as soon as you've determined this guy is only there because he is running a Coca-Cola stand on the side of the road, and this one was sitting on his front stoop, let them go." What's more, he said, "celebratory fire is pretty common over there." So what if the guy firing the machine gun out his car window wasn't shooting at anyone? "They arrest him," Deland said. "He's got a fourteen-year-old son in the car with him? They arrest *him*. For what? Didn't know what to do with him, couldn't leave him on the street. Now we can't get him out of jail."

Camp Ganci was supposed to address this problem at Abu Ghraib. Officially, it was meant to hold Iraqis suspected of strictly civilian crimes, so that prisoners of genuine military concern could be concentrated in Camp Vigilant. But in practice the distinction between criminal and military prisoners had always been sloppy, and it often seemed meaningless as the prison population grew. Even when Deland got judges to throw out groundless charges, and found lawyers to take release orders to the prison, the soldiers at the gate would tell them no.

There were exceptions, of course. Every week, some prisoners got to see a judge or a lawyer, and some got released, but the process appeared increasingly arbitrary. "What we kept hearing was, they have intelligence value," Deland said. "Well, hell, anybody on the street has got intelligence value. You can talk to them and see if they know anything. Don't count me just as a humanitarian that just wanted to help these poor people, although I did. There were also pragmatic reasons. We didn't have enough space for the bad guys. Why tie it up with the good guys?"

Deland was proud of the work his tiny team had accomplished with local contractors. But as his time in Iraq ran out, and the country grew more treacherous—by the day, it seemed—the prospect of Iraqi self-government grew more remote. Deland feared that the rebuilding of Iraq's civilian criminal justice system was being sidelined when it had only just started, and he felt "a terrible frustration."

"I grew up on John Wayne and Roy Rogers and all that stuff in the forties that developed certain ideas in your mind," he said, and at first he had seen Iraq as it was reflected in its wasted prisons—as an open frontier, almost a blank slate. Running the corrections academy gave him a new perspective. "We tend to look at things through American eyes," he said. "You should look at them through the other side's eyes. They saw this differently. They had no experience in the rule of law. It astounded us. Then you thought about it for a while. Why did it astound us? You're not just fixing wires. You're changing an entire culture. Corrections aside, I don't think the American government had any idea exactly how enormous the project was going to be. Everybody focuses on, 'Oh, there was no weapons of mass destruction when you got there; you must have crappy intelligence.' Well hell, there was a whole lot of reasons to say we didn't have good intelligence. We didn't know anything about the country, hardly, when we got there."

The map shows one Iraq, but Deland was simplifying when he spoke of one Iraqi culture. The country was a tangle of cultures—ancient and modern, sectarian and secular, each with its clans, tribes, regions, and classes, its codes and its creeds—and with Saddam's overthrow, all that he had stamped down sprung up: the violently thwarted passions of humiliation and revenge, exclusion and ambition, ideology and greed, political feuds and private vendettas. The occupation, too, was fundamentally fragmented, a grab bag of uncoordinated agendas, with snarled and conflicting lines of authority and accountability, tugged this way and that by opportunistic local allegiances, and hobbled by political calculations that often had less to do with Iraq than with Washington bureaucracy and careerism. There was a great deal at stake for America, of course, but never as much as there was for Iraqis. Everyone knew that sooner or later, individually and collectively, the Americans would get to go home—or have to—leaving the war's spoils to forces beyond their control. Until then, the big, vague idea was to put Iraq back together, not according to a unified vision, but piece by piece, so for the most part nobody really knew what anybody else was doing. And, in the absence of civilian control, as things continued to fall apart, the only coherent imperative was military.

3.

—————

U.S. ARMY DOCTRINE on the handling of prisoners in wartime adheres to the Geneva Conventions. In fact, the pertinent Army regulation (AR 190-8) says that if military doctrine and the Geneva Conventions ever appear to diverge or conflict, Geneva is the higher authority. And the Geneva Convention Relative to the Treatment of Prisoners of War, commonly known as the Third Geneva Convention, is unambiguous: prisoners of war are not criminals or pariahs, but simply enemy assets that have been neutralized by their removal from combat. They are fighters like the soldiers who have captured them instead of killing them, and when the war is over, they must be freed. Until then, the Third Geneva Convention requires that prisoners be "entitled in all circumstances to respect for their persons and their honor."

The Third Geneva Convention is thorough, and for a legal document it is exceptionally clear and straightforward, not least because one of its provisions requires that its full text be made available to all prisoners of war to read in their own language. It says that upon their capture, prisoners of war must be speedily transferred "to camps situated in an area far enough from the combat zone for them to be out of danger," and they must never be held in any place "exposed to the fire of the combat zone." They must obey the laws of the army that holds them, and they must be granted the legal protections of those laws. They must be housed in camps "under conditions as favorable as those for the forces of the detaining power who are billeted in the same area," and with respect for their military rank. They must be given shelter that is entirely dry and adequately lighted. They must also be provided with adequate food, clothing, and medical care, as well as sanitary toilet and shower facilities. They must not be subjected to any physical or mental injury or coercion; they are not obliged to divulge any information to their captors other than name, date of birth, rank, and service number; they may not be used as hostages, nor may they be paraded or otherwise displayed as trophies, as they must be protected not only from violence and intimidation, but also from insults and public curiosity. They may not be held in penitentiaries. They may not be held in secret locations. They are entitled, as soon as they are captured, and any time they are relocated, to send cards to relatives, stating where they are being held, and the condition of their health. They may receive mail, including care packages containing everything from food to books, devotional articles, scientific equipment, examination papers, musical instruments, and sports outfits; they may wear their uniforms and medals and badges of rank and nationality; they must be allowed to engage in athletic activity. Their labor may be used for nonmilitary purposes, and they must be paid for it. And so on.

The Third Geneva Convention presumes a conventional war between the armies of sovereign states. And, in the beginning—the six weeks of blitzkrieg when Americans and their allies fought Saddam's forces for military domination of the country—the invasion of Iraq was such a war. During that time, thousands of Iraqi prisoners of war were taken, and most of them were held far behind the front lines at Camp Bucca, in the sandy southern desert outside the port of Umm Qasr, two miles from the border with Kuwait. Then, on May Day, the president of the United States gave the word that major combat operations had ended.

The full import of this declaration was largely eclipsed by its triumphalist staging: the commander in chief landing in a fighter jet aboard an aircraft carrier, the USS *Abraham Lincoln,* emerging in a full combat flight suit and aviator goggles, giving a thumbs-up to the cameras, and posing amid sailors in orange jumpsuits, before delivering his address beneath a red, white, and blue banner stamped with the legend MISSION ACCOMPLISHED. The bravado, and the tone of premature self-congratulation, became the story of the speech, especially as the war escalated over the ensuing months and years. But the text of the president's remarks conveyed a more complex message.

Even as he proclaimed victory, and "the arrival of a new era" of Iraqi freedom, reconstruction, and political transition, the president made it clear that the war was not over. Only he didn't call the fight in Iraq a war. He described it as one battle in the war on terror that began on September 11, 2001. This was the core of his message: half the speech was devoted to the long war on terror, and just one sentence to the fact that Saddam Hussein and much of his top leadership remained at large in Iraq. He did not speak Saddam's name, referring to him only as "the dictator," but he named Al Qaeda four times and September 11 three times, even though Iraq had no connection to either. On the same day, in Afghanistan, the secretary of defense announced, much more quietly, that "major combat activity" had also ended in that country, where U.S. forces had originally claimed victory and installed a new government eighteen months earlier. What did it mean?

FIVE DAYS AFTER the September 11 attacks the vice president emerged from a thirty-six-hour meeting with the president and his national security team, and told the TV newsman Tim Russert that America's new war on terror would not only be fought on the battlefield, but also by working "the dark side." He said, "We've got to spend time in the shadows in the intelligence world. A lot of what needs to be done here will have to be done quietly, without any discussion, using sources and methods that are available to our intelligence agencies."

Russert pursued the vice president's lead. "There have been restrictions placed on the United States intelligence gathering, reluctance to use unsavory characters, those who violated human rights," he said, and asked, "Will we lift some of those restrictions?"

"Oh, I think so," the vice president said. He anticipated "a very thorough sort of reassessment of how we operate and the kinds of people we deal with," and said: "If you're going to deal only with sort of officially approved, certified good guys, you're not going to find out what the bad guys are doing. You need to be able to penetrate these organizations. You need to have on the payroll some very unsavory characters if, in fact, you're going to be able to learn all that needs to be learned in order to forestall these kinds of activities. It is a mean, nasty, dangerous, dirty business out there, and we have to operate in that arena. I'm convinced we can do it. We can do it successfully. But we need to make certain that we have not tied the hands, if you will, of our intelligence communities in terms of accomplishing their mission."

Over the next several months, the vice president's legal counsel, David Addington, presided over the production of a series of secret memoranda, which argued against several centuries of American executive practice and constitutional jurisprudence by asserting that the president enjoyed essentially absolute power in wartime, including the authority to sanction torture. That November the president issued a military order, declaring that the prosecution of the war on terror created a state of "extraordinary emergency" under which any foreign citizen could be detained, at home or abroad, solely on the basis that he, the president, determined that the person "has engaged in, aided or abetted, or conspired to commit, acts of international terrorism" against U.S. targets, or "has knowingly harbored" such a person. The order explained that anyone taken into custody on these terms would be a military prisoner, but would not have the standing of a POW, and would be subject to trial by a military tribunal ungoverned by "the principles of law and the rules of evidence generally recognized in the trial of criminal cases in the United States." Then, in January 2002, the president decided that the Geneva Conventions did not apply to any prisoners taken in the war against Al Qaeda and the Taliban in Afghanistan, whose fighters and active supporters he classified collectively as "unlawful combatants."

The secretary of state contested this decision, and the president's legal adviser, White House Counsel Alberto Gonzales, drafted a memo exploring the arguments for and against denying POW status to an entire enemy force rather than on a case-by-case basis. On the positive side, Gonzales found that the decision preserved "flexibility" in the prosecution of "a new kind of war" that "renders obsolete Geneva's strict limitations on questioning of enemy prisoners, and renders quaint some of its provisions," such as a POW's right to athletic uniforms and scientific instruments. The decision also preserved flexibility for the future, Gonzales said, establishing a precedent that could come in handy during conflicts "in which it may be more difficult to determine whether an enemy force as a whole meets the standard for POW status." What's more, Gonzales said, the decision "substantially reduces the threat of domestic criminal prosecution under the War Crimes Act," a law in the U.S. code that makes violations of the Third Geneva Convention by American citizens, including public officials, a war crime, punishable by anything from a fine to the death penalty. Gonzales showed real concern about the War Crimes Act, making reference to the unpredictability of independent counsels, who are generally appointed to conduct criminal investigations of high public officials, notably presidents.

On the downside, Gonzales observed that "since the Geneva Conventions were concluded in 1949, the United States has never denied their applicability to either U.S. or opposing forces engaged in armed conflict, despite several opportunities to do so." Breaking with this tradition, he said, would mean that the United States could not invoke Geneva to protect its own forces, and it "would likely provoke widespread condemnation among our allies and in some domestic quarters," while perhaps encouraging "other countries to look for technical 'loopholes' " to avoid Geneva in future conflicts. Finally, he said, denying POW status to enemy fighters "could undermine U.S. military culture which emphasizes maintaining the highest standards of conduct in combat."

After weighing these negative concerns, Gonzales rejected them as "unpersuasive." The Justice Department and the Pentagon agreed. And the president stuck to his decision, laying it out in February 2002, in a formal memorandum—"Subject: Humane Treatment of Al Qaeda and Taliban Detainees"—addressed to the vice president, the secretary of state, the secretary of defense, the attorney general, the chief of staff to the president, the director of central intelligence, the assistant to the president for national security affairs, and the chairman of the Joint Chiefs of Staff. "Of course," the president said, "our values as a nation, values that we share with many nations in the world, call for us to treat detainees humanely, including those who are not legally entitled to such treatment. Our Nation has been and will continue to be a strong supporter of Geneva and its principles. As a matter of policy, the US Armed Forces shall continue to treat detainees humanely and, to the extent appropriate and consistent with military necessity, in a manner consistent with the principles of Geneva."

In the war on terror, then, adherence to the Geneva Conventions was no longer the law but a choice of the commander in chief. In the Iraq war, however, Geneva remained in effect—as law—even after the

May Day declaration of the end of major combat, and by midsummer the great majority of the POWs seized during the invasion had been sent home. But hundreds of them remained in military custody, while new prisoners continued to be taken in the course of military operations. These captives, who could no longer be said to serve the army of an enemy state but were deemed to have intelligence value or to pose a threat to occupation forces, were now classified as "security detainees"—a label that had gained currency in the war on terror to describe "unlawful combatants" and other prisoners who had been denied POW status and were held indefinitely, in isolation and secrecy, without charges or judicial recourse, under exceptionally harsh conditions.

BRIGADIER GENERAL JANIS KARPINSKI of the Army Reserves said she first heard the term "security detainee" when she arrived in Iraq in the summer of 2003 as the commander of the 800th MP Brigade, in charge of the fifteen military detention camps in the country. Karpinski, who had never run a prison before, kept being corrected by Army intelligence and judiciary officers when she called her wards "prisoners." She didn't think much of it. The military has its own language, a technocratic pidgin, heavy with acronyms and legalese, which blends euphemism and hyperspecificity in a code that is alien to the untrained ear. With every new mission there was new lingo, and Karpinski was quick to adapt. But, in time, she came to understand that calling someone a security detainee was "far more than just word-smithing." She said, "It was meant as a convenience to sidestep the law, to sidestep the requirements of the Geneva Conventions."

Karpinski was right that the designation security detainee, or security internee (the terms were used interchangeably), is nowhere explicitly defined in law. And yet, it was from the Geneva Conventions that the occupation authorities in Iraq derived the justification for holding prisoners in this category. The fourth convention, which extends Geneva's regime of rights and protections to civilians in wartime, includes a few lines in Article Five that create an exception for anyone "detained as a spy or saboteur, or as a person under definite suspicion of activity hostile to the security of the Occupying Power." Such captives are still to be treated with humanity, and they are covered by nearly all of Geneva's usual provisions. But, the convention says, in the name of "absolute military security" or "imperative military necessity," they may be held incommunicado and indefinitely, so long as their cases are reviewed by the occupier from time to time— "if possible every six months."

That is all the fourth convention has to say about the matter. It is as general and open to interpretation as the third convention's rules on POWs are particular and rigorously prescriptive. The International Committee of the Red Cross, in its longstanding commentary on Geneva, describes the critical loophole created by Article Five of the fourth convention as uncharacteristically "involved," "open to question," and "regrettable." "What is most to be feared," the ICRC says, "is that widespread application of the Article may eventually lead to the existence of a category of civilian internees who do not receive the normal treatment laid down by the Convention but are detained under conditions which are almost impossible to check. It must be emphasized most strongly, therefore, that Article Five can only be applied in individual cases of an exceptional nature, when the existence of specific charges makes it almost certain that penal proceedings will follow. This Article should never be applied as a result of mere suspicion."

By the time that General Karpinski assumed her command at the end of June 2003, the CPA had already done what the Red Cross feared, issuing a document under Ambassador Bremer's signature,

called Memorandum Number Three, which invoked the Fourth Geneva Convention as providing "an appropriate framework" for "the
ongoing process of security internee management." Bremer's memo
effectively defined as security detainees everyone taken into military
custody who was not explicitly charged as a criminal under Iraqi law,
and it said that they could be held for as long as eighteen months at
a stretch—or, for those under the age of eighteen, twelve months. The
memo said nothing about who had the authority to decide in the first
place that a person's captivity met the standard of "imperative military necessity." That was left to the soldiers and commanders of units
who picked them up.

American soldiers, however, are rarely trained in the provisions of
Article Five of the Fourth Geneva Convention, although many of
them did know that in Afghanistan a security detainee was someone
to whom Geneva did not apply. So General Karpinski wasn't alone in
her confusion about the laws that applied to the prison camps she was
supposed to run. At Camp Victory, the occupation headquarters in
Baghdad, at Central Command in Tampa, Florida, and back in Washington, too, opinions on the status of prisoners in military custody in
Iraq in the summer of 2003 were endlessly finessed and refinessed to
accommodate the conflicting but increasingly conflated legal and rhe-
torical frameworks of the war waged in the name of the liberation of
Iraq and the war on terror.

ON JULY 22, 2003, two days after Deputy Secretary of Defense Wol-
fowitz visited Abu Ghraib, a special operations forces assault team
called Task Force 20, dedicated to capturing or killing "high-value
targets," descended with a contingent of the 101st Airborne on a
house in Mosul, where an informant had said they would find Sad-

dam's sons, Uday and Qusay Hussein. After a four-hour battle, the Americans entered the house and announced that they had killed both men as well as Qusay's fourteen-year-old son, Mustapha.

The next day Captain Carolyn Wood of the 519th Military Intelligence Battalion, which was based in Saddam's hometown, Tikrit, accompanied several of her colleagues on a scouting mission to Abu Ghraib. The 519th had received a Warning Order, giving them advance notice of plans for Operation Victory Bounty, an impending nationwide sweep to round up members of the Fedayeen Saddam, the paramilitary arm of Saddam's Ba'ath Party. In the Warning Order, the occupation's central command instructed the 519th to establish interrogation operations at Abu Ghraib, and the day after the advance team's visit, the first MI unit deployed to the prison to set up its tents and get ready for business.

Captain Wood was not impressed by the prison, which reminded her of Camp Cropper, where she had spent the month of June. Cropper had originally been set up as an interrogation center for the occupation's most-wanted Iraqis, including the top fifty-two whose faces appeared on a deck of cards issued by the Army, with Saddam as the ace of spades. But Wood found it crammed with "low-value detainees" who had been picked up for petty offenses. The tented camp, which was built to hold two hundred prisoners, held seven hundred to a thousand, some of whom, Wood said, "were what was referred to as 'fifty-meter detainees,' because they had been in the general vicinity of the target of a U.S. raid and been picked up essentially for being in close proximity."

Wood had seen worse conditions during the invasion, as she hopscotched north from Kuwait, from one temporary holding camp to another, where the prisoners were kept in big wire cages with meager water rations and no tents. Still, on June 9, MPs at Camp Cropper got rough with an unruly prisoner, and a small riot broke out in the camp. One of the guards responded by shucking his camouflage shirt and flexing his muscles at the angry captives, provoking the riot to a frenzy. The MPs feared they would be overwhelmed, and their Quick Reaction Force fired on the crowd, wounding five prisoners. An investigation by the MP platoon leader concluded that the shooting was in self-defense, and blamed the escalation and outcome of the incident on the shooters' obstructed sight lines and lack of nonlethal rounds, the camp's unclear chain of command, and its inadequate and outdated SOP (standard operating procedure). Captain Wood found that the Military Intelligence mission also suffered from the camp's disorder. She said, "Cropper lacked facilities for proper interrogation operations" and "sufficient logistical support," and when officers expressed their frustration and their concerns about "the disgruntled mood of the detainees," they got no response from their superiors. Still, Cropper did have running water and steady electricity, and it sat comfortably within the security perimeter of Baghdad International Airport, where the military had a powerful communications center and soldiers could be relatively comfortable—none of which could be said for Abu Ghraib.

Major David DiNenna, the commander of the 320th MP Battalion, had similar misgivings when he made a scouting trip to Abu Ghraib early that summer. The move was under way to make the prison the central military detention depot of Iraq, and DiNenna had been tapped to be its chief operations officer. Abu Ghraib sat solidly inside the Sunni Triangle, Saddam's home turf, and the center of increasingly violent resistance to the occupation. "I was kind of skeptical of operating a facility in between Fallujah and Baghdad," DiNenna said. "That was not the prime location to me." The prison took its name from the adjacent city of Abu Ghraib, a Ba'ath party stronghold with a population of a million or more, over which American forces had only nominal control, and DiNenna argued that it would be wiser to concentrate the prison mission at Camp Bucca, where he had been based for several months. Bucca was one of the most secure places in the country. "It's nothing but desert. You can build forever," he said. "But it became a transportation issue—how to move the prisoners if they had to go to trial or be released in the Baghdad area." DiNenna was ordered to install himself at Abu Ghraib with the first contingent of his troops in July. That month there were twenty-five mortar attacks on the prison, and sometimes the shrapnel wounded prisoners in Camp Vigilant. Meanwhile, bulldozers were preparing the ground for Camp Ganci, a much bigger target.

The new camp was constructed according to a modular design, with rectangular, triple-strand concertina-wire enclosures meant to house five hundred prisoners each, and wide corridors between them for guards to patrol. At first two sections were built, but the bulldozers leveled space for at least eight more to be added as needed. You couldn't help wondering: if it had been impossible to control a few hundred rioting prisoners in Camp Vigilant without shooting at them, what would it be like when Ganci filled up? DiNenna worried that securing Abu Ghraib, and providing convoy protection for prisoner and supply transports, would require so many of his soldiers that he would be left shorthanded as the prison expanded and he needed more guards. On his scouting trip he had put in a request for a K-9 unit—as in "canine"—for Abu Ghraib, and he hoped it would come soon. "I had military working dogs at Camp Bucca," he said. "They're an extremely effective asset. Most people realize they cannot argue with a dog. The presence of a dog has a tremendous effect on prisoners, so they're a force multiplier."

CAPTAIN WOOD UNDERSTOOD the desire for dogs. She had graduated from the U.S. Army Intelligence Center and School at Fort Huachuca, Arizona, and served for ten years as an MI interrogator and human

intelligence collector. She had done two tours with the NATO stabi-
lization force in Bosnia-Herzegovina, and before coming to Iraq she
had spent six months as the operations officer of the interrogation
center at Bagram Air Base in Afghanistan. There, in a Soviet-era
warehouse, her team had been under heavy pressure from Washington
to extract "actionable intelligence" from several hundred prisoners
who were classified as unlawful combatants. On her arrival, Wood had
issued a new interrogation policy to induce these prisoners to talk by
allowing a variety of techniques that had no precedent in Army
doctrine: isolation for up to thirty days; nakedness; shackling in pain-
ful stress positions; sensory deprivation; and the use of barking
dogs to induce extreme fear. MP guards were given the task of admin-
istering many of these harsh tactics, and some of them accepted their
new license with zeal. On Wood's watch, three prisoners were beaten
to death.

Autopsies found the killings at Bagram to be homicides. In two
of the cases, medical examiners said that the dead prisoners, who had
been hung by their arms from the rafters while they were worked
over, were so destroyed that their legs would have had to be amputated if they'd survived. One of the murdered men was also determined to have been an innocent civilian who was wrongly arrested.
An Army investigation eventually found that violent abuse was blatant and routine at Bagram, and that guards and interrogators who
had a taste for beating prisoners, stripping them naked, kicking their
genitals, stepping on them, making them lick soldiers' boots, slamming them against walls, pouring water down their throats until they
choked, or hanging them in handcuffs from doors and ceilings could
do so without fear of reproach.

Wood was awarded a Bronze Star for her service in Afghanistan,
and promoted from first lieutenant to captain. In light of her background, she said, "I consider myself very knowledgeable of interrogation operations and techniques." At Abu Ghraib, in the first week of

August 2003, she was appointed officer in charge of interrogation operations. Once again, she decided that the Army's intelligence and interrogation Field Manual (FM 34-52, issued in 1992)—a hundred seventy-one pages of dos and don'ts, including a four-page, double-columned glossary of acronyms—was obsolete and inadequate.

"The interrogation environment in Iraq was challenging because the current U.S. Army interrogation training and doctrine is rooted in and geared toward a conventional, Cold War threat and not toward the Arab mind-set," Wood said, and she went on: "We were moving from a tactical to an operational or insurgent environment, and it increasingly felt to me like my experience in Afghanistan. I did not want my folks to lose sight of their boundaries and their left and right limits. I saw the situation moving to the Bagram model. Pressures were increasing from overpopulation, the mission creep from bona fide security detainees to others who probably really didn't need to be detained for a long period, and the realization that Iraq was evolving into a long-standing mission. I increasingly felt the need to draw on my experience in Afghanistan. We had used sleep adjustment and stress positions as effective techniques in Afghanistan. . . . I used my best judgment and concluded they would be effective tools for inter-rogation operations at Abu Ghraib. Because the winds of war were changing, and the mounting pressure from higher for actionable in-telligence from interrogation operations, I requested more options than FM 34-52 provided."

So Wood saw Abu Ghraib as a feature of the war on terror. It is unclear from her rhythmic, if-this-then-that reasoning why an in-creasing number of prisoners of no interest to her created a need to treat those of interest more harshly. But she was speaking in retro-spect, and it is not always possible to filter the confusions of the time from the confusions of hindsight. She was certainly clear about what she did next. With the help of a colleague, she got hold of the Inter-rogation Rules of Engagement used by Task Force 20, the special operations force that killed Saddam's sons, and, Wood said, "essentially plagiarized it"—"changing the letterhead" and "incorporating general editing"—before submitting it to her brigade command for approval as the rules of engagement for MI at Abu Ghraib. Task Force 20 consisted of a few dozen commandos from various divisions of the military, as well as members of the CIA's covert paramilitary arm, and was kept on twenty-four-hour alert to conduct manhunts at the behest of the president or the secretary of defense. Its activities were obscured by extreme secrecy, and its rules of engagement were never made public, but they were understood to be as unfettered as rules can be—notable for what they permit rather than what they forbid.

Wood's brigade did not respond to the proposed new interrogation rules, so Wood submitted them directly to the office of Major General Barbara Fast, the MI commander for Iraq, at Camp Victory. An officer on Fast's staff advised Wood to pursue approval "through command channels rather than intelligence channels," and she sent the rules on to the office of Lieutenant General Ricardo Sanchez, the commander of all ground forces in the occupation. Soon after that, in the last week of August, two military lawyers came to see her, an American and an Australian, who said her proposal looked fine, and would be "pushed higher" for command approval. "The Australian lawyer even commented that the techniques were rather soft," Wood said.

In the meantime, as Camp Ganci began to take in a new wave of prisoners from Operation Victory Bounty and other sweeps, Wood told her MI team to stick to the old field manual, but to feel free to augment its procedures with stress positions for forty-five-minute stretches, and sleep deprivation regimes, which entailed keeping prisoners awake for all but four hours in every twenty-four, over periods of seventy-two hours. Once again, it was left to MP guards to enforce these regimes, and Wood said, "I did not, nor did any MI personnel to my knowledge, have a conversation or provide written instruction to the MPs as to how to exactly implement the procedure."

IN MID-AUGUST, at about the same time that Captain Wood sent her proposed interrogation rules for Abu Ghraib to Camp Victory, a military intelligence officer on Sanchez's staff, Captain William Ponce of the Human Intelligence Effects Coordination Cell, sent an e-mail to MI unit commanders in Iraq, asking them to provide lists of "individuals who we have in detention that fall under the category of 'unlawful combatants.' " Ponce described this category, with reference to the Geneva Conventions, as including "spies, saboteurs, or civilians who are participating in the hostilities," and he suggested, inaccurately, that such captives were not protected by Geneva. He noted that the MI command was unaware of any rules of engagement that pertained to them, and he urged interrogators to provide him immediately with an "interrogation techniques 'wish list' " to help craft such rules. Ponce concluded his message on a hortatory note: "The gloves are coming off gentlemen regarding these detainees. Col. Boltz"—Colonel Steven Boltz, the deputy MI commander in Iraq— "has made it clear that we want these individuals broken. Casualties are mounting and we need to start gathering info to help protect our fellow soldiers from further attacks. I thank you for your hard work and your dedication." And he signed off, "MI always out front!"

    "Meanwhile," General Janis Karpinski said, "we're holding these prisoners, many of them without any evidence other than the one-page arresting report by some young soldier from one of the infantry or armored divisions that said, 'Caught looting.' " Or else, she said, "You'd have a target individual, and a good grid coordinate on his last known location, and the divisions or the brigades would put an operation together to go and apprehend this individual. Well, if he's in the middle of a card game or a dinner and he's got thirty of his closest friends around him, they're not always clear who the individual is. They just know that this is the grid coordinate location. So they arrest everybody there."

Karpinski sat on a review-and-appeal board that was established in August to examine the files of Abu Ghraib prisoners who might be eligible for release. The board met at Camp Victory under the direction of General Fast. Karpinski said she rarely saw more than the flimsiest hint of any association with insurgent activity in the files, and by way of example she told the story of a man who had been held at Abu Ghraib for a month when his case came up for review. "He and his neighbor had lived side by side for years. There was some jealousy between them, normal, neighborly jealousy. Just after the war was over, this individual sold a parcel of land, and he went out and bought a generator and a pickup truck. When he came back to his house with the generator in the back of the pickup truck, the neighbor said, 'Aha!' And as soon as he saw some coalition soldiers, he grabbed them and said, 'My neighbor all of a sudden has a pickup truck, and he has a generator, and he got that money from the Fedayeen, or the Ba'athists, for giving information away on you guys.' So they arrested him, and they arrested his two sons. They released the two sons after about three weeks. But they kept him as a security detainee." The board decided to release the man. "By the time he got back, of course, everything had been looted from his home," Karpinski said. Still, that man was lucky. At the first meeting of the review board, Karpinski said, forty prisoners' files were examined and debated over the course of four hours, and thirty-five of the prisoners were denied release. That was typical, she said: Military Intelligence called the shots, and nobody wanted to find out later that a terrorist had been set free.

Colonel Marc Warren, the senior legal adviser to General Sanchez, also sat on the prison review board, and he, too, described the files as

"thin." He said the documentation they contained was often ran-
domly assembled and improperly filled out, and he said that this was
a "great frustration" to General Fast. But, Warren said, "the board
was trying to find an appropriate balance between release and security,
and we took the side of security. We did not want to take a chance
based on what we didn't know. Unfortunately, we didn't know much
from an intelligence standpoint."

"Well, OK," Karpinski said. "It's against the law, but they held
them. And the next night, there was a hundred more. And the next
night, there were fifty more. And the next there were three hundred
more. And it went on and on and on, until we had thousands of them
being held out there without any reason or any discussion about why
they were being held. And they were all tagged as security detainees.
I mean that literally. Each one of them comes in with a tag that's attached to some part of his clothing, and it says, 'security detainee.' "

As the general charged with running military prisons in Iraq,
Karpinski also had the mission of assisting the CPA in setting up
civilian prisons, and Abu Ghraib was the biggest and busiest of her
operations in both respects. But it was hardly the only one. She had
a lot of other places to be around the country on any given day—from
Camp Bucca way down south, to Camp Ashraf in the far north (where
she was responsible for six thousand exiled Iranian rebels from the
Mujahedin-e Khalq who had surrendered to American forces and were
being held under the guard of Bulgarian soldiers). And in Baghdad
there was no end of meetings at Camp Victory. By all accounts, including her own, Karpinski did not spend much time at Abu Ghraib.
She would escort important visitors on their tours—congressional
delegations, say, or American network news reporters—and she would
come for command meetings. But there was a war on, and Karpinski
said she quickly realized that nobody at Camp Victory and none of
the commanders running combat operations wanted to be bothered
about prisoners. Soldiers had to take them, and they had to have a

place to hand them off as quickly as possible. That place was Abu Ghraib, and all anybody wanted from it was intelligence.

"People have their priorities," Karpinski said. "And for General Sanchez and the battalion commanders it was the war fighters—it was not prison operations. I don't want to, but I understand that mindset." Still, she said, "One of the effects of policing up people that are completely innocent was that their families are annoyed. So they join the insurgency to get even—if you took my brother, I'm going to take one of your soldiers. So the insurgency, as a result of all of these raids and the detention, was increasing."

4.

THERE HAD BEEN NO PRISONERS at the hard site when McCotter and Deland said their good-byes, but a first batch was soon transferred from Camp Ganci and installed under the watch of Iraqi guards and MP overseers in the eight-man cells of the second cell block—Tiers 2A and 2B. The prisoners selected were the prisoners for whom the hard site was intended: criminal suspects or convicts whose cases were under the purview of Iraq's civilian courts. The first cell block was another story. It was made up of single-occupancy cells that had caught the eye of Colonel Thomas Pappas, the military intelligence brigade commander in Baghdad. Pappas wasn't happy with the MI setup at Abu Ghraib. Nobody was. To interrogate a prisoner properly you need to be able to regulate his environment in a manner that is conducive to his cooperation. At the very least, you have to be able to keep the prisoner apart from others, protected from influence for as long as the interrogation is active. In the tented camps of Abu Ghraib that was impossible, and as soon as the hard site was open for business, Pappas arranged with the CPA to start holding high-value MI prisoners on Tier 1A. General Karpinski didn't object, and the tier was placed under the exclusive guard of MPs. It was strictly off limits to Iraqi cops and corrections officers, and to most Americans, too.

The MI move to the hard site took place just as Major General

Geoffrey Miller, the commander of the prison and interrogation camp at Guantánamo Bay, Cuba, arrived in Iraq to discuss what he called the "current theater ability to rapidly exploit internees for actionable intelligence." Gitmo, as the Cuban camp is known, was America's preeminent prison for the war on terror, reserved for prisoners to whom Geneva protections were denied. Most of the inmates there had been captured in and around Afghanistan by American forces, or by local officials eager to collect the five-thousand-dollar bounty the United States was offering for alleged Al Qaeda and Taliban associates; and many of these prisoners had undergone fierce interrogations at Bagram and other Afghan camps, or in various secret prisons operated by American intelligence agents around the world, before being shipped to the Caribbean. There, they were kept in extreme isolation, caged and frequently hooded and chained, in a seemingly permanent legal limbo.

Many prisoners at Gitmo had been there for a year and a half already without being told why, and in the two weeks before General Miller flew into Baghdad, at least twenty-three of them had attempted suicide in a mass protest. Army doctors later said that these prisoners hadn't really wanted to die, so the Pentagon reclassified their efforts to hang or strangle themselves as "manipulative self-injurious behaviors." But this episode had been kept secret, and when Miller visited Abu Ghraib on September 7, 2003, with an entourage of seventeen past or present colleagues from Gitmo, he came as something of a superstar of what he liked to call the GWOT—the global war on terror. He enjoyed the reputation of being a hard man for hard times, held in high esteem at the White House and the Pentagon.

The secretary of defense was also in Iraq, and he had dropped by Abu Ghraib the day before to tour Saddam's death house and torture chambers, and to pose for photographs with soldiers. Then he flew away; he said he didn't want to see anything else. But Miller was all business. His appearance coincided with a command decision to shut

down Camp Cropper and consolidate its intelligence operation at
Abu Ghraib, making the prison the MI interrogation center of Iraq.
Miller visited Tier 1A, and told the MI team that he was there because General Sanchez wanted him to explain how things were done
at Gitmo.

A regular military prison is run by the Military Police, according
to Army doctrine, but at an interrogation center like Gitmo, Miller
explained, the interrogators ran the show. That meant the MPs worked
for them, treating the prisoners according to the demands of their
interrogation regimes. After all, in their training, interrogators are
encouraged to speak of the place they house their prisoners as an
"inn," and to call their prisoners "guests." MP guards, in turn, are
seen as the "innkeepers"—although MPs more often refer to their role
as "babysitters"—who look after the prisoners between interrogation
sessions. Only it is the interrogator who sets the terms of this room
service, allowing or denying creature comforts, so that the prisoner
understands that his condition depends entirely on his relationship
with the all-powerful person who periodically summons him to a
meeting in the interrogation booth. Even then, it is an MP who con-
ducts the prisoner to and from the interrogation, allowing the interrogator to remain at all times only an interlocutor, and never the
direct agent of the conditions he imposes. This scenario may play out
in a grand château or in the most primitive basement lockups and
improvised field camps—it doesn't matter: whatever the setting, the
interrogator's ideal is an atmosphere of total control.

Taking over Tier 1A, then, was just the first step for MI. "It is
essential," Miller wrote in a report on his mission to Abu Ghraib,
"that the guard force be actively engaged in setting the conditions for
successful exploitation of the internees." General Karpinski remem-
bers Miller making his case more plainly in person. She said he told
soldiers at the prison, "The first thing I noticed is that you're treating
the prisoners too well. You have to have control, and they have to

know that you're in control. You have to treat the prisoners like dogs."
In his report, however, Miller repeatedly called for strict rules and
standards for interrogators and guards, and by way of an example, he
provided General Sanchez's legal staff with a copy of the Gitmo interrogation rules, a list of approved "counter-resistance techniques in the
War on Terrorism," signed by the secretary of defense.

THE GITMO RULES had emerged from a protracted spate of legal im-
provisation by the framers of the war on terror that followed the
president's decision to set aside the Geneva Conventions in Afghanistan. Once it was established that the humane treatment of prisoners
in the war on terror was optional, the question became: If we opt not
to, what is allowed? So the White House asked the Justice Department for an opinion as to just how far an interrogation, unbound by
Geneva, could go without violating the UN's Convention Against
Torture and Other Cruel, Inhuman or Degrading Treatment or Punishment. The answer came, in the summer of 2002, in the form of a
fifty-page, single-spaced memorandum, signed by Assistant Attorney
General Jay Bybee, which basically said not to worry: only "the most
extreme acts" qualify as torture, and they must be committed with
the "precise objective" of inflicting pain "equivalent in intensity to
the pain accompanying serious physical injury, such as organ failure,
impairment of bodily function, or even death."

The Bybee memo offered further reassurance by noting that international legal decisions on harsh interrogation practices "make
clear that while many of these techniques may amount to cruel, inhuman or degrading treatment . . . there is a wide range of such techniques that will not rise to the level of torture." For example, in 1978,
the European Court of Human Rights ruled in the case of *Ireland v.
the United Kingdom* that making a prisoner stand spread-eagled and on

tiptoes with his hands against a wall high above his head and all of his weight on his fingers "did not occasion suffering of the particular intensity and cruelty implied by the word torture." *Ireland* reached the same conclusion about hooding prisoners, subjecting them to loud noise, and depriving them of sleep, food, and drink pending or during interrogation. The Supreme Court of Israel, too, ruled that such practices and worse—"the forceful shaking of the suspect's upper torso, back and forth, repeatedly, in a manner which causes the neck and head to dangle and vacillate rapidly"—did not cross the threshold of torture. And, the Bybee memo stressed, neither the Convention Against Torture nor U.S. law against extraterritorial torture imposed criminal penalties for "cruel, inhuman, or degrading" acts.

So the mood in Washington was permissive in the fall of 2002, when General James Hill of the Southern Command, which was responsible for Guantánamo Bay, wrote to the Joint Chiefs of Staff, saying, "Despite our best efforts, some detainees have tenaciously resisted our current interrogation methods." Hill proposed a new set of more aggressive "counter-resistance techniques," and in early December, the secretary of defense approved eighteen of the practices on Hill's list, including the use of stress positions, isolation for up to thirty days, removal of clothing, twenty-hour interrogations, forced shaving of facial hair, the use of dogs to induce phobia and stress, and "the use of mild, non-injurious physical contact such as grabbing, poking in the chest with the finger, and light pushing."

Then, five weeks later, in mid-January 2003, the secretary rescinded his approval of these methods, although he said that they might still be used in specific cases, if he received a request with "a thorough justification" and "a detailed plan" for their implementation. At the same time, the secretary commissioned a working group, composed of representatives from all major departments of the military except the Military Police, to produce a comprehensive study of the legal and policy options for breaking the resistance of unlawful combatants under interrogation in the war on terror. The working group's report was delivered in April, and formed the basis of a new memo from the secretary, laying out a more restrained set of rules for Gitmo interrogators.

The April rules allowed twenty-four techniques for breaking a prisoner's resistance. Seventeen of them were established practices drawn from the MI interrogators' field manual. These included: Incentive/Removal of Incentive (providing a reward or removing a privilege, for instance, the Koran); Emotional Love and Emotional Hate (playing on a prisoner's love or hatred for an individual or group); Fear Up Harsh (significantly increasing the fear level); Fear Up Mild; Reduced Fear; Pride and Ego Up (boosting the ego); Pride and Ego Down (attacking or insulting the ego); Futility (invoking a prisoner's feeling of futility); We Know All (pretending to know already everything the prisoner refuses to tell); Establish Your Identity (tricking the prisoner into revealing who he is by pretending to mistake him for someone else); Repetition (continuously repeating the same question); Mutt and Jeff (teaming up on the prisoner with a friendly and a harsh interrogator); Rapid Fire (asking questions in rapid succession without allowing for answers); and Silence.

The other seven techniques were: Change of Scenery Up (altering the interrogation setting to a more pleasant location); Change of Scenery Down; Sleep Adjustment (reversing sleep cycles from night to day, but not sleep deprivation); False Flag (pretending to be from a country other than the United States); Environmental Manipulation (adjusting temperature or introducing an unpleasant smell); Dietary Manipulation; and Isolation (for up to thirty days).

The secretary of defense required that he be given advance notice of the use of four of the approved techniques: Removal of Incentive; Pride and Ego Down; Mutt and Jeff; and Isolation. But, at the same time, he reiterated his invitation to commanders in the field to send

him written requests for the use of any other methods they might see
a need for, case by case. Nothing was absolutely ruled out.

COLONEL MARC WARREN, General Sanchez's legal adviser, said that his
officers reviewed the Gitmo rules with MI and "scrubbed them to ensure compliance with the Geneva Conventions," then took the secretary
of defense's April memo and "modified it as our own." In fact, the unsigned first draft of Sanchez's Interrogation and Counter-Resistance
Policy, which Warren's office circulated on September 10, the day
after General Miller left Iraq, was largely a verbatim transcript of the
Gitmo rules. But the Sanchez draft said that the rules applied to
prisoners of war as well as security detainees. This stood out, because
the requirement, which the secretary of defense had imposed on interrogators of unlawful combatants at Gitmo—that he should be given
advance notice before the use of certain techniques—was reserved by
Sanchez only for interrogations of POWs, and there were no POWs
at Abu Ghraib.

What's more, in drafting the rules, Colonel Warren's team had
incorporated aspects of the proposed interrogation policy that Captain
Carolyn Wood had copied from Task Force 20 and submitted in August. So, to the extent that the Sanchez draft differed from the Gitmo
rules, it was significantly more permissive. In addition to the techniques allowed at Gitmo, the draft rules for Abu Ghraib allowed the
use of muzzled military working dogs to exploit "Arab fear of dogs,"
sleep deprivation, sensory deprivation, yelling, loud music and light
control, deception by means of false statements and false documents,
and stress positions, limited to an hour at a time and four hours a day.
And, of course, the draft said that any other techniques not listed
could be submitted for approval. In Iraq, however, requests for such

approval, and advance notice of reserved techniques, were to be sent to Sanchez, not the Pentagon.

Four days after the draft policy went out, it was replaced by a different version, signed by Sanchez. Sleep deprivation had been dropped from the list of approved tactics, and the use of dogs, stress positions, and noise and light control had been added to the group of practices that could only be used after notice was given to Sanchez. But once again the reservation of these methods applied only to POWs, making it a moot point at Abu Ghraib. Sanchez's rules were now official policy, and Captain Wood said she had the MI interrogators at the prison take turns reading them aloud, while others followed along. Then she made them sign statements saying they had read and understood them. She also made a computer slide with a list of all the approved approaches and, in bold type, a list of safeguards: "Approaches must always be humane and lawful. . . . Detainees must NEVER be touched in a malicious or unwanted manner. . . . The Geneva Conventions apply." Finally, at the bottom of the slide, Wood created a red box with the message in big red letters: "Everyone is responsible for ensuring compliance. . . . Violations must be reported immediately." Wood printed out the slide, and posted copies around MI work areas—"as a constant reminder," she said.

Just two weeks after the Abu Ghraib rules went into effect, Sanchez's legal shop sent out a new, revised draft version of the policy, which trimmed the list of allowed techniques to eliminate changes of scenery, dietary and environmental manipulation, sleep adjustment, false flag, dogs, sensory deprivation, loud noise and light control, deception, and stress positions. These changes appeared to restrict the options of interrogators, but other changes had the opposite effect. For instance, isolation, which was no longer listed as an approved technique, was now described as "segregation," and presented not as a special approach but as a standard practice for prisoners under interrogation. The new draft also shed any reference to POWs, and along with it any requirement that advance notice of the use of specified techniques be given to Sanchez. In addition, detailed cautionary notes about the possible conflict of several techniques with the Geneva Conventions—cautions that had been carried over from the Gitmo rules—were gone. To be sure, the new draft still said that the Geneva Conventions applied in Iraq, but the rules granted interrogators more license than their colleagues at Gitmo were given to deal with prisoners denied the Geneva Conventions.

A week later, yet another draft was dispatched for review, identical to the last except for some subtle and barely discernible editorial fine-tuning. The mid-September rules remained in effect, however, for one more week. Then, on October 12, after a final bit of editorial tweaking, the new policy was made official and distributed over Sanchez's signature. Although the list of approved interrogation techniques had been significantly shortened over time, Captain Wood said, "It was explained to me (I cannot remember by who, but the guidance was from higher) that those approaches removed from the 14 Sep version were not necessarily out of reach." So when she remade her slide, she simply listed those techniques in a separate column, and indicated that they had to be run by Sanchez for approval. She did not say, however, whether she made all of the interrogators who had signed off on the earlier rules sign off on the new ones.

What a mess. In the course of a month five different versions of the interrogation rules—the three unsigned drafts, and the two official policies—had been put into circulation at Abu Ghraib. Some of the changes along the way were substantial, but they were never explicitly identified. You had to scrutinize the succeeding documents side by side to detect all their differences, and they all looked enough alike that you could easily assume you'd already read one when you'd actually read the other. And there was more to these documents than their lists of interrogation techniques. From one to the next, much of what Colonel Warren called the surrounding "verbiage"—the law-

yerly framework discussing the premises and implementation of the
rules—had been substantially reworked. For instance, the first draft
of the first policy, alongside its discussion of POWs, included vesti-
gial references to unlawful combatants from the Gitmo rules. Simi-
larly, the first and second drafts of the second policy, after citing the
Fourth Geneva Convention as the grounds for classifying civilians as
security detainees, said that security detainees could be denied all
Geneva protections "where the exercise of such rights would be prej-
udicial to the security of Iraq." These passages, the first misleading
and the second just wrong, disappeared in the official versions of the
policy. But the confusion about the law among those who were laying
it down for Abu Ghraib suggested that the interrogation rules were
not really rules but a kind of guesswork, and that they invited exceptions, which certainly fit with the fact that interrogators were being
allowed—even encouraged—to do so much that wasn't in their hand-
book, so much that was even restricted at Gitmo, so much they were
not trained to do.

There was no time for training, and nobody to provide it, and the
October 12 policy, which remained in effect for seven months, offered
no guidance for the use of specific interrogation methods. Colonel
Warren had the impression that the MI commanders rather liked it
that way. "I believe that MI doctrine suggests that use of approved
approaches should be left to the imagination of the interrogator,"
Warren said. "I believe that it is possible that the guys at the bottom
weren't looking at the policy that we had issued from the top." And,
he said, "I recall everyone being very tired by this time, and a lot of
activity was going on."

IN THE WEEKS AFTER GENERAL MILLER'S VISIT, the MI team at Abu
Ghraib grew at great speed as new officers kept arriving with new

briefs to reorganize the operation. Miller had called for the establish-
ment of a state-of-the-art, secure communications and information
technology system for Abu Ghraib, and new equipment and techni-
cians soon showed up to make that happen. Miller had said that
women and children in the tented camps needed to be segregated,
and in short order they were installed on Tier 1B of the hard site,
while more high-value MI prisoners were transferred to 1A. Then the
interrogators and analysts of the 325th MI Brigade started moving in
from Camp Cropper, and they had to be integrated with the 519th
MI team that was already there. At Gitmo, Miller said, there were
behavioral science consultation teams of Army psychiatrists and psy-
chologists to assist with interrogations, and military lawyers to help
define the limits of acceptable treatment of prisoners, so these, too,
were on their way.

   "I do believe that the Miller visit propelled Abu Ghraib to become a 'mini-mo,' " Captain Wood said. But Abu Ghraib was already
a much bigger prison than Gitmo, and the inmate population was
growing rapidly. By the end of September there were as many as three
thousand prisoners at Abu Ghraib, nearly ten times as many as there
had been in early July, but the number of soldiers to look after them
had only increased slightly. There was no way to keep up, and the
more prisoners there were, the more the demand for intelligence grew.
"People were on edge and under pressure," Colonel Warren said. General Sanchez, he said, "was under intense pressure." Warren was told
about calls coming in from Washington, and the message was: produce, produce. Everybody wanted to know: What was the intelligence? Where was the intelligence? So what MI wanted at Abu
Ghraib, MI got.

   Major David DiNenna, the MP operations officer for the prison,
couldn't believe it. He'd been asking for a secure communications
center since he got to the prison in July. "We had to fight to get the
basic secret connections," he said. "We, as an MP battalion running

a confinement facility with three different facilities—Camp Ganci, Camp Vigilant, and the hard site—were not given the same resources as the MI folks. They had a signal trailer all to themselves. We had to share another signal trailer with them." In DiNenna's experience and understanding of Army doctrine, MPs were supposed to run prisons without any interference from other branches of the military. But he had been asking for more troops, and more outdoor lighting for the tent cities, as well as military working dogs, since he got to Abu Ghraib in June, and he couldn't get a fraction of what he needed. Even the most basic supplies were hard to come by—jumpsuits for prisoners, toothbrushes, soap.

DiNenna wasn't happy, either, about the subordination of MP guards to MI interrogators. "There were two major missions being conducted at Abu Ghraib," he said, "the confinement of prisoners being our mission and intelligence gathering being the MI mission. The two don't go together or they don't cross over. MPs secure, house, and protect prisoners for MI. MPs do not get involved in interrogations of any sort. But intelligence gathering became the priority in theater. There was such a push for intelligence. And I understand this to a degree—they needed to stop the attacks."

5.

LIEUTENANT COLONEL STEVEN JORDAN, a reserve officer serving in the Army's Intelligence and Security Command, arrived at Abu Ghraib on September 17, and he was amazed by the squalor of the prison. "Just a lot of nothing," he said, "a lot of dust, a lot of sand, wild animals, wild dogs, huge cats—I've never seen cats that big in my life. And the sand spiders or camel spiders, sand fleas, the occasional snake here or there, or what have you. I couldn't believe that soldiers were being housed in such conditions." Most of the soldiers at Abu Ghraib at the time were living in a concrete warehouse they had reclaimed from the ruins of the prison laundry. The only vacant room Jordan found there was a cemented-over latrine. It was a fetid chamber, but by means of bleach and incense he managed to tame the lingering stench to a level he deemed tolerable— no fouler, anyway, than the rest of the place—and by nightfall he'd moved in.

Then somebody out in the darkness began shooting mortars over the prison wall. Jordan's latrine shook from one explosion, and another, and another. There may have been a fourth, he could never remember for sure. He was scared. Each exploding shell seemed louder and nearer than the last. Jordan, who was forty-six, had only been in

Iraq for a few days, but he had spent more than half his life in the military—fourteen years on active duty, ten in the reserves—and he'd never come under attack before. The bombs that night fell on open ground and did no harm. But Jordan wasn't reassured. In the morning everyone was talking about the time in August when a similar barrage, three mortars, had splashed into the camps, killing a handful of prisoners and wounding more than forty badly enough to require medical evacuation to a hospital.

The Military Intelligence team was also working in tents near the hard site, while another solid prison compound stood nearby, locked and empty. It made no sense. Jordan had been sent to Abu Ghraib by General Fast to establish a Joint Debriefing and Interrogation Center, an umbrella office for coordinating intelligence gathering and intelligence reporting. He had no interrogation training or experience—his background was in civil affairs—but as the highest-ranking resident intelligence officer at the prison, he was now in charge of the effort to exploit high-value prisoners at Abu Ghraib, and he thought a good place to start would be to cut the locks off those unused hard buildings and move the MI operations indoors. Jordan made inquiries and learned that the CPA had claimed the compound, and planned to refurbish it once the hard site was finished. But nobody could say when that would happen, and Jordan said he could use those buildings as they were—right away. The response from the CPA was: That's not your lane; stick to intel reporting.

Jordan didn't like being rebuked, but he didn't think about it again until shortly after nightfall on September 20, his fourth day at the prison, when he and Chief Warrant Officer Ed Rivas and Major Mike Thompson were meeting with Colonel Pappas at the Military Intelligence command tent, and a mortar round fell just inside the prison's south perimeter wall. The boom and shudder made them dive flat to the ground, and they were picking themselves up to scramble

for cover when Jordan saw the orange flash of a second explosion—
and then nothing.

IT MIGHT HAVE BEEN THREE SECONDS, or it might have been three
minutes, before Jordan came to and found Chief Rivas crouched over
him, tugging at his shirt collar. The world appeared dark. Rivas
looked like he was saying something, or maybe shouting, but at first
Jordan couldn't hear, and when sound returned it was just babble to
him. Finally words took shape. Rivas was saying, "You're hit. You're
hit. Are you okay, sir?"

"No, man," Jordan said. "I'm on fire." He touched his right side,
where it burned. Everything there was wet and sticky. He thought
his canteen must have burst, and in the same instant he knew he
hadn't been carrying his canteen. He heard himself saying, "You
don't got to worry about me, I'll be fine, I'll be good," but even as
he spoke he was thinking, "I'm bleeding out, I'm dying here in the
Iraqi desert." Jordan realized he was regaining his senses; there was
the smell of cordite in the air from the explosion, there were the
sounds of soldiers yelling for medics and the moaning of soldiers lost
in pain. A wild panic gripped him, a frantic wish to run for cover
before the next mortar fell. Just then Chief Rivas hauled him up and
over several strands of concertina wire and dragged him to a medic
station.

They got him on a gurney and cut away his shirt. A piece of metal
shrapnel was stuck in his side. The medics snapped it out. The pain
was such—the heat, the hurt—that when a medic said, "Hey, sir,
you're going to be all right" it occurred to Jordan that this was exactly
what you'd tell a dying soldier to ease him out of life. Then he heard
from the radio chatter that fifteen soldiers were wounded and med-

evac helicopters were being called in, and he knew he wasn't dying. He didn't want to be flown out. He wanted to be with his soldiers.

"I'm good," he said, but when he started to get up a puddle of blood appeared at the bottom of his gurney. Nobody could see where it came from. Jordan was shoved back down, and there were hands all over him again. Jordan's own hands went to his groin and his heart. Both were intact. The wound was in his calf, another piece of shrapnel, a little one, the size of birdshot. He hadn't noticed it beneath the pain in his ribs. As soon as it was bandaged, he got up and went outside. There were wounded all around the blast site—soldiers bleeding from their heads, soldiers who looked as if they might lose an arm or a leg.

Amid the devastation, Jordan saw that he'd been lucky. And he wasn't the only one. A dozen Americans were awaiting medevac, and the wonder of it was that they hadn't been killed. The second mortar had crashed through the side of the MI signals tent and detonated against a field table, two and a half feet above the ground, and because mortar blasts blossom up and out, and most of the soldiers in the tent were off duty, sitting or lying down, playing video games and cards, much of the worst of it had sprayed right past them. Still, two men had been caught standing at the moment of impact, Sergeant David Travis Friedrich and Specialist Lunsford Brown.

Friedrich's right side was ripped open; Jordan came upon him as a triage team was trying to get an IV in him, and his veins were draining too quickly to allow the needle purchase. There was nothing for Jordan to do, so he went to see if he could be of use to someone else. He found Brown in agony. Jordan hadn't known anybody at Abu Ghraib for more than a few days, but he felt a connection to Brown, who was Colonel Pappas's driver. They had shown each other photographs of their kids. Brown's was a three-and-a-half-month-old girl. The pictures were all Brown had seen of her, but he had a home leave coming in two weeks, which he spoke of nervously—wary, as any soldier, of getting his hope up. Now his back was shredded and he feared that he was dying, and Jordan couldn't help him either.

By the time the helicopter arrived, Sergeant Friedrich had bled to death. Jordan helped load his body into the ambulance that took him to the landing pad, and a little later in the night Colonel Pappas came and told the troops that Specialist Brown, too, had not made it. "I kind of blame myself for their deaths," Jordan said, "because I didn't knock the locks off those buildings and push to move those soldiers into hardened facilities."

Jordan returned to the shredded MI tent to study the bloodied ground. "I could see where Sergeant Friedrich had been standing," he said. "He had just walked out of that tent, and come around the side when that round hit, and he took a portion of the blast. You could see the pattern of the shrap-metal—and what he took was coming right for myself and Mike Thompson and Chief Rivas and Colonel Pappas. Had that mortar not hit that table, who knows how many more folks would have been dead. Had Friedrich not been standing where he was at, there was some significant-size chunks of shrap-metal that I know would have ended my time on earth. And there's been a couple of times I've thought, 'Hey Lord, if you're really there, how come you didn't just take me out and leave Friedrich?' I don't know, he's never answered me back. It's not something that you can explain away. If he wasn't standing where he was, I wouldn't have additional time with my older two children. And I wouldn't have my youngest son."

IMMEDIATELY AFTER FRIEDRICH'S DEATH was confirmed, while Brown was still among the wounded, the MP battalion at Abu Ghraib issued a Serious Incident Report, which listed the casualties and noted that shortly before the mortars struck, two white pickup trucks had been spotted near the prison, one of which fit the description of a truck that might have been involved in previous attacks. The prison's Quick Reaction Force was dispatched in pursuit, and returned before long with such a truck and its driver and passenger in custody. Members of the Internal Reaction Force, MPs trained in riot control and prisoner searches, met the party at the prison gate and took charge of the suspects—a male and a female, as soldiers say. According to sworn statements later given to the Army's Criminal Investigative Division (CID) by two of these MPs, Sergeant Gregory Spiker and Sergeant First Class Daryl Plude, a couple of Military Intelligence officers soon arrived on the scene, and one of them went straight for the male suspect, shouting profanity at him and knocking him to the ground with a punch to the back of his head.

"The suspect was handcuffed, on his knees and a towel wrapped around his head," Spiker said. "The MI soldier kept yelling, 'Eyes down, get up,' while knocking the suspect back down." Plude said the soldier screamed at the suspect—"What the fuck are you looking at?"—as he shoved his face in the dirt. At that, both MPs said, their superior officer, First Lieutenant David Sutton, the commander of the Internal Reaction Force, told the MI soldier that his violence was unnecessary, and the soldier replied that he was a professional and knew his business. Sutton said that he didn't look professional, and reminded him that the suspect might be innocent. The MI soldier ignored him, and a second MI soldier came over —"a very large stocky soldier," Plude said—and yanked the suspect off the ground. Spiker said the second soldier put an armlock on the Iraqi's neck, and the first soldier hit him in the stomach. The MI soldiers then dragged the man off to their Humvee, where Plude said the second soldier beat his back and head, while screaming at him to get in the truck. There were more blows, and Plude had the impression that the suspect was bleeding from his lip, but it was night and he was unsure. Plude asked the soldiers to identify themselves, and they told him they were from the 519th MI company. "I then realized," he said, "that these were soldiers from the unit that had been attacked."

Spiker said that Sutton joined Plude in a loud argument with the MI soldiers, and that the MI men ended it by driving away with the suspect. Later that night, Major DiNenna, the prison's chief of operations, summoned Sutton and Plude to a meeting with the MI officer in charge, a first sergeant named McBride. According to Plude, McBride "told us that this had never happened and that he had people that were wounded and everyone was upset." Plude said, "We explained to them that during our many years of law enforcement you never send a suspect back to a group of officers that were directly affected by an incident because you don't know what they might do and that this case was exactly the same." McBride replied that he would handle the matter, and the MPs told him they were going to make sworn statements and let investigators handle it.

In all, five MPs made sworn statements describing the beating of the Iraqi suspect, and five MI officers made sworn statements saying that there had been no abuse. By the time these statements were passed on to the CID, the Iraqi suspects had been questioned, found to have no connection to the mortar attacks, and let go; and in the absence of a victim, the CID determined that there was insufficient basis to pursue the case.

"PEOPLE ALWAYS WORRY about being killed, of course. But people don't really think about what happens if my buddy is killed and I have to watch," Sergeant Andrew Stoltzman said. Stoltzman was in Iraq with the MI unit that suffered the heaviest casualties in the September 20 attack, so he had known Sergeant Friedrich and many of the wounded. But Stoltzman wasn't at Abu Ghraib that night. "Originally nobody from our company was supposed to go there until the beginning of October," he said. "Then our command structure decided—nope, we're going to send part of you two weeks early."

Stoltzman thought it was a good idea to consolidate MI operations at one address. But Abu Ghraib? Even before the deadly attack, he said, the move cast a gloom over his company. "We had this idea that something bad was going to happen. We knew they were being mortared quite often there, and we just decided that we weren't going to make it." And after the attack, as he brooded over his buddies' fate, Stoltzman almost wished that he had been there—to be a part of the loss that had become a part of him.

"It's a very weird feeling," he said. "I don't know if it's guilt, because to me guilt is, I did something wrong and I got away with it. And that's not how I feel with this." But just as Lieutenant Colonel Jordan kept reliving the instant of the blast when Friedrich stepped between him and death, Stoltzman could not stop asking, "Why did they have to go early? Had they not gone early, they wouldn't have been hit." He said, "I am so glad that I came home alive and with all my body parts—I can never be more thankful—but you always wonder, why wasn't it me? You always have this in the back of your mind. Who was in charge that really decided? I believe in God, and I have a strong relationship with Jesus, and that's the only thing that keeps me from going insane about it—that it was out of my control, and it was just not my time."

When he finally got to Abu Ghraib with the second wave of his company, Stoltzman had another, more pressing anxiety: "How are the rest of our comrades going to look upon us? Are they going to view us the same as before, thinking us as equals, and comrades and friends? Or are they going to look at us as people who missed the tragedy and are no longer equals because we didn't have the same experience that they did, and now they have their own clique?" He did not have to worry for long. On his first night at the prison, a mortar smacked into the concrete wall of the company's sleeping quarters and blew up its generator. After that, he said, "We were accepted very well."

PART 2

DURING

The past is inaccurate.

—CZESLAW MILOSZ

6.

SPECIALIST SABRINA HARMAN of the 372nd Military Police company, a United States Army Reserves unit out of Cresaptown, Maryland, arrived at Abu Ghraib on October 1, 2003, and wrote a letter home to her wife:

Kelly
First day at the prison. Its 9:00 pm and we can hear shots—no white lights are allowed to be on at night no leaving the building after dark. I hope we aren't here long! We drove in and two helicopters were landed taking prisoners off. I'm scared of helicopters because of the dream. I think I wrote it down before. I saw a helicopter and it looked like the tail was swaying back and forth then it did it again then a huge flame/round shot up and it exploded. I turned around and we were under attack, I didn't have my weapon (gun) so all we could do was hide under these picknick tables. So back to the prison . . . we get to our buildings and I step out of my truck right in front of a picknick table.—I almost freaked out. I have a bad feeling about this place. I want to leave as soon as possible! We are still hoping to be home X-mas or soon after.—

I love you.

I'm going to get some sleep.

I'll write you again soon.

Please don't give up on me!

            Sabrina

Like many young reservists, Harman had never imagined she'd see war, and Iraq often felt unreal to her; like a dream, she said. Then she had that dream—about a gunman shooting at a helicopter from a date palm, while she hid, unarmed, beneath a picnic table—and it was all too real. It was the only dream she ever remembered having in Iraq. "And it kind of came true, two or three weeks later," she said. "Down the road, they started shooting helicopters from date trees."

That was in Al Hillah, where the 372nd MPs had been stationed since they got to Iraq in mid-May. Having sat out the "shock and awe" phase of the invasion at Fort Lee in Virginia, they were sent in through Kuwait right after the president declared that major combat was finished—and in Al Hillah, during that first summer of the war, it was. The MPs felt safe walking the streets; they made friends with Iraqis, played with their kids, shopped in their markets, shared meals at their outdoor cafés. The company's headquarters, in an abandoned date-processing factory, was minimally fortified, and never attacked. The company's mission was law and order, to provide combat support for the 1st Marine Expeditionary Force, which controlled the city, and to train local policemen for duty under a new national government. The MPs understood their presence to be temporary—maybe three months, at most six—a stopgap operation; their expectation, on arrival, was that America would hand the country over to democratically elected Iraqis by summer's end, then get out of the way.

To Harman, the assignment felt like a peacekeeping mission, not a tour of combat, and she wasn't complaining. She was known in the unit as someone who hated to see or do violence. "Sabrina literally would not hurt a fly," her team leader, Sergeant Hydrue Joyner, said. "If there's a fly on the floor and you go to step on it, she will stop you." Specialist Jeremy Sivits, a mechanic in the company's motor pool, said, "We'd try to kill a cricket because it kept us up all night in the tent. She would push us out of the way to get to this cricket, and would go running out of the tent with it. She could care less if she got sleep, as long as that cricket was safe." That made Sivits laugh, but he worried that she wouldn't survive a firefight. Joyner agreed. "As a soldier, you can't allow your heart to get in the way sometimes, because the moment you do, you may get killed, or may get someone else killed," he said. "Sabrina, I think, would have made a better humanitarian than a soldier, and I don't mean that in a negative way." Sivits couldn't figure why she'd joined the military. "She was just too nice to be a soldier," he said.

Harman said she became an MP because the Army would help pay for college, and because she wanted to become a cop. Her dad and her brother were cops. Her idea was to become a forensic photographer. Pictures had always fascinated her—taking them and being in them. She made an album of the snapshots people took of her: a baby propped beside the dog on a green plaid sofa; a diapered toddler in a blue knit cap sitting beside a yellow telephone, her mouth wide open with mirth; a little girl—maybe four or five—with perfectly combed and bobbed bangs, kneeling in an elaborately frilled dress, white stockings, and white gloves on a green carpet against a studio backdrop of rampantly blooming cherry trees; a girl laughing, a girl riding a pony, a girl with a puppy, a girl with a stuffed animal, a girl with a horse, a girl with a big old dog; a blurry girl with long hair and bangs bending over a blurry table to blow out the candles of a blurry birthday cake; a girl ready for Halloween, looking out through the eyeholes of a homemade black dog costume; a girl at the beach, a girl under a Christmas tree; a teenage girl, heavily made-up, with big hair in a big perm, all wings and waves; a teenage girl, ponytailed and kneeling on the grass beneath a weeping willow tree, in a uniform of blue-plaid kilt and yellow polo shirt, holding a field hockey stick; a teenage girl with head shorn to a close, boyish crop, wearing dungarees and boots and a loose, oversized flannel shirt beneath a loose black leather motorcycle jacket; a young woman squinting in a sun-blasted parking lot, wearing full camouflage—helmet, flak jacket, cargo pants—and carrying a riot baton. It was an ordinary life in pictures, except for one thing: the directness with which she met the camera, eye to eye, looking frankly through the lens as if she were the one taking the picture.

She liked to look. She might recoil from violence, but she was drawn to its aftermath. She could look at pretty much anything, and when others would want to look away she'd want to look more closely. Wounded and dead bodies fascinated her. She made no secret of it. "She would not let you step on an ant," Sergeant Javal Davis said. "But if it dies, she'd want to know how it died." And taking pictures fascinated her. "Even if somebody is hurt, the first thing I think about is taking photos of that injury," she said. "Of course, I'm going to help them first, but the first reaction is to take a photo."

In July she wrote home to her father, "On June 23 I saw my first dead body. I took pictures! The other day I heard my first grenade go off. Fun!" She paid a visit to the Al Hillah morgue, and took pictures: a body, just arrived and drenched in undimmed blood; mummified bodies, smoked by decay, blackened here and ashen there; extreme close-ups of their ghastly faces, their lifeless hands, the torn flesh and bone of their wounds; a punctured chest, a severed foot. The photographs are ripe with forensic information. About Harman, they tell us only that she wasn't squeamish, and they suggest that she was enthralled.

She also had her picture taken at the morgue, leaning over one of the blackened corpses, her sun-flushed cheek inches from his crusted eye sockets. She is smiling—a forced but lovely smile—and her right hand is raised in a fist, giving the thumbs-up. But for the setting, she is a vividly wholesome-looking twenty-six-year-old. Another photograph from Al Hillah shows that same thumbs-up picture of Harman at the morgue taped to a wall at the date factory, below a sign that says AUTHORIZED PERSONNEL ONLY! TRESPASSERS WILL BE VIOLATED, and a decal of the American flag stamped with the Web address of Black Hawk Industries ("the world's finest tactical gear"), and a tampon stained to look used. Soldiers' humor. If the picture troubled anybody, nobody gave Harman any trouble about it.

"I kind of picked up the thumbs-up from the kids in Al Hillah," Harman said. "Whenever I get into a photo, I never know what to do with my hands, so I probably have a thumbs-up because it's just something that automatically happens. Like when you get into a photo, you want to smile." There are at least twenty photos from Al Hillah in which she appears in the identical pose—same smile, same thumbs-up: bathing in an inflatable wading pool; holding a tiny lizard; standing at the foot of a wall that bears a giant bas-relief of Saddam (the button of his suit jacket is bigger than her head); fooling around with her buddy, Specialist Megan Ambuhl, who is giving her the finger and flashing a tongue stud; holding a tiny figurine of Jesus; holding a long, phallic melon; mounting the ancient stone lion of Babylon at the ruins of King Nebuchadnezzar's city; leaning over the shoulder of an MP buddy who is holding a Fanta can on top of which sits a dead cat's head; and so on.

The cat's head was another of Harman's gags. She had a kitten that was killed by a dog, and since it had no visible wounds, she performed a rough autopsy, discovered organ damage, and then she mummified its head. She gave it pebbles for eyes, and photographed it in various inventive settings: on a bus seat with sunglasses; smoking a cigarette; wearing a tiny camouflage boonie hat; floating on a little pillow in the wading pool; with flowers behind its ears. She took more than ninety photographs and two short videos of it. The series, in its weird obsessiveness, achieves a dark comedy. At one time or another at least fifteen of Harman's fellow MPs posed for photos with the cat head, including the company's deputy commander, Captain Christopher Brinson, and several other senior officers. More than a dozen Iraqi men and boys also took the time to have their pictures taken with it. The cat head had become a fetish object, like the dead cat that Tom Sawyer and Huckleberry Finn barter over—a scene that Norman Rockwell illustrated in a folksy print, entitled: "Lemme see him, Huck. My, he's pretty stiff!"

"She's a happy-go-lucky person," Specialist Sivits said of Harman. "She likes to have fun. She's fun to be around. I've never seen an ounce of anger out of that girl." And much of her photo album from Al Hillah looks like a fantasy travel brochure for post-Saddam Iraq: here she is, skin aglow and beaming her radiant smile, her short curls golden and eyes startlingly blue, amid swarms of joyous Iraqi children— children clambering into her lap, children throwing arms around her, children mobbing her in the streets; here she is welcomed into local homes, sipping little glasses of coffee with head-scarfed women and mustached men in dishdashas, gathered beneath ceiling fans; here she is visiting the antiquities, with a Bedouin and his camel at the ziggurat of Borsippa, and with fellow soldiers at the Ishtar Gate of Babylon; and here she is in camouflage, with her arm around a pregnant woman swathed in black—her hand on the future-full belly, the woman grinning.

Harman bought her Iraqi friends clothes and food and toys. She bought one family a refrigerator, and made sure it was stocked. "A few of us called her Mother Teresa," Sergeant Jeffery Frost said, and Sergeant Joyner said, "The Iraqi kids—you couldn't go anywhere without them saying, 'Sabrina, Sabrina.' They just loved themselves some Sabrina. She'd get these kids balloons, toys, sodas, crackers, cookies, snacks, sweet rolls, Ho Hos, Ding Dongs, Twinkies, she didn't care. She would do anything she could to make them kids smile."

But while Al Hillah was an uncommonly welcoming place to be an American troop in the summer of 2003, the welcome was brittle. The Americans weren't bringing the Iraqis what they had promised: a new order. The war wasn't over, Iraq had no government, the liberators had become occupiers, and the occupation was slapdash, improvised, and inadequate—at best a disappointment, and more often an insult. So, in the fever heat, month after month of a hundred ten and a hundred twenty degrees, alienation set in. Frustration gave way to hostility, hostility gave way to violence, and by summer's end the violence was increasingly organized. It was demoralizing. Every Iraqi might be the enemy. What was the point of being there, unwanted? Nobody from the 372nd was killed in Al Hillah, but on patrols there was shooting, in the night there were explosions, and Harman had her nightmare. At least the picnic tables had seemed to her purely fanciful, the random furniture of dreamscapes, until she got to Abu Ghraib.

AFTER FOUR MONTHS IN AL HILLAH, the 372nd MPs had thought they were done with Iraq and about to go home—half the company had already pulled back to Kuwait—when the word came down that they were redeploying to the prison. For the sake of security, the order was given, as always, at the last minute. All that any of the MPs knew about the place was that it was on the front lines: officially designated Forward Operating Base Abu Ghraib.

To get there you had to travel some of the deadliest roads in the country, heavily bombed and frequently ambushed. The MPs received proper Interceptor vests just in time for the trip, replacing the twenty-five-year-old Army surplus flak jackets without ballistic plates, which they'd been lucky not to need in Al Hillah. But their Humvees were still thin-skinned; none had been up-armored to shield against the IED booby traps and rocket-propelled grenades that had left the road-sides cluttered with wreckage. When the convoy stopped in a small town along the way to wait for stragglers, all anyone could do to buf-fer the fear was pray or curse.

"You die if you stop," said Tim Dugan, a civilian interrogator who worked at Abu Ghraib that fall. On his way there from the airport, his driver had almost run over some kids who looked liked they might be trying to make him slow down for an ambush.

"We seen a sign saying 'Fallujah'—right there, next town over—and we're like, 'Yo, we're right in the heart of it now,' " Sergeant Javal Davis said. "Downtown Baghdad is right to the back wall. Al Ramadi, the other hot-spot town, is right up to the west of us, not too far. We're right in the heart of the insurgency."

The prison squatted on the desert, stark and vast, a wall of sheer concrete traced with barbed wire and picketed by watchtowers. "Like something from a Mad Max movie," Davis said. "Just like that—like, medieval. We went through the walls, and it's nothing but rubble, blown-up buildings, dogs running all over the place, rabid dogs, burnt remains. The stench was unbearable—urine, feces, body rot." Then there were the prisoners, clad in orange, crowded behind concertina wire. "The encampment they were in when we saw it at first looked like one of those Hitler things almost," Davis said. "They're there, in their little jumpsuits, outside in the mud. Their restrooms was running over. It was just disgusting. You didn't want to touch anything. What-ever the worst thing that comes to your mind, that was it—the place you would never, ever, ever, ever send your worst enemy."

The MPs were told to make themselves at home in one of Sad-dam's old prison blocks, a compound ravaged by looters and invaded by the desert: the sand lay several inches deep in places, mixed with decomposing trash. Moving in meant digging out and sweeping up, and when you'd purged the debris—weird stuff, some of it, for instance used syringes, that just made you wonder—what you had left were prison cells. The military term of art for the place where soldiers sleep and bathe and eat on base is LSA, which means Life Support Area, and at other forward operating bases around Iraq, an LSA meant climate-controlled tents and a mess hall, electricity and hot water, a gym and Internet café, phones, satellite television, a PX shop, fast-food joints. A proper LSA is an outpost of the motherland, and it affirms the sense of pride and tribe that is essential to morale and discipline. At Abu Ghraib, when the 372nd MPs arrived, showers were wooden sheds with drums of cold water propped overhead. The unit had no field kitchen, so chow was combat rations—MREs, meals ready to eat—breakfast, lunch, and dinner in a cardboard box: chicken, pork, pasta, beef patty, omelette, sandwich, chicken, pork, chicken.

Nobody had expected luxury after Al Hillah, but the MPs' morale was low to begin with—all anybody really wanted to know was when they were going home—and there was something about living in cells at Abu Ghraib that never stopped feeling wrong. "We had some kind of incinerator at the end of our building," Specialist Megan Ambuhl said. "It was this huge circular thing. We just didn't know what was incinerated in there. It could have been people for all we knew, bodies." Javal Davis was not in doubt. "It had bones in it," he said, and he called it the crematorium. "But hey, you're at war," he said. "Suck it up or drive on." That was a mantra in Iraq. Of course you couldn't drive on. And, parked in a prison cell at Abu Ghraib, you couldn't help but feel outcast and forsaken.

The autumn nights were getting cold in the desert, down to forty degrees, which felt colder in a concrete box where the wind blew in through empty window frames. From those windows in some of the cells you could look out over the prison's perimeter wall into the windows of an apartment complex in the city of Abu Ghraib, and the people in those apartments could look back at you. As they unpacked their kit in their new quarters, the MPs were told that snipers sometimes made use of this arrangement to shoot into the prison. The trick was not to make yourself a target: stay away from the windows, keep your lamps dim and covered—don't cast a shadow.

7.

ONE OF THE FIRST THINGS the 372nd MPs were told as they arrived at Abu Ghraib in early October was that two MI guys had just been killed, and it didn't take long before they had their own but-for-this and but-for-that stories of near misses. "A few nights after we got here," Sabrina Harman wrote to Kelly, "we were sitting in a meeting, heard three thumps then an explosion." A firefight ensued. "Next day," Harman wrote, "found out it was an IED (bomb planted in a coke can wired to a clicker) blew up a vehicle (no one hurt), then they chased down the three men that did it and killed them."

It was said that Abu Ghraib was the most-attacked American base in Iraq at the time, and it may have been. There were days and nights that fall when no mortars hit the prison, but not many; and between the mortars there were rocket-propelled grenades and small-arms fire. The prison certainly made an obvious target for insurgents: immense and immobile and poorly defended, an outpost of the military occupation in its most despised aspect—literally holding Iraqis captive.

"Mortars. Rockets," Javal Davis said. "They would go right to that field across from the prison, and jerry-rig up some PVC pipe, or have some guys in a pickup truck driving down the road dropping them in a tube, shooting them at you. And you'll hear it. *Thunk. Chhh. Boom.* You're walking around in your compound. Next thing you know, all you hear is *shoooooo-boom.* Incoming! Everyone was yelling, Incoming! *Boom.* Incoming! Incoming! You've got to run for hard cover."

"Everything is so quiet, and then all of a sudden stuff just starts exploding, and everything gets frantic," Jeremy Sivits said. "Everything goes crazy. You're running around, trying to get cover. You're bumping into people. You lose track of what you're doing." And hard cover was not a guarantee of safety: some mortars could pierce concrete. "One pierced the roof of the hard site," Javal Davis said. "Pierced the roof, went right to the floor—but it didn't explode. Soldiers in there were like, 'Holy crap.'"

At first the attacks came at nightfall, around the time that the muezzins' call to prayer was broadcast from loudspeakers atop nearby minarets. "When the mosque was playing, that was 'mortar o'clock,' " Sabrina Harman said. "There was a loudspeaker right behind our compound. It sounds beautiful. In Al Hillah it was kind of soothing and relaxing, but the mortars don't sound nice with it. When they were praying, that's when you knew you were going to get hit at Abu Ghraib."

But with time, the bombardments ceased to adhere to such a predictable schedule. "We were pretty sure—as sure as we could be—that we were pretty safe during the daytime," Andrew Stoltzman said. "Then I remember brushing my teeth in the morning, and all of a sudden mortars started coming in. It brought a whole new set of worries." And Harman said, "I was more afraid of walking outside or going to take a shower. I pretty much didn't. I would use baby wipes. I kind of went infantry for the time I was there, maybe shower once or twice a month if I had to. The showers were outside. They were made of wood, and if a mortar hit, you were going to die. You had to go to the showers and the bathroom with your flak vest on. If I could've peed inside, I probably would have."

"One time, a rocket attack took out an entire motor pool from the 320th MP company," Javal Davis said. "All their trucks, done—it went through the glass, busted all their tires. There was a couple of guys in the port-a-johns. One guy got peppered down his leg. Luckily he was in the farthest one down. If he was in the port-a-john at the end, he'd have been dead on the john. That was his nickname—I called him Dead Man on the John. It was kind of funny." Then he said, "It wasn't funny at all." At Abu Ghraib, Davis said, even sleep was no refuge. He hated the thought that he could be killed without knowing it: "I always used to say, 'God, if I go out, if I have to die, don't take me in my sleep. I want to feel it.' "

The soldiers had bomb shelters, and a drill to follow during an attack: run, grab your body armor, run, crowd into the shelter, and wait. After a while, hardly anybody bothered. Fatalism set in. "If you get hit, you get hit," Harman said. "There was really nothing you could do if they got lucky." And Tim Dugan, the civilian interrogator, said, "The best way to function about this stuff is, you got to consider yourself dead. If you come back, you're just a lucky bastard, but while you're there, if you consider yourself already dead, you can do all the shit you have to do and not be worried about it."

As Lieutenant Colonel Jordan had learned, survival can be as accidental as death, and for the most part, the mortars fell on empty space: nobody was hurt, no property damaged. In fact, after the September 20 attack, no soldiers were killed or seriously wounded inside the prison in 2003, but the randomness and imprecision of the persistent shelling only heightened the sense that nowhere was safe. "You were just on pins and needles, wondering when it was going to happen," Megan Ambuhl said. "Then, if it didn't happen for a day or two, you're waiting for it to happen, wondering why it hasn't happened. So it was just as much stress if it didn't as when it did."

———

"IT'S NOT LIKE WE COULD SHOOT BACK," Sabrina Harman said. "Not without orders, you couldn't shoot back. It wasn't like a prisoner. You could shoot them, which doesn't make sense. But if they're shooting from outside the compound, you can't."

The order to return fire was only given when MPs in the watchtowers had direct visual contact with someone attacking the prison. "You can't see if he's shooting from two miles away from a tube," Javal Davis said. "All you hear is the thump of the round being shot, and you have to wait for it to hit, that's it. Once they found out that all we could shoot up was parachute flares, it was, Hey, thanks for lighting up our position, now we'll just continue pounding the hell out of your compound. And to be jerk-offs about it, they started shooting up parachute flares just to mess with us. Because they knew that we couldn't shoot back."

In late September, a contingent of the 82nd Airborne arrived at Abu Ghraib to help defend the prison, but the mortar attacks only increased. "One time I was in the guard tower, listening on the radio," Davis said. "We had a counterambush team from the 82nd Airborne out in the field. They were patrolling, they were taking fire, they were on the radio, calling in for fire. Denied. 'Sir, we're taking hits, we're getting hit, we have men down. We need indirect fire support like right now.' Denied. 'Sir, goddamn it, we need indirect fire support, we need it now.' 'You better watch your tone on this radio, you're talking to a colonel,' or whatever he was. Denied. That night, we had two guys got killed. They came in, their truck was riddled with bullets, and one of the soldiers lost his leg from the knee up because his truck got shot head-on by a rocket-propelled grenade.

"After a while, the fear goes away, and you just get angry," Davis said. Then he said, "You know those games when you go to the fair and you got the little duck running across and you got to shoot it with the air pistol?" At Abu Ghraib, he said, everybody was that bird—not a sitting duck, who is enviably unaware of being hunted. "You've got to keep moving," he said. "You can barely sleep. You're always thinking."

Of course, the prisoners in the tented camps couldn't move. Their helplessness was absolute. And as mortars kept falling on Abu Ghraib, prisoners kept getting killed and maimed. These casualties were promptly recorded in Serious Incident Reports on the military security networks. Then the dead were removed and their remains were sent to a morgue, while the wounded were treated at the prison clinic or, if the damage was severe, evacuated to a hospital before being returned to the camps. The Americans running the prison knew that it was their duty to protect their prisoners, and they knew that at Abu Ghraib that was impossible. It was a crime to hold prisoners in such conditions. But there they were, and the understanding among the soldiers was that if these prisoners weren't there, they might be the ones firing the mortars.

During their orientation at Abu Ghraib, some of the 372nd MPs were given a tour of the outdoor camps by guards from the company they were replacing. "They brought these two guys forward, saying, 'Tell them what you told us,' " Megan Ambuhl said. "They told us that they were here to kill us, and that's what they would attempt even inside the prison." That was the message, she said: "Don't turn your back on anybody, because they're all possible terrorists, even the children."

THE 372ND MPS ASSUMED that they had been sent to Abu Ghraib because it was dangerous. They were combat MPs, trained to support the operations of front-line forces—to conduct route reconnaissance, escort convoys, run patrols, go on raids. They were heavily armed and traveled with a fleet of heavy vehicles. "We're trigger pullers," Javal Davis said. "We're out on the battlefield. We do everything that infantrymen would do except go straight into combat. So we thought we were going to go kick some behind around the prison and help them out. But that's not what happened. Once we got there, they told our guys, No—we're going to be prison guards."

The new assignment bewildered the company. Combat units don't run prisons. That is the province of another cadre of MPs—internment and resettlement MPs—who are schooled in the Geneva Conventions. The 372nd MPs had no such training. A couple of them had experience as corrections officers back home, but the rest didn't know the first thing about prison work. Their company commander, Captain Donald Reese, was a window-blinds salesman in civilian life. How could he lead his troops on a mission he didn't know how to perform? Reese told the MP operations chief at Abu Ghraib, Major DiNenna: It's not right, this isn't our job, we don't have the soldiers for it.

DiNenna understood. He didn't have the soldiers either. The prison kept expanding; construction was incessant as new compounds were added to Camp Ganci and Camp Vigilant, and new cell blocks were opened at the hard site to accommodate the daily truckloads of new prisoners rounded up by the 4th Infantry Division's increasingly aggressive and indiscriminate security sweeps. The inmate population nearly doubled in October, and DiNenna's forces were overwhelmed, working around the clock in twelve-hour shifts, with no days off. It wasn't unusual to have as few as three MPs guarding a compound of five hundred prisoners in the outdoor camps. Combat MPs, too, were desperately overextended running perimeter security and road protection for supply and transport convoys in the face of intensifying insurgent attacks. And most of the MPs were reservists, who had to be

sent home after twenty-four months, so those who had been mobilized in the aftermath of September 11 were starting to leave. Unlike
the regular Army, the Reserves had no system to replace soldiers who
timed-out. When DiNenna lost a troop—that was that.

Running Abu Ghraib required a siege mentality: DiNenna was
making cooks and mechanics and supply troops pull MP duty, and
now he was about to lose an entire internment and resettlement company. The 72nd MPs, a National Guard unit that had been guarding
Camp Vigilant and the hard site, were going home to Nevada, and
DiNenna told Captain Reese that the 372nd had to take their place.
"I made the recommendation that he use his civilian correctional officers, put them in charge of the hard site prison—because they understand the concept and the process of how you operate a jail
cell—and they would train the other MPs who worked with them,"
DiNenna said. "And that's how it was." Or, as Javal Davis put it, "A
major outranks a captain, so we were prison guards now."

A sergeant of the 72nd MPs led the soldiers whom Reese assigned
to the hard site on a tour of the place. He showed them the CPA cell
blocks for Iraqi criminals, and the Military Intelligence block, where
the high-value prisoners were held on Tier 1A. "That's when I saw
the nakedness," Javal Davis said. "I'm like, 'Hey, Sarge, why is everyone naked?' You know—'Hey, that's the MI. That's what the MI does.
That's the MI thing. I don't know.' 'Why do these guys have on
women's panties?' Like—'It's to break them.' "

"They had a guy that had his back against the bars, and they
had bent him over and handcuffed him to the bottom part of the
bars," Sergeant Jeffery Frost said. "So he couldn't stand up straight,
and he wasn't allowed to sit down, either." One of the 72nd MPs
told Frost that this was the way to deal with uncooperative prisoners: "Just have them stand there for an hour or so. Or have them
stand there naked. And if you wanted to go ahead and completely

strip them, have a female do it, because that would be even more humiliating."

"Guys naked," Davis said. "Guys in women's panties. Guys handcuffed in stress positions, in isolation cells, no lights, no windows. Open the door, turn the light on—'Oh my God, Allah.' Click, turn the light off, close the door. It's like, whoa, what is that? What the hell is up with all this stuff? Something's not right here."

A DELEGATION OF THE INTERNATIONAL Committee of the Red Cross visited the MI block of the hard site between October 9 and 12, 2003, and had much the same reaction as Javal Davis. The Geneva Conventions require that ICRC delegates be given unrestricted access to military prisons, to monitor conditions, and to interview prisoners in private. At Abu Ghraib, however, they reported that there were "many obstacles" to their mission, "imposed, apparently at the behest of Military Intelligence," and what they were permitted to see did not please them. On Tier 1A they found a number of prisoners naked in their cells, and immediately alerted Lieutenant Colonel Jerry Phillabaum, the MP commander at the prison. Phillabaum later told Army investigators that he took the matter straight to Lieutenant Colonel Jordan, and that Jordan advised him that keeping prisoners naked was a common practice on the MI block. But the prisoners were given clothes for the remainder of the ICRC visit, and the delegates were able to talk to them and learn how they were handcuffed painfully, held naked in bare, lightless cells, paraded naked down the hallways, verbally and physically threatened, and so forth. The Red Cross was not reassured when MI officers explained that these abuses were part of the interrogation "process," and the delegates were indignant to learn that there were some prisoners whom they would not be allowed to see at all. They broke off their visit in a deadlock with the prison authorities, demanding that Geneva be respected when they returned to complete their tour later in the month.

The 372nd MPs took over from the 72nd three days later, on October 15. On the night shift, which ran from four in the afternoon until four in the morning, Staff Sergeant Ivan "Chip" Frederick was named the noncommissioned officer in charge of the whole compound; Javal Davis was the NCOIC of Tiers 1A and 1B; Megan Ambuhl was his junior officer, with particular responsibility for 1B, which housed women and children as well as the MI overflow from 1A; and there was one MP assigned to each of the other cell blocks, plus a runner who filled in wherever help was needed. That made seven MPs for as many as a thousand prisoners, and Sergeant Frederick was the only one who had ever worked in a prison.

By way of on-the-job training, the new guards had spent a couple of days shadowing their predecessors on their rounds. Frederick was surprised when he saw one of the 72nd MPs reach into a cell, grab an elderly prisoner by his long white beard, and yank him forward into the bars. The prisoner, who was known as Santa Claus, was said to be mentally unstable, but nobody objected to his treatment. He had been whining, and the first rule on the tier was no talking. Besides, Frederick said, he "didn't hit the bars hard."

Beyond such instruction by example, Frederick said, his orientation had consisted of being told how to turn the water and electricity on and off. There was no mention of the Geneva Conventions or U.S. military doctrine on internment or interrogation. There were no written regulations for the MI cell block, and when Frederick asked for a copy of the prison's standard operating procedure, all he got was the MPs' one-page rules of engagement, which described the steps for escalating the use of force in a dangerous confrontation:

shout, show, shove, shoot. "It had nothing to do with handling the detainees," he said.

"That's it—one piece of paper," Megan Ambuhl said. In contrast, she said, "Sergeant Frederick explained to me that the standard operating procedure at his prison in Virginia would have been as high as him, and he's six foot at least. Every little situation will be outlined in an SOP. But we were put into a situation where we had no training, we were vastly outnumbered, and we were given lots of responsibilities that we didn't have any knowledge about how to carry out. It was like putting you into an operating room and saying 'Okay, go ahead and do open-heart surgery. And hope you do a good job of it. And by the way, I'm not going to train you for it. And I'm not going to give you any procedures to do it. And if you do it wrong, well, then you're going to face consequences for it. Wait a minute, we'll give you one piece of paper, one general rule—use a knife, maybe some antiseptic. Good luck.' "

FOLLOWING HIS VISIT TO ABU GHRAIB from Guantánamo Bay in early September, Major General Geoffrey Miller had urged the Baghdad command to "develop a comprehensive set of detention physical security SOPs for MPs" and "conduct training for detention center leadership and staff on the implementation of these procedures." To that end, Miller said he had provided General Sanchez's headquarters with a copy of the Gitmo SOP, a two-hundred-and-thirty-seven-page book, published under his signature, which dictated step-by-step the way MPs should execute every task in their assigned routine and how they should respond to every manner of possible emergency, from attempted or actual suicides to power outages, hostage situations, fratricide (the killing of one U.S. soldier by another), mass casualty incidents, and destructive weather.

There is no record of what General Sanchez's office did with the Gitmo SOP. But Sanchez's interrogation policy for Abu Ghraib gave interrogators total authority over their prisoners, and by extension over MPs as well. On its first page, the policy states: "The interrogator should appear to be the one who controls all aspects of the interrogation, to include the lighting, heating and configuration of the interrogation room, as well as the food, clothing and shelter given to the security internee." And, on the last page, the policy puts the onus for developing an MI-friendly SOP for Abu Ghraib on the MP units themselves: "Interrogation operations are never conducted in a vacuum; they are conducted in close cooperation with the detaining units. Detention regulations and policies established by detaining units should be harmonized to ensure consistency with the interrogation policies of the intelligence collection unit."

But Sanchez's interrogation policy, which was addressed to the MI brigade, was never distributed to MPs. And MP units don't write SOPs; they follow them. The Gitmo SOP made that clear. It came from the commander, and its table of contents alone ran over more than four tightly spaced two-column pages. The mission was defined, the command structure was mapped, and the responsibilities of every class of soldier explicated. The bureaucracy of record keeping and reporting was spelled out. MPs were told how to search a cell, how—and how not—to search a prisoner's Koran, what to do with keys and with prisoners' laundry, how to oversee a prisoner's haircut, how to micromanage visits by Red Cross delegates, how to deal with medical problems, how to conduct a Muslim funeral, how to enter and leave a gate, how to administer incentives and rewards, how to administer disincentives and punishments, how to avoid contact with prisoners' bodily fluids, and what to do if you fail. There were charts and tables, diagrams and maps, and a fifty-page appendix that presented sample copies of every form of paperwork that MPs were responsible for in running the prison.

An orthodox SOP leaves nothing to the imagination, and as Ambuhl settled into her job, it occurred to her that the absence of a code was the code at Abu Ghraib. "They couldn't say that we broke the rules because there were no rules," she said. "Our mission was to help MI, and nobody ever said, 'This is your SOP.' But that was in a sense what it became, because our job was to stress out the detainees, and help facilitate information to the interrogators, and save the lives of other soldiers out there."

8.

STRESSING OUT THE PRISONERS was hard work. There were different regimes for different MI prisoners. For instance, Javal Davis said, "Cell seven, no sleep. Or, wake up four o'clock, go to bed one o'clock, wake up three o'clock, go to bed five o'clock, wake up—like that, up and down, up and down, up and down." An MI prisoner on a seventy-two-hour sleep deprivation program was supposed to be allowed four hours' sleep for every twenty hours awake. Lieutenant Colonel Jordan heard his soldiers discussing the possibilities: "You could let them sleep for four hours, be up for twenty hours, and be up for another twenty hours, and give them four hours of sleep. So they could be up for forty hours, but they get four hours on either end."

It was up to the MPs to keep the prisoners from nodding off. "The Military Intelligence people would come up there, and say, 'Hey, play music at this time, play it loud,'" Javal Davis said. "If they fall asleep, throw water on them, wake them up. Slam the doors, run up and down with garbage cans, bang on them, make sure they stand up when you walk by, don't sit down, things like that. That was the verbal standard operating procedure. Take the megaphone and stick it right at the door for individual treatment, and just play music, and

cut the lights off and on so they won't know what's up, what's down—
just totally disorient them."

The instructions came largely anonymously, since the prisoners'
MI handlers at the hard site wore "sterile" uniforms, with their name
and rank tags removed or taped-over, or no uniforms at all, just un-
marked T-shirts and sweatshirts. The MPs had no way to tell who the
handlers were, or where they stood in the hierarchy of authority. Javal
Davis said he only knew the nicknames of the two men who most
often told him what to do on Tier 1A: Big Steve, who Davis figured
was nearly six and a half feet tall and must have weighed about two
hundred seventy pounds, and Gitmo Guy. "He told us what he did
over in Guantánamo Bay," Davis said. "Like in Guantánamo Bay, they
don't have no rights, no Geneva Convention, blah blah blah. We were
thinking, Wow—OK."

Most of the MI handlers were soldiers, like Gitmo Guy. But there
had been little demand for Army intelligence missions in the late
twentieth century, and MI's ranks were thin when the Iraq war began.
So, even as more MI soldiers kept arriving, making Abu Ghraib the
largest single MI operation since World War II, scores of civilians on
hire from private security firms in Virginia were brought in to supple-
ment their ranks: interrogators and analysts on the payroll of CACI
International (Big Steve was one of them), and Arabic interpreters
supplied by the Titan Corporation. Although many of these civilians
were veterans with more experience than the MI soldiers at the prison
(and they were all much better paid), they had no standing in the
military chain of command. Nevertheless, they were integrated into
the interrogation "tiger teams," composed of an interrogator, an analyst, and an interpreter, that were assigned to each prisoner.

The directions the MPs were given often seemed as deliberately
vague as the identities of the men who gave them. Sleep manipulation
schedules were supposed to come in writing, and they frequently did,

but the particulars were largely left to the MPs' imagination. Sergeant Jeffery Frost, who worked the day shift on Tier 1A, said, "It was all just word of mouth—MI telling the MPs to soften up a prisoner before they got interrogated, which would involve anything from making them do PT, physical training, just so they got pretty exhausted before they would go to their interview, to just yelling at them for quite a few minutes to shake them up."

The Military Police like to say that MP stands for multipurpose. On Tier 1A that notion was given new meaning. "At first we were supposed to have been babysitters, then we got moved up into condition setters," Davis said. "We got implemented into the plan." And it made him angry, after serving six years as an MP and making sergeant, to be doing MI's dirty work, with nobody watching his back. "Whenever we raised a question, or asked anything to our chain of command pertaining to that particular cell block, the answer would always be, 'Oh, well, that's MI, just do what they tell you to do,'" he said. "The lines were crossed and blurred, just messed up. It was a total leadership failure. We depend on our leaders to make the right decisions, to make our jobs easier. Our leaders failed us, and left us out to dry."

And it wasn't just MI giving orders. Some of the prisoners on the tier were being held by the CID, while still others were being held under the auspices of OGA—"other government agencies"—an acronym that is usually a euphemism for the CIA, but was also used at the prison to describe various other secretive or clandestine investigative outfits, such as the Defense Intelligence Agency, the FBI, Taskforce 121, or Taskforce 6-26. "We called them the ghosts, because you never knew who they are," Javal Davis said. "They didn't wear name tapes. They were allowed to have facial hair, allowed to have beards." OGA prisoners were, in turn, known as ghost prisoners. They were never formally admitted to the prison, or assigned prisoner numbers,

but rather spirited in, usually by night, installed on Tier 1A, interrogated for a day or two, then spirited away. The MPs were supposed
to take care of them, but they weren't supposed to acknowledge their
presence in any official paperwork. "You know—Here's this guy, don't
log him in," Javal Davis said. "Just put him in a cell, and don't mark
it. When the Red Cross comes, hide him somewhere."

With as many as ten OGA ghosts at a time on a tier of forty to
fifty prisoners, the most ordinary routines of guard duty, like the head
count, could quickly get out of whack. "They existed, but didn't
exist, if that makes any sense," Sergeant Joyner said. "They were there,
but weren't there." He didn't like juggling fictional numbers of actual bodies, so he brought a log book to the Tier 1A office, and alongside the official count, the MPs started jotting down the true
count—including the OGA holds, who were sometimes simply referred to as "others." The log quickly became a housekeeping chron-
icle of prisoner feedings and showers, haircuts and cell searches,
disciplinary problems and medical emergencies, power outages and
plumbing failures. This litany can be nightmarish. There is no end of
vomiting and lice, of violent fits subdued, of suicides threatened or
thwarted, of shanks discovered and razor blades wielded. But it is as
a shift-by-shift record of the otherwise undocumented and often
murky comings and goings and demands of the MPs' new bosses, and
of the intimate involvement on the tier of senior MI and MP officers,
that the log is most telling.

In military slang, the first law of survival is CYA: cover your ass.
Joyner started the log because he thought there was wisdom in it.
"Who knows?" he said. "They might be trying to come after me."
And on nearly every page there are notes like these:

> We are holding an inmate in cell 15 for MI. . . . He is not on the
> count. Will only be here overnight after he speaks with MI in the
> morning should be returned to Vigilant.

FBI are interrogating OGA #8 in the stairwell

The 4 new OGAs are in 2, 4, 6 and 8 they are to have no contact
with each other or anyone else—they are not to sleep or sit down
until authorized by OGA personnel also we were informed that all
four are neither hungry nor thirsty.

Attempted again to strip out the following . . . and PT them as per
instruction passed down by Sgt Joyner from Col Jordan but these
were changed by Capt Brinson to have them placed in jumpsuits and
placed in cells. Having them stand in their cells would be their PT.

OGA in—they are going to speak with OGA in 1A-38 over the
next couple of days and needs to be on a disruptive sleep program.

Spoke with LTC Jordan about moving MIs in 1A to make space.
MIs also came here and said to give special treatment to inmate . . .
who was brought in this morning.

ON OCCASION, THE MPS WERE TOLD to treat a prisoner kindly—give
him a better meal or a pack of cigarettes—as a reward or incentive for
cooperation in interrogation. But mostly what interrogators wanted
when they asked for "special treatment" was punishment: take away
his mattress; PT him; keep him awake; take away his clothes. "It was
normal procedure for MI to say, This guy wears panties for a day, or
wears panties for three days, or until he decides to cooperate with us,"
Frost said. There was a big cardboard carton of panties in the supply
cell on Tier 1A, each pair in a plastic slip cover. "They were pink,"
Frost said. "They were almost like a bikini panty. It wasn't a thong,
but it wasn't a full bottom panty either. It was one that showed like

half the cheek. It was like a seventies bikini bottom. So it was kind of skimpy, and it didn't really look well on men."

Frost thought the business with the panties was "kind of odd, but it kind of made sense." He figured that if the idea was to unman someone, a pink panty might be more effective than nakedness. "I've never been trained or read anything on interrogation," he said. "But I would assume humiliation is a tactic for getting someone to cooperate." Not that anybody cared what he thought. "We had no say over anything that they told us to do," Frost said. "It was understood that what MI said went." Still, when it came to the details of PT or sleep deprivation, he said, "A lot of it was at our discretion." You could have prisoners do push-ups or a squatting duck-walk for twenty minutes at a stretch, or you could play a siren through a megaphone, or you could yell in their faces until you wore yourself out, too.

"I started out playing rap music," Javal Davis said. "I'd stick the megaphone to the little speaker, and I'd play rap music for my whole shift, just as loud as I can. I played this song called 'Hip Hop Hurray' over and over and over again. 'Hip hop hurray, ho,' that's what it sounds like. After a while, the Iraqis were saying, 'Hey, ho.' So I put on heavy metal music. I put on Metallica, 'Enter Sandman,' this very loud song." Davis wore ear plugs and noise-canceling headphones, cranked up the volume, and played the sinister lullaby all night: "Sleep with one eye open . . . If I die before I wake / Pray the Lord my soul to take / Hush little baby, don't say a word / And never mind that noise you heard."

"They were screaming, 'Ah, I don't like it,' " Davis said. "But after a while, they were numb to that. I guess they were so deaf from the guitar, the A chord, that they were able to sleep. So I put on country music. That worked. They couldn't stand it. Like, 'Oh my god, Allah, Allah! Cut it off!' So that was the music for me. It was Clint Black. I don't remember the song. All I know is it was slow. He was talking about 'my doggie' or something. They have a lot of fans, country music, but not in that cell block. By the time the interrogators would come to take them out of the cells, they were more than ready to go."

Usually, when a prisoner's tiger team wanted to go to work on him, the MPs would strip-search him and escort him to a small compound called Site Wood, or simply Wood, which stood just outside the tier—six or eight interrogation booths made of plywood, with plastic chairs and a plastic table, a metal eye ring in the floor to which shackles could be fastened, and one-way glass windows for observers to look in from the corridor. But, especially at night, some interrogators preferred doing their business right on the tier, in the cells, or in the showers, or in a chamber under the stairs. "They put a sheet up over the door and for hours and hours and hours, all you would hear is screaming, banging, slamming, and just more screaming at the top of their lungs," Davis said. "When they were done eight, ten hours later, they'd bring the guy out, he'd be halfway coherent, or unconscious. You'd put him back in the cell and they'd say, 'OK, this guy gets no sleep. Throw some cold water on him. We'll be back for him tomorrow.' "

THE MPS ON THE MI BLOCK never learned the prisoners' names. Officially, they referred to their wards by their five-digit prison numbers, but the numbering system was confusing: some prisoners had been given more than one number as they were moved from camp to camp on their way to Abu Ghraib, and some had separate MI numbers that didn't match the MPs' database. Besides, the numbers were meaningless; they told you nothing about a person, which made them hard to remember. So the soldiers gave the prisoners nicknames based on their looks and their behavior. A prisoner who made a shank and tried to stab someone was Shank, and a prisoner who got hold of a razor blade and tried to slash an MP was called Slash. A prisoner who kept spraying himself and his cell with water and was always asking for a broom was Mr. Clean. A prisoner who repeatedly flooded his cell was Swamp Thing.

There was a man they called Smiley, and a man they called Froggy, and a man they called Piggy, and a man they called Twitch on account of his facial tics. There was a man with no fingers on one hand, only a thumb, who was called Thumby—not to be confused with the enormous man called the Claw or Dr. Claw, because one of his hands was forever frozen in a half-clenched curl. The man they called Santa Claus was also called Snowman, and there was a gaunt man they called Gus, but nobody knew why that name had stuck, and he was also sometimes called Mr. Burns, after the skinny villain on *The Simpsons*. There was the man they called Taxi Driver, because he'd been arrested while driving a cab, and there was Gilligan, whom Sergeant Hydrue Joyner said looked just like his television namesake, only Iraqi—"all you needed was the little hat to put on him."

Sergeant Joyner was in charge of the day shift on Tier 1A, and he took credit for giving many of the prisoners their nicknames. "I had one guy whose breath just stank. I called him Yuck Mouth. We had a guy—probably the tallest Iraqi I've ever seen—and his nose kind of looked like Big Bird off *Sesame Street*. I called him Big Bird. I had Trap Jaw, because he had real sharp teeth, looked like he could chew a brick. I had one that I called Gomer Pyle. That was strictly for my entertainment right there. He was a big white Iraqi. I didn't know they had them like that, big white Iraqis." The nicknames made the prisoners more familiar than their numbers ever could, and at the same time the nicknames made them into cartoon characters, which kept them comfortably unreal. "It was jail but, you know, you can still laugh in jail," Joyner said. "It's not a crime, I hope."

Javal Davis was all for laughs, and he enjoyed gallows humor as much as the next guy. The problem was that when you spend your nights doing nasty things to people, you've got to endure them yourself. You could jack yourself up for it—Davis had violence in him, and he found that whaling on men toward whom he had no personal animus could work him into a mounting, generalized rage—but aggression could only get you so far before the depression caught up with it. There were so many ways to torment a prisoner according to MI's demands, and for the most part there was nothing funny about them.

"Smells," Davis said. "Put them in a cell where the toilet is blocked and backed up. It smells like urine and crap. That would drive you nuts." And then there was food. You could keep shifting a prisoner's meal times, or simply withhold meals. The prisoners ate the same MREs that the guards ate, but you could deny them the spoon, and all the fixings. "If you got Salisbury steak, they got the Salisbury steak, not the rice that comes with it, not the hot sauce, not the snack, not the juice—the Salisbury steak, and that's it," Davis said. "They were starving by the time they'd get interrogated. And it would be, 'OK, we'll give you more food if you talk.'"

You could also inflict pain. "You had stress positions, and you escalated the stress positions. Forced to stand for hours at a time. Stand on a box. Hold a box out straight. Hold bottles of water out to your sides. Do the electric chair, put your back to the wall, and bend your knees ninety degrees to hold yourself. Handcuffs behind their backs, high up, in very uncomfortable positions, or chained down," Davis said. "Then you had the submersion. You put the people in garbage cans, and you'd put ice in it, and water. Or stick them underneath the shower spigot naked, and open a window while it was like forty degrees outside, and watch them disappear into themselves before they go into shock."

And, of course, you could combine these treatments. "Mohammed in cell sixty-eight is giving them problems and they decided that they're going to keep him up," Megan Ambuhl said. "And they want him standing. And they only want to allow him fifteen minutes' sleep every four hours, or something like that. And during that fifteen minutes, they're probably going to come interrogate him, or that's when he's going to get food. They're only allowed to have their MRE for, like, fifteen minutes—I'm not sure of the exact time—but by the time he came back, that time was up. So his food was gone and he was back on time to be up."

It was "Gitmo from the get-go," Davis said. "I didn't invent any of these things. These were presented to us. I didn't jump out of the bed in the morning saying, 'Hey, I want to go smack up a detainee,' or, 'Hey, I want to throw ice on people,' or, 'I want to play loud music.' Who would have thought of something like that?"

JAVAL DAVIS HAD JOINED the Army Reserves in 1994, when he was in college. He was impressed by the ROTC drill he saw—"the saluting, about-face, that looked kind of sharp, the rank and file, the order and everything"—and he said, "I was expecting to learn a career field, get some benefits for college, get a step ahead of my peers, get discipline, become a man." He thought it was both an honor and honorable to serve his country, and he was willing to die protecting its freedoms. "Especially after 9/11," he said. He was born and raised in Roselle, New Jersey, just across New York Harbor from the World Trade Center towers. He had won county and state championships in the hundred-ten-meter high hurdle, and he hoped one day to be a

Roselle policeman, or a New Jersey state trooper. "And to see that happen on my own soil," he said. "It turned it up a notch."

But after four or five nights of running Tiers 1A and 1B of the Abu Ghraib hard site, he said, "I just wanted to go home." Instead, Sergeant Frederick transferred him to one of the CPA cell blocks, Tiers 3A and 3B, where he was in charge of four hundred prisoners who had been arrested as criminals but, for the most part, had never been charged or given a court date, and who were as angry about being there as he was. "So I improvised," Davis said. "I got me a detainee who speaks English. I said, 'Tell them everything I'm saying. You all live in a cell. I live in a cell. You all are eating bad food. I'm eating bad food, too. You all want to go home. Hell, I want to know when I'm going home, too. I don't even know when I'm going home. You all are locked up. I'm locked up, too. You all can't see your family. I can't see my family.' From that point, they started to relate with me."

To gain respect and burn off some energy, Davis would strip to the waist and work out in front of his new wards. He could do thirty pull-ups in a set, and a hundred push-ups, and when he was done he'd let a few prisoners out at a time and offer cigarettes to anyone who could do better. He didn't have to give away a lot of cigarettes, but he said the prisoners appreciated it. He organized regular prayer hours for them, and with time, he learned passable Arabic, and they appreciated that, too. Still, sometimes when the prison was under attack and the bombs were falling, the prisoners on the tier would start chanting: "Our souls, our blood, we'll sacrifice for you, oh Saddam." That was one thing Davis would not tolerate. It scared him, he said, and he responded by making sure the prisoners were scared enough of him to cut it out.

Davis had a reputation for yelling at prisoners just as loudly and abusively on his new post as he had on the MI block. Some of the

MPs at the hard site said that he would tell prisoners in vivid terms about how he'd been having his way with their wives and their mothers, and that he threatened to do the same to them. There was also a story about how he drew his gun, took out the bullets, and counted them off, telling prisoners, This one's for you and this one's for you. Sergeant Frost and Sergeant Frederick both told these stories, and Frederick said that from time to time, when they were in-processing new prisoners, Davis would punch one or another of them in the kidneys.

Davis didn't talk about these things, but he didn't pretend that he'd left his anger or his violence behind on the MI block. In fact, he kept going back there. He wasn't the only soldier who had no official business on Tier 1A who liked to stop by to hang out for a while in the course of a night. There was always hot coffee in the office, and a good supply of pogie bait—snack food, cheese and crackers, ramen noodles, all the side dishes and extras that had been stripped out of prisoners' MREs—and 1A was where the action was. Davis hadn't forgotten how shocked he was when he first saw it. "But then," he said, "over time—seeing it every day, day in and day out, and then seeing the MI guys and some of the OGA guys coming in, laughing and joking like it's funny—after a while it became the same thing for myself. Like, man, look at that guy. I bet you don't want to blow up Americans now. I bet you don't want to come shoot at us now. You go from a compassionate guy, saying, 'Hey, don't put that guy in no panties, that's a grown man, what the hell are you doing?' to 'Yeah, you're in the panties now, brother. Don't you feel ashamed now?' "

Davis felt that what he did and saw on the MI block was morally wrong. "But it was reaffirmed and reassured through the leadership— we are at war, this is Military Intelligence, this is what they do—and it's just a job," he said. "So you become numb to it, and it's nothing. It just became the norm. You see it—that sucks. It sucks to be him.

And that's it. You move on." He told himself it was still far better for an Iraqi to be an American prisoner on Tier 1A than for an American to be captured by Iraqi insurgents. And he said, "Anyone who's not in that situation will not understand. If you were there, then most likely you'd understand. That's how I had to look at it."

9.

SABRINA HARMAN ALSO FELT herself growing numb at Abu Ghraib, and at the same time she kept being startled by her capacity to feel fresh shocks. "In the beginning," she said, "you see somebody naked, and you see underwear on their head, and you're like, Oh, that's pretty bad—I can't believe I just saw that. And then you go to bed and you come back the next day, and you see something worse. Well, it seems like the day before wasn't so bad."

Harman was a runner on the night shift at the hard site, filling in where an extra hand was needed. She started out on one of the Iraqi criminal cell blocks. "I really don't remember the first day," she said. "I remember the first day of working in Tier 1A and 1B. I guess the first thing that I noticed was this guy—he had underwear on his head, and he was handcuffed backwards to a window, and they were pretty much asking him questions. That's the first time I started taking photos." This was the prisoner the MPs called Taxi Driver. He was naked except for the underpants on his head. The position he was in—his hands bound behind his back and raised higher than his shoulders, forcing him to bend forward with his head bowed and his weight suspended from his wrists—is known as a Palestinian hanging, on account of its use in Israeli prisons. Later that evening, Taxi Driver was moved to a bed, and Harman took another picture of him there. Then she saw another prisoner, lying on his bed fully dressed, and she photographed him, too.

As far as Harman knew at the time nobody else had taken any pictures on Tier 1A. Later, when she saw a photograph from a few days earlier of a naked man in the corridor, handcuffed to the bars of a cell door, she wasn't surprised. Sergeant Frederick had a camera, and so did Corporal Charles Graner, who had just been brought in to replace Javal Davis as the officer in charge of the night shift on the MI block, and by the end of Harman's first night the three of them had taken at least twenty-five photographs. Most of these pictures show solitary naked prisoners in stress positions, cuffed to the bars of their cells, or stretched and bent forward and backward over bunk beds, with their hands bound to the far railings. Some of the prisoners are hooded with sandbags, some with underpants. One naked man is lying face-down, arms unbound, on a concrete floor. Several photographs show a row of prisoners in orange jumpsuits doing push-ups in the hallway, and in one Sergeant Frederick can be made out, standing in the background. But nobody in any of these photographs appears to be aware of the camera. The pictures have a stark discomfort to them, a sense of silence and an absence of any discernible attitude, which gives them the quality of stolen glimpses of men rendered into hellish statuary.

Harman said she began photographing what she saw because she found it hard to believe. "If I came up to you, and I'm like, 'Hey this is going on,' you probably wouldn't believe me unless I had something to show you," she said. "So, if I say, 'Hey this is going on, look I have proof,' you can't deny it, I guess." That was the impulse, she said: "Just show what was going on, what was allowed to be done."

———

ON THE SAME NIGHT that she started shooting pictures at the hard site, Harman wrote home:

> KELLY,
>
> The days are long here, 12 hour shifts. The prison has been quiet for the past two nights. The night before that another IED went off. No one was killed but it destroyed another Hmvv. None of our unit has been in the mix of the mortars or IEDs. Not yet. Im afraid to leave the prison to go south to use the phones, they plant those IEDs on the roads and set them off as you pass. The sound is unforgettable . . .
>
> The prisoners we have range from theft to murder of a US soldier. Until Redcross came we had prisoners the MI put in womens panties trying to get them to talk. Pretty funny but they say it was "cruel." I don't think so. No physical harm was done. We've even got Sadams sons body guard here. . . . Boy did he fail his job. It sucks working with the prisoners because they all have something wrong. We have people with rashes on their bodies and who-ever is in the cell with them start to get it . . . I spoke too soon, its 3am, there's a firefight outside. Its never going to be calm here! We have guys with TB! That sucks cause we can catch that. Some have STDs. You name it. Its just dirty!
>
> The food <u>sucks.</u> I live off cup o noodles, that's my meals. The meals they serve are T-REX which is out of a box. If I do come home, boy am I going to eat!

The next night Harman was back on the MI block, and she wrote again:

October 20, 03—12:29am

Kelly,

The lights went out in the prison so here we were in the
dark—in the prison. I have watch of the 18 and younger
boys. I hear, misses! Misses! I go downstairs and flash my
light on this 16 year old sitting down with his sandal
smacking ants. Now these ants are Iraqi ants, LARGE! So
large they could carry the family dog away while giving you
the finger! LARGE. And this poor boy is being attacked by
hundreds. All the ants in the prison came to this one boys
cell and decided to take over. All I could do was spray
Lysol. The ants laughed at me and kept going. So here we
were the boy on one side of the cell and me on the other in
the dark with one small flashlight beating ants with our
shoes. . . . Poor kids. Those ants even Im scared of.

So that was the start of my shift. They've been stripping
"the fucked up" prisoners and handcuffing them to the
bars. Its pretty sad. I get to laugh at them and throw corn at
them. I kind of feel bad for these guys even if they are
accused of killing US soldiers. We degrade them but don't
hit and that's a plus even though Im sure they wish we'd
kill them. They sleep one hour then we yell and wake
them—make them stay up for one hour, then sleep one
hour—then up etc. This goes on for 72 hours while we fuck
with them. Most have been so scared they piss on themselves.
Its sad. It's a little worst than Basic training ie: being naked
and handcuffed . . .

But pictures were taken, you have to see them! A sandbag
was put over their heads while it was soaked in hot sauce.

Okay, that's bad but these guys have info, we are trying to get them to talk, that's all, we don't do this to all prisoners, just the few we have which is about 30–40 not many.

The other night at 3, when I wrote you, the firefight . . . 3 killed 6 injured—Iraqis.

. . . Its time to wake them again!!!

And later that same day, on her next night shift, Harman wrote:

Oct 20, 03
10:40pm

Kelly,
Okay, I don't like that anymore. At first it was funny but these people are going too far. I ended your letter last night because it was time to wake the MI prisoners and "mess with them" but it went too far even I can't handle whats going on. I cant get it out of my head. I walk down stairs after blowing the whistle and beating on the cells with an asp to find "the taxicab driver" handcuffed backwards to his window naked with his underwear over his head and face. He looked like Jesus Christ. At first I had to laugh so I went on and grabbed the camera and took a picture. One of the guys took my asp and started "poking" at his dick. Again I thought, okay that's funny then it hit me, that's a form of molestation. You can't do that. I took more pictures now to "record" what is going on. They started talking to this man and at first he was talking "I'm just a taxicab driver, I did nothing." He claims he'd never try to hurt US

soldiers that he picked up the wrong people. Then he
stopped talking. They turned the lights out and slammed the
door and left him there while they went down to cell #4.
This man had been so fucked that when they grabbed his
foot through the cell bars he began screaming and crying.
After praying to Allah he moans a constant short Ah, Ah
every few seconds for the rest of the night. I don't know
what they did to this guy. The first one remained handcuffed
for maybe 1½–2 hours until he started yelling for Allah. So
they went back in and handcuffed him to the top bunk on
either side of the bed while he stood on the side. He was
there for a little over an hour when he started yelling again
for Allah. Not many people know this shit goes on. The only
reason I want to be there is to get the pictures and prove
that the US is not what they think. But I don't know if I can
take it mentally. What if that was me in their shoes. These
people will be our future terrorist. Kelly, its awful and you
know how fucked I am in the head. Both sides of me think
its wrong. I thought I could handle anything. I was wrong.
Sabrina

NOBODY CALLED SABRINA HARMAN Mother Teresa at the Abu Ghraib
hard site. But even on the MI block she retained her reputation as the
blithe spirit of the unit—obviously not a leader, and yet never a true
follower, either; more like a tagalong, the soldier who should never
have been a soldier. The first word that came to Graner when he
thought about Harman was "innocent." That was certainly how she
conceived of herself, even while she steeped in the corruption of Tiers
1A and 1B. So, in her letters from those first nights, as she described

her reactions to the prisoners' degradation and her part in it—ricocheting from childish mockery to casual swagger to sympathy to cruelty to titillation to self-justification to self-doubt to outrage to identification to despair—she managed gradually to subtract herself from the scenes she sketched. By the end of her outpourings she had repositioned herself as an outsider at Abu Ghraib, an observer and recorder, shaking her head, and in this way she came clean to her wife. In this way she preserved her sense of innocence.

Harman said she wanted to be there to get pictures, and she imagined herself producing an exposé—to "prove that the U.S. is not what they think." The idea was abstract, and she had only a vague notion of how to see it through, or what its consequences might be. She said she intended to give the photographs to CNN after she got home from Iraq and out of the army. But she did not pretend to be a whistle-blower-in-waiting; rather, she wished to unburden herself of complicity in conduct that she considered wrong, and in its cover-up, without ascribing blame or making trouble for anyone in particular. And, at the outset—during her first weeks at the hard site—when she photographed what was being done to prisoners, she did not include her fellow soldiers in the pictures. In these images the soldiers are the unseen hand in the prisoners' ordeal; as with crime-scene photographs, which show only victims, we are left to wonder: who done it?

"I wasn't trying to expose actual individuals," Harman said. "I was trying to expose what was being allowed"—that phrase again—"what the military was allowing to happen to other people." In other words, she wanted to expose a policy; and by assuming the role of a journalist she had found a way to ride out her time at Abu Ghraib without having to regard herself as an instrument of that policy. But it was not merely her choice to be a witness of the dirty work on Tier 1A. It was her role. As a woman she was not expected to wrestle prisoners into stress positions or otherwise overpower them, but rather, just by her presence, to amplify their sense of powerlessness. She was there as an instrument of humiliation. "There were times," Graner said, "where I had a prisoner out and was PTing him, and if they were semiclothed or nude, I'd have her with me or within the vicinity just so they'd know—Hey, here's a female and, you know, she's watching—the way we were supposed to be doing that."

The MPs knew very little about their prisoners or the culture they came from, and they understood less. But at Fort Lee, before they deployed, they were given a session of "cultural awareness" training, from which they'd taken away the understanding—constantly reinforced by MI handlers—that Arab men were sexual prudes, with a particular hang-up about being seen naked in public, especially by women. What better way to break an Arab, then, than to strip him, tie him up, and have a "female bystander," as Graner described Harman, laugh at him? American women were used on the MI block in the same way that Major David DiNenna spoke of dogs—as "force multipliers." Harman understood. She didn't like being naked in public herself. To the prisoners, being photographed may have seemed an added dash of mortification, but to Harman, taking pictures was a way of deflecting her own humiliation in the transaction—by taking ownership of her position as a spectator.

Her letters to Kelly functioned in the same way. "Maybe writing home was a release, to help me forget about what was happening," she said. Then, moments later, she said, "I put everything down on paper that I was thinking. That's the only way I can remember things, is letters and photos." The remarks sound contradictory, but Harman seemed to conceive of memory as an external storage device. By downloading her impressions to a document she could clear them from her mind and transform reality into an artifact. After all, she said, that was how she experienced the things she did and saw done to prisoners on Tier 1A: "It seemed like stuff that only happened on TV, not something you really thought was going on. It's just something that you watch and that is not real."

REAL OR UNREAL, participant or bystander, degrader or degraded, overstimulated or numbed out—Harman may have meant no harm, but she seemed to understand that in the malignant circumstances of the MI block that hardly made her benign. Unable or unwilling to reconcile her most disturbing and her most appealing actions and reactions, she sought her equilibrium in equivocation. When she wrote of "both sides of me," she said, "It was military and civilian—the tough side and the non-tough side. You battle out which one is stronger. You're trained to be tough. I was right out of basic, and you're just trained to do what you're told, and to not let things affect you. You're supposed to set all emotions aside, because this is war. I think it's almost impossible. It is emotional."

Megan Ambuhl, who was Harman's best friend and roommate at Abu Ghraib, agreed that emotion was inescapable. But Ambuhl's emotion fed her toughness, and she said she had no quarrel with the brutal practices of Tier 1A: "Not when you take into account that we're being told that's helping to save lives, and you see people are coming in from right outside the wire with their body parts missing, and they need to know who's doing it so they can stop it—and these are your battle buddies." Ambuhl regarded Harman as a little sister, in need of protection. "She was just naive, but awesome," she said, "a good person, but not always aware of the situation." Harman, in turn, called Ambuhl "Mommy," and accepted the verdict of naiveté with equal measures of solace and regret.

Harman's problem was that she wanted to be tough and she wanted to be nice, and she said, "I shouldn't have been there. I mean,

I didn't do what I was supposed to. I couldn't hit somebody. I can't stomach that, ever. I don't like to watch people get hit. I get sick. I know it's kind of weird that I can see a dead person, but I don't like actual violence. I didn't like taking away their blankets when it was really cold. Because if I'm freezing, and I'm wearing a jacket and a hat and gloves, and these people don't have anything on, and no blanket, no mattress, that's kind of hard to see and do to somebody—even if they are a terrorist." In fact, she said, "I really didn't see them as prisoners. I just saw them as people that were pretty much in the same situation I was, just trapped in Abu Ghraib. I told them that we were prisoners also. So we felt how they were feeling."

It was easier to be nice to the women and children on Tier 1B. But, Harman said, "It was kind of sad that they even had to be there." The youngest prisoner on the tier was just ten years old—"a little kid," she said, "he could have fit through the bars, he was so little." This child was not a suspected criminal or terrorist. Rather, like most of the other kids and many of the women there, he was being held as a pawn in the military's effort to capture or break his father. "If we can't get the insurgent leader, we took their kid," Javal Davis said. " 'OK, Akbar, I have your son—your son is in jail, turn yourself in, and we'll let your son go.' I call that kidnapping, but that's what we did."

Megan Ambuhl spoke of the kids as "hostages," and she told the story of a prisoner on Tier 1A—one of Saddam's former generals—whose son was being held in one of the tented camps: "They brought his son in from the outdoor area, and they explained to him that he couldn't say anything, and threatened him: 'Just stand there.' Then they pulled the general out of his cell with a hood on and walked him up to the cell where his son was. They took the hood off, so he could see that his son was there, and then they put it back on and took him away, and they were just gonna use the fact that they had his son, and he knew it." It was Ambuhl's understanding that this practice was one of the more effective ways to make prisoners talk. "Their imagination about what you might do to their child," she said, "will be a pretty motivating factor for somebody."

Still, Harman enjoyed spending time with the kids. She would let them out to run around the tier in a pack, kicking a soccer ball, or she would enlist them to help sweep the tier and distribute meals—special privileges, reserved only for the most favored prisoners on the MI block. The kids never gave her trouble. "They were fun," she said. "They made the time go by faster." Of course, she didn't like seeing children in prison "for no reason, just because of who the father was," but she didn't dwell on that. What was the point? "You can't feel, because you'll just go crazy, so you just kind of blow it off," she said. "You can only make their stay a little bit acceptable, I guess. You give them all the candy from the MREs to make their time go by better. But there's only so much you can do or so much you can feel."

On Tier 1A, instead of candy, Harman liked to sneak cigarettes and doses of Tylenol or ibuprofen to prisoners who were being given a hard time. Small consolations, but these gestures gave her comfort, too, and it pleased her that prisoners sometimes turned to her for help. One night, at the end of her first week at the hard site, Harman was passing through Tier 1A when a prisoner who was handcuffed to his cell bars with his hands over his head called out to her. Sergeant Joyner, who had cuffed the man like that at the end of the day shift as a punishment for talking, had instructed Sergeant Stephen Hubbard, who was substituting for Graner on the tier that night, to uncuff him after twenty minutes. Joyner even wrote the instruction in the log, but Hubbard had ignored it. Six hours had passed. The prisoner was in pain. "His hands were really cold and clammy," Harman said. "I went over to Hubbard and I asked him why the guy was like that. He just said, 'If you have a problem with it you go uncuff him,' which I did." Harman then reported Hubbard to Joyner, and Joyner reported the matter to Frederick, and Frederick banned Hubbard from the tier.

But Harman saw, or had a hand in, many scenes as bad as that strung-up prisoner's plight without complaining. She was generally as forgiving of her buddies as she was of herself. When toughness failed her, and niceness was not an option, Harman took refuge in denial. "That's the only way to get through each day, is to start blocking things out," she said. "Just forget what happened. You go to bed, and then you have the next day to worry about. It's another day closer to home. Then that day's over, and you just block that one out." At the same time, she faulted herself for not being a more enthusiastic soldier when prisoners on Tier 1A were being given the business. She saw other MPs going at it without apparent inhibition, and all she could say was, "They're more patriotic."

10.

IN ADDITION TO RANK AND GRADE, all Army personnel are classified according to something called the Military Occupational Structure, an alphanumeric code that indicates their levels of training, qualification, and clearance for specific job assignments. Corporal Charles Graner's MOS code was 71L, a low rating, which meant he lacked the basic security clearance to wear an MP armband or serve as a military policeman with custody over prisoners. The Army runs or stumbles on such technicalities of doctrine and protocol, and an MOS 71L shouldn't have been allowed even to visit the MI block. But when Sergeant Frederick put him in charge of the night shift on Tiers 1A and 1B, nobody cared.

Of course, nobody wore armbands or any such insignia on the MI block. Sterile uniforms were the style, stripped of all identification. As Graner understood it, anonymity was a security measure: if you're dealing with terrorists, you don't want them to know who you are. "There could be repercussions at home," he said. But he couldn't stand the Iraqi habit of calling out "Mister, Mister"—insistently, like they were the cops, or in pleading tones, like street beggars. "If you wanted my attention, you called me 'Sir,'" he said. He had picked up sufficient Arabic to make his wishes known, and a number of the prisoners on Tiers 1A and 1B also spoke serviceable English. Still, to make sure that there was no misunderstanding, Graner replaced his regulation name tag with a patch in Arabic that said "The Sir."

"My first impression of Graner was that he was an arrogant, loud, and obnoxious type person," Sergeant Frederick said. That was back in Virginia, at Fort Lee. Graner was new to the unit. He was an ex-Marine, a Desert Storm vet, now a Pennsylvania corrections officer, a grown man with more spark in his eyes than most of the kids in the company. He made sure he was noticed, talking up his exploits with women, full of attitude, a gung-ho soldier, and at the same time a prankster (he liked to tell the one about how he spiked a rookie prison guard's coffee with mace); he came on as a bit of a bad boy, not a misfit but a maverick, always ready to take a poke at pomp and hypocrisy, and he didn't care who heard him.

Never mind regulation spit shines and grooming and the official sexlessness of the Army: Graner liked a little hair on his head and a bit of bristle in his mustache, and pretty soon he had a girlfriend in the unit, Private First Class Lynndie England, and he let it be known that he took authority on his own terms—when it earned his respect. Frederick, who loved a fiercely starched and creased uniform, said, "The best I can explain is, he knew the rules, but he would always look for a way around the rules to explain why he did or didn't do something."

Frederick's initial take on Graner hadn't changed entirely, but in Al Hillah the two men became friends. They moved out of the date factory—"it was screaming hot in there, and the birds would shit on you," Frederick said—and set up a tent on the loading dock of an adjacent building, where they installed a TV and a DVD player and surround sound. Frederick had the higher rank, but he was relatively unassertive, more of a go-along-and-get-along officer than a natural leader, and he felt the excitement in Graner's unruliness. He told the story of a night in Al Hillah when there was a blackout: the soldiers had to find their way around with phosphorescent chem-lights, and Graner declared Naked Chem-Light Tuesday.

"He pulled his shorts out, broke a chem-light, poured the liquid into his shorts, on his penis and everything, then paraded himself around," Frederick said. Nobody else went that far, but the idea caught on. "We were using the chem-light liquid to put marks on people and watch them glow—like smiley faces, skeletal heads, stuff like that," Frederick said. Even First Sergeant Brian Lipinski, who was always on Graner's case about his thing with Lynndie England, was there, and Frederick said, "Pretty much everybody was laughing and trying to relax." That was Graner: balls out, taking the lead.

IT WASN'T ALL GOOD TIMES in Al Hillah. Out on security patrols, when the tension was high, some of the MPs became a law unto themselves and made Iraqis feel their power. Sergeant Jeffery Frost talked about the time that some guys from the unit who got cut off in traffic hauled the offending driver out of his truck with a gun in his face and knocked him around before continuing on their way. And once, during an altercation at a gas station, Frost said, Javal Davis punched out an older Iraqi. "But if we went to our chain of command and said, 'Hey, this is happening,' nothing would get done about it." In July, Specialist Jeremy Sivits wrote home to his dad, a veteran of three tours in Vietnam, and asked what to do when a senior NCO he admired went berserk. During a night patrol Sivits had watched as the unnamed officer confronted an Iraqi policeman and "choke slammed" him against a truck. Sivits had wondered which of the two men he should be ready to shoot. "I tell you," he wrote, "this WAR play hell on you're mind." Sergeant Frederick didn't need to be told. He said he'd gone on a raid in which a bunch of Iraqis were taken

captive and lined up on their knees with their hands on their heads
and foreheads pressed to a wall. One of the prisoners wouldn't shut
up, and Captain Brinson had gone over to talk to him, when—
smack!—Specialist Matthew Smith hit the prisoner in the head. The
blow was loud, "so hard it shocked me," Frederick said. He was surprised that nobody pulled Smith away or even objected.

None of these incidents involved Graner, who seemed more interested in sex than in violence, and Frederick said he assigned him to
the MI block because of his experience as a prison guard. But Graner
however found that his civilian training wasn't of much use at Abu
Ghraib. "I had come in with a correctional officer's mind-set of care,
custody, and control, and I'm going to do the least amount of work
possible and get paid for it because that's what corrections officers
do," he said. "And that lasted for about a day, and then I met Big
Steve." Big Steve was the CACI contract interrogator whom Javal
Davis identified as one of his primary MI tutors on Tier 1A. His
proper name was Steven Stefanowicz, he was a former petty officer in
the Navy, and he had never conducted an interrogation before he arrived at Abu Ghraib in October with a six-figure salary. But his im-
posing physical stature gave him an aura of authority. "He seemed
like he was in charge," Graner said. "You know, he walked into the
room, he commanded the room." So when Big Steve told him to get
with the program, Graner listened.

Big Steve wanted to see Taxi Driver and a couple of other prisoners—Smiley and Piggy—broken, and he explained what that meant:
the yelling, the nudity, the manhandling. Graner was reminded of the
popular television series *24,* whose post–September 11 hero is regularly forgiven for committing crimes, including torture, in the cause
of protecting America from terrorism. He said he told Big Steve, "We
don't do that stuff, that's all TV stuff," and Big Steve told him that
Taxi Driver had been involved in the plot to blow up the UN headquarters in Baghdad in mid-August, which killed the UN envoy,

Sergio de Mello, and twenty-one others. That "tugged on the heart-strings," Graner said. Nevertheless, he said, he checked with his company's deputy commander, Captain Brinson, to make sure he should be doing Big Steve's bidding, and he said Brinson told him, "On 1A, we work for MI—our mission is to support MI."

Graner said that Lieutenant Colonel Jordan and Chief Warrant Officer Ed Rivas—MI's "big people involved in the block"—told him the same thing: "Whatever you're doing is OK." Jordan was on Tier 1A "basically every day," and Chief Rivas also checked in regularly, so they both saw "everything that went on," Graner said, and "everything seemed to be fine." Graner said that he was always asking what was allowed, and Rivas instructed him to take his lead from Sergeant James Beachner, the MI interrogator whom Javal Davis had known only as Gitmo Guy. Graner credited Beachner with teaching him how to use stress positions, and how to use women to humiliate Arabs, and how to cause them pain without injury, and how to smack them around. He said that Beachner told him "the gloves were coming off," and that meant: "Don't be afraid to use force with the prisoners. They don't expect you to use force in dealing with them because we're Americans, and we treat everybody nice."

GRANER WAS A QUICK STUDY. During one of his first shifts on the tier, an MI prisoner was brought in from Camp Vigilant. His handlers said they'd be back to collect him for interrogation in the morning, so Graner didn't bother putting him in a cell. "We just had him out and PT'd him the whole night," Graner said, and by PT he meant everything from deep knee bends to low crawling naked up and down the tier. MRE cartons were always handy: a prisoner could be made to stand still on one until he fell off, or to hold one out in front of him until its weight became unbearable. And whatever the drill was, he'd be yelled at. In a full-on PT session, he might get shoved or slapped around, too. Graner wore the prisoner from Vigilant out, and he said, "Supposedly MI got good results from him." After that it became a routine: for every new prisoner on the tier the first night was "hell night." This was Graner's idea, and he came to regret it. "It takes a lot of energy to yell and scream at somebody, and it gets old real fast," he said, and added, "Eventually we had all lost our voices."

Still, he kept coming up with new tricks to keep the prisoners on edge. One of the first things Frederick remembered seeing Graner do at the hard site was walk a hooded and handcuffed MI prisoner into a tall pole that was sticking out of the ground. Frederick saw the collision coming, and told Graner to watch out, but he kept going straight for the target. "It wasn't as if he pushed the detainee," Frederick said. "He just allowed him to walk right into it. The pole hit him to just one side of the sternum, but it didn't hit him in the face. Afterwards, Graner yelled at the detainee for running into the pole."

Frederick let it slide. The only time he remembered telling Graner to cool it at the hard site was after an escape from one of the Iraqi criminal cell blocks. Two prisoners had got out their cell window on Tier 3A. Frederick was standing in the corridor with the escapees' two remaining cellmates when Graner showed up. "He went over to one of the detainees and hit him in the face with his elbow, like a hard rushing blow, mostly with his forearm," Frederick said. "The inmate just took it. As Graner went to strike the other detainee, I yelled at him to stop, and he did. He then started helping me get information and search the building. I never really ever said anything to Graner, because I was more involved with finding out facts about the escape, and I forgot about the incident."

So Frederick could give an order and Graner would obey it, but when it came to the MI block, Frederick said that it was his understanding that Lieutenant Colonel Jordan ran the show, and he didn't interfere. On the contrary, Frederick said, he tried to help out. One night he came onto the block while Specialists Luciana Spencer and Armin Cruz of MI were interrogating the prisoner called Froggy in the Tier 1B shower. "The MI guys were yelling and they were throwing tables around, and I came in and asked them if they wanted me to yell at him," Frederick said. "Cruz said, 'Yes, go ahead.' So I started yelling at him." Then Graner arrived and turned on the shower and soaked Froggy, who was wearing a jumpsuit and had a sandbag over his head. At that point, Frederick said, Cruz and Spencer left the prisoner with the MPs, and Graner stepped out and returned with some pepper.

"He lifted the detainee's hood up and blew the pepper into the detainee's eyes," Frederick said, and went on, "The detainee didn't yell or anything. He was shaking his head and moving around. To me, it looked like it was burning his eyes. Then me and Graner started hitting him with an open hand. It wasn't hard, kind of like in wrestling. I believe we only hit him in the chest. I don't recall us hitting him anyplace else." They kept hitting him for a while—"I only thought it was about five minutes," Frederick said—and at some point, Frederick also clamped his forearm around Froggy's throat in a headlock. "But," he said, "I wasn't choking him out or anything like that."

Graner remembered the scene somewhat differently. He said that Spencer and Cruz complained that they weren't getting anything out of Froggy, and asked the MPs to "rough him up" for five minutes, at which point they would come back, pretend to be surprised, and to throw the MPs out, then resume their interrogation. He also said he'd sprayed Froggy with mace, not pepper, and that he and Frederick had gone at him with "elbows and knees" as well as "just slapping him around and throwing him into the wall, throwing him in between the two of us." He called this a fear up harsh approach, except for the mace, which was his idea.

It was "all fun and games," Graner said, until Froggy started fighting back. Then it became "serious." A fighting prisoner meant that the use of force could be called self-defense. You could kill a prisoner in self-defense, but mace made that unnecessary. And it went without saying that if you maced someone for the hell of it you could always claim it was in self-defense. If anybody asked, it was your word against a suspected terrorist's. But it was unlikely to come to that. Graner said that Sergeant First Class Shannon Snider, who was Frederick's immediate superior, had come on the scene while they were beating up Froggy in the shower. Sergeant Snider was the MP in charge of the entire hard site, day and night, and neither Frederick nor Graner recalled him taking any special interest in what they were doing. "It was just kind of a normal night on 1A-1B," Graner said.

FOR ALL HIS ZEAL on the job, Graner said that he didn't like spending his nights abusing prisoners, and that "from the get-go" he had asked to be given a different assignment. He knew that four MPs were facing courts-martial for beating and kicking several prisoners at Camp Bucca during the early days of the occupation, in mid-May. The accused, who were charged with ganging up on prisoners after subduing them on the ground, said that they were defending themselves against assault. Their battalion commander, Colonel Jerry Phillabaum, was now the MP commander at Abu Ghraib, and he was not an inspiring leader: just as Graner started work at the hard site, Phillabaum, who had been complaining of stress, took off, on orders from General Karpinski, for two weeks of R & R in Kuwait. The MPs on the MI block were only vaguely aware of his absence, but they couldn't help noticing how, when trouble came, the troops who snapped in the thick of the action got sent to the brig while the brass got a holiday. Graner felt that he was being set up for "disaster" on Tier 1A. "But they're telling us to do it," he said, and every time he asked to be transferred,

the answer from his superiors was "No. We hear you're doing a fan-
tastic job for MI. They need you over there. We can't pull you. They're
short of people."

Not long after he started working the tier, Graner said, his company commander, Captain Reese, stopped by and asked him if he was
having more fun than if he were at home. Graner remembered telling
him, "I don't find this fun," and, "It's illegal." He said he had warned
Reese on at least three separate occasions, "We're going to get in
trouble for it," and that Reese told him: "MI knows what they're
doing. Don't worry about it." Nobody else seemed concerned, either.
"Captain Brinson was real big on bringing people around and showing them what we were doing," Graner said. JAG officers—members
of the prison's legal team—and medics were frequent visitors to the
tier as well, and they took what they saw in stride, or suggested slight
modifications to this or that prisoner's treatment. Many of these visits were noted in the log. For instance, when a prisoner who was being
kept standing and handcuffed to his cell bars started to suffer from
swollen feet, a medic, Sergeant Reuben Layton, advised the MPs to
rearrange him and handcuff him to the bars sitting down.

There was nothing in the log, however, about the time during
Graner's first week on the block when he asked Sergeant Layton for
help because he found the prisoner called Smiley lying limp in his
cell. Graner wanted Smiley on his feet so that he could yell at him for
a while, but Smiley was unresponsive. This was a recurrent problem
with Smiley—"he would just come in and out of it, just vegging out,"
Graner said—so he called for a medic. Layton showed up, examined
Smiley, and found nothing wrong with him. Later on they found out
that Smiley had cancer, but they didn't know that at the time. They
assumed he was malingering and, Graner said, "Layton grabbed him,
threw him up against the back of the wall, charged his pistol, put it
in his mouth, started yelling at him." Nobody was supposed to carry

a gun on the tier, but there it was, and it made Smiley responsive—
"real quick," Graner said.

He hadn't reported Layton because, he said, "nothing happened."
Then again, Graner never reported anything that happened on the
tier—not exactly, not formally. But he always kept his camera handy,
figuring that when he saw anything "unusual" or "off the wall," it
would be good to take photographs. "He was a picture person," Frederick said. "He was normally proud of the picture he took." And when
Graner liked a picture, he liked to show it. Specialist Joseph Darby,
an MP with the 372nd who worked in the operations office of the
prison, remembered the first time he saw one—on an October morning, an hour or two before dawn. "I'm sitting on a pile of lumber out
in front of the building I live in, and Graner's getting off work as I'm
going to work," Darby said. "He walks over with his camera, and he
pulls up a picture, and he goes, 'Check this out, Darb.' I said, 'What's
up?' He shows me a picture of an inmate chained to his cell, naked,
with a bag over his head, and water on the floor, which really didn't
strike me that much as abuse, because the inmate wasn't chained in
any weird position. The prisoner handcuffed to a cell—that's common
practice. It's like being handcuffed to a car door."

Darby talked about the picture as if the prisoner's nakedness was
invisible to him. The only thing that struck him as unusual was the
puddle at the man's feet, but there was an overturned water bottle
lying in it, which seemed to explain it. Graner made Darby see it
differently: "Graner looked at me and said, 'The Christian in me
knows it's wrong, but the corrections officer in me can't help but love
to make a grown man piss himself.' Then he walked away. As he was
walking away, I said, 'Dude, you're sick.' And then my ride came, and
I went to work, and I never thought anything else about it." From
Darby's response there was no way to know if he believed Graner was
telling the truth or putting him on. He said he wasn't sure: "I thought

maybe it was just bullshit. There wasn't anything going on with the inmate. It was standard procedure."

Around the same time, Graner showed several of his pictures of naked, trussed, panty-hooded prisoners to some men from his unit who were hanging around at their living quarters: a staff sergeant, a sergeant first class, a lieutenant—all of them his superior officers. Like Darby, they worked in other parts of the prison, so what they were seeing was news to them. There is no official record of their response, and that tells you something. It told Graner that what he was doing was acceptable. That didn't mean it was right—"Was all this stuff wrong?" he said, "Hell yeah"—but it meant he wasn't keeping a secret.

11.

PRIVATE FIRST CLASS LYNNDIE ENGLAND'S cell at Abu Ghraib was small and, of course, it stank. "It stank all over Iraq," she said. "You walk into that country—I mean, Jesus, it smells like oil and shit, diesel fuel, smoke, and piss. I swear to God, you would be driving down the highway and there would be one of those pumper tankers that suck the stuff from their little hole-in-the-floor potties, and they would just be letting it out on the side of the road. It would pool up—it was disgusting." Her bunk wasn't as bad as that, but it wasn't much of a refuge in the chilly desert darkness—just a place to sleep. Most nights England preferred not to sleep rather than to go back there.

By day she was a clerk in the prison administration. She worked 10:00 A.M. to 10:00 P.M., doing in-processing. As new prisoners were delivered to Abu Ghraib, England told them where to sit and when to move to the next chair while other clerks entered their particulars into computers and prisoner numbers were assigned to them. Then she took their fingerprints and scanned their irises, printed out and laminated their ID bracelets, and attached the bracelets to their wrists. It was assembly-line work, and there was a lot of it. Some days, there'd be hundreds of newly captured Iraqis, and England would have to work around the clock. But, as a rule, if the prison wasn't under attack when she got off, she headed over to the hard site to hang out with Corporal Graner and the other MPs on the night shift.

Graner and Iraq: for England the two experiences were inseparable, at times indistinguishable. The year before, in November, the unit was on a drill weekend in Maryland, preparing to mobilize, getting shots, getting records in order. England was doing her thing, administration, when he presented himself—the new guy. He'd got himself transferred from another reserve outfit because he wanted to go to Iraq. He gave England his paperwork and she in-processed him. "All I knew was he was an ex-Marine and he was volunteering. I didn't look at him twice," she said. "He looked twice at me, though. I mean, I didn't notice it then, but people started telling me about it. He would follow me around. Like, I smoked and he didn't. He started smoking so he could go out there in the little smokers' group so he could talk to me."

England wasn't accustomed to such attention. Specialist Jeremy Sivits remembered another weekend with the unit, in the summer of 2001, the first time he'd been activated; he was getting ready to go to Bosnia, and he was talking to his sergeant at the smokers' pit. "There was somebody standing there with a pair of boots and a pair of jeans and a Carhartt jacket and a Kentucky hat on, short haircut. I said, 'Who's the new dude?' She turned around and said, 'I'm not a dude.'" That was Lynndie England. "Really a down-home country girl, worked hard, always nice, very well-mannered," Sivits said. "Just an easygoing person. Pretty much all of us were. But you could tell by the look in her eyes when she'd see different places—this girl has never been anywhere besides her hometown."

England had enlisted when she was seventeen, and she'd gone through basic training during her last summer of high school. She'd always wanted to be a soldier and to serve her country, and basic training had put that desire on trial. In basic, you couldn't get away with anything; they broke you down and built you back up into a person whose actions and inactions had consequences for an entire system. Discipline meant respect, and that worked both ways. This was the principle of command responsibility: every soldier is accountable to and for her buddies, and every officer is accountable for the welfare and good conduct of his soldiers, and if they're in trouble you're in trouble. It was simple as that—basic collective self-interest: you answer to your officer so he doesn't have to answer for you, in every hierarchy and sub-hierarchy, at every link in the chain of command.

England admired this order of duty. She saw its justice and felt its reward, and she'd found it strange to return to high school as an MP. "Like when the teacher leaves and people are acting up, I kept wanting to say, 'What are you doing? You're going to get us smoked.' Because in basic, if we acted up, everybody got punished—we got smoked together. I kept thinking how immature everyone was." She took pride in feeling different. Plus, she was working nights in a chicken-processing plant, a world of feathers and blood and gizzards and rotten pay, and a reservist's tuition benefits were her only hope of going to college—especially after she got fired for complaining that management was cutting corners on health and safety regulations. "I was in the military," she said. "I made it through basic. I was part of a unit. I was part of something that a lot of people want to be a part of."

Three years later she still looked underage, short and slight, more like a soldier's little sister than a soldier. The other MPs were always saying: Does your mom know you're not in school? Does your mom know you're out this late? She didn't mind. Kidding was the normal way for soldiers to show affection—so it took a number of drill weekends for her to register that Graner wasn't just kidding. "It was a game," England said. "He played me." One weekend at the barracks, she was alone in her room, and suddenly she heard bluegrass music blaring. She loved bluegrass so she followed the sound, and it led her straight to Graner. "He told me later, 'You came to me,' " she said.

"He knew what he was doing. He would find out from people what I liked and what I was interested in. It was never about him—he would always try to put everything on me. For instance, he had a truck, and it was a manual. I didn't know how to drive stick. So he taught me, just because I was curious. He bought me clothes. He bought me drinks, food. I'd never been to the beach, so he takes me to Virginia Beach."

Graner was divorced. England was married. "That's what was holding me back from maybe having a relationship with him," she said. "Because I'm the type of person that dates one person at a time." She liked her husband—everybody in her family did—but she felt stress and disconnection at home, aggravated by the prospect of deployment. She talked to Graner about it, and he listened. She'd say, I don't need this, and he'd say, Well, no, you don't need that. She'd say, We're just friends, and Graner would say it back to her. We're not really compatible as husband and wife would become: you're not really compatible as husband and wife. And she found this steady echo persuasive.

"Graner," she said. "He's really charming. If you didn't know him and you just meet him, you'd be drawn into him. In a crowded room, he'd be the one to look at. He would draw the attention. If the attention is not on him, he'll get it there. That's what he does. He thrives on that. If you're not paying attention to him, he'll make comments about you. Whatever you want to hear, he'll say it. And I was what? Twenty years old when I met him. He was thirty-four. He had fourteen years more experience than I did. He knew what to say, what to do, how to act. I finally suckered in around the end of February."

IN THE LAST WEEK OF FEBRUARY 2003, the 372nd MP company was activated and mustered at Fort Lee, in Virginia. Instead of occasional weekend encounters, England and Graner were now around each other all the time. "Everyone tried to tell me, he's too old for you, he's a bad guy, I don't think you should be messing around with him," she said. "But I didn't believe them because I believed him." England filed for separation from her husband, and told him she wanted a divorce. She and Graner talked of getting married themselves, and having a bunch of kids. One weekend they drove to her hometown, Fort Ashby, West Virginia, to visit her family. But her parents had gone to Kentucky, and in their absence England's husband was at the house. That was too weird for England, and Graner wanted to go to his home in Uniontown, Pennsylvania, so they drove up there for the night, then down to Kentucky to see her folks. By the time they got back to Fort Lee, they had traveled about a thousand miles. It was a heady, hurtling spring, with the war on TV—waiting to go, in love.

Graner and England made no secret of their romance, but its consummation made it an outlaw affair. Under the Uniform Code of Military Justice, adultery is a crime subject to court-martial; you can be jailed for it, and the regulations say you're married until you're divorced; separation doesn't count. Unmarried soldiers aren't supposed to have sex with each other on duty, either. "It wasn't allowed in the military, period," England said. But hanging around at Fort Lee and waiting for orders wasn't like basic training. It was more like going back to high school. Soldiers coupled up and soldiers partied down and nobody got smoked. If you fell short on a training qualification—missed a few shots on the firing range, say, or were overweight for your height and age—the chances were that you'd get told to work on it, but not held back. The Army needed soldiers for Iraq; most units were looking to build their rosters up, not bust soldiers out for getting sloppy on the eve of war. "It was a cat-and-mouse game to us, so they wouldn't catch us," England said. "Because we were told we couldn't be together like that. The higher-ups, first sergeants, platoon sergeants, they knew what was going on. But, as long as they didn't see it, it wasn't happening, so to say."

The thing was, Graner liked to be seen, and he liked England to be seen with him. He was always taking pictures of her and e-mailing them to his friends, or showing them around in the unit. "He thought I was hot—and, you know, I'm with a twenty-year-old," England said. "It was a guy thing." One night at Virginia Beach, he took pictures while they had sex, and he had her expose herself for more pictures, posed beside a sleeping buddy of theirs—gotcha pictures to show the guy when he woke up. "I objected to the sex pictures," England said. "He still took them." Afterward, he hid his camera so she couldn't delete the pictures. She got used to it. She said, "He had the power." And she said, "I was young and I guess I was blind by love."

Digital cameras meant that lots of people were taking and swap-ping all sorts of pictures of everything. If you didn't like it you didn't have to look. And when they got to Iraq, Graner gave England a reason for recording his exploits: when he told people about them, he said, he didn't like to be doubted. As a Marine, he'd served in the first Gulf War, and when he came home with his stories, he felt they were greeted with skepticism. He didn't go into detail, but his main beef was with the Veterans Administration. When he'd gone in complain-ing of the symptoms of post-traumatic stress, he'd been shown the door. "He would have nightmares and headaches, stuff like that," England said. "He tried to get medicine or something from the VA, and when the VA looked at his paperwork, his headquarters unit wasn't in a combat zone, even though his platoons were, and that's where he was. They didn't have the proof. They didn't believe him. So they didn't give him the help that he needed. This time around he said that he was going to have proof of whatever he saw and went through. He wanted to take pictures of everything, because then there would be evidence that it happened. So I was like, OK, makes sense to me. And whenever he wanted me to grab his camera to take a pic-ture when he couldn't, I did it."

They took a lot of pictures in Al Hillah, but nothing that would
interest the VA, just "happy snaps" of themselves and their buddies
goofing around in off-hours: skinny dipping in the pool of one of
Saddam's palaces; pissing on his portrait; playing with a kitten; posing with their weapons; sleeping at their desks; looking at pictures of
naked pinup girls; mooning the camera; drinking beer; going fishing.
Three of these things—pets, porn, and alcohol—were strictly forbidden under General Order Number One for all American troops in the
Iraqi theater, but there they were. Nobody seemed to care. When
Graner set up house in the tent next door to the date factory, England
all but moved in with him there. Senior officers kept telling them to
knock off the relationship, but they didn't. Graner raised more ire
when he painted the words "Po White Trash" on the back of his
Humvee. Besides, Specialist Megan Ambuhl was seeing one of Graner's roommates, and she was at the tent almost as much as England
without getting hassled about it. So it hardly seemed like a big deal
to England, when she got to Abu Ghraib, to set out after curfew to
be with her man. Officially, England wasn't authorized to set foot on
the MI block—she wasn't on duty and it wasn't her post; she wasn't
even a guard—but to her, the hard site at night was the natural place
to be. After all, she said, "The only thing that kept us going was
hanging out with our buddies."

TEN P.M., WHEN ENGLAND GOT OFF WORK at Abu Ghraib, was the
midpoint of the night shift on Tiers 1A and 1B. By then the prisoners had been counted, fed, showered, and bedded down or trussed up
in stress positions for the evening, and if the tiers were quiet, she'd
usually find Graner and Ambuhl in the little office the MPs had set
up by the top of the stairs between the tiers, watching movies on
Graner's laptop. They watched a lot of war movies on the night shift,

and lots of old *M*A*S*H* and *South Park* episodes, and it seemed like any time there wasn't a DVD on, Ambuhl was at the computer playing spider solitaire. Sabrina Harman used to joke that Ambuhl should get charged with dereliction of duty for playing that game. First Sergeant Shannon Snider, the MP officer in charge of the hard site, would often be there, playing alongside her. The office was nothing special—a corner of a corridor, walled off with sandbags and plywood—but Graner had a coffeemaker there, and Frederick dropped by regularly to shoot the shit between his rounds. It was the closest anywhere at Abu Ghraib came to the old tent on the loading dock at Al Hillah. During the slowest hours of the night, England often curled up in an empty cell nearby and caught a nap. But if there was work to be done, she tagged along.

On the night of October 24, when England showed up at the tier she found Graner and Ambuhl getting ready to take a prisoner nicknamed Gus out of the hole—a solid-doored, windowless, lightless, waterless, toiletless, unfurnished, concrete isolation cell reserved for prisoners who were out of control, or whose interrogators prescribed a stint of total sensory disorientation. It was Gus's first day on the tier, and he'd been in there since he arrived. Graner had an MI prisoner who was supposed to be put in the hole after his usual 2:30 A.M. PT regimen, and he wanted to clean it up first. Prisoners tended to soil the place during their stays.

The word on Gus was that he had been picked up by occupation troops a few days earlier and had wound up in Camp Ganci, where he had acted out, shouting insults and threats at the guards. Then he threw rocks at them, so they took him to the hard site. The move did not subdue him. "He was spitting, he was naked, and he kept saying he hated Americans and he wanted us to die," England said. "He would try to grab us through the bars, and I guess that was one of the reasons why he was in solitary." To extract a genuinely dangerous prisoner from a cell, you'd normally want two or three men who knew how to handle themselves in a fight. But Gus was scrawny, and there was no such team available, so Graner took a cargo tie-down strap, put his camera in his pocket, and told Ambuhl and England to follow him.

"I was immediately behind him and Megan was behind me," England said. "We went downstairs. When he opened the door Gus was in there. He was naked. He wouldn't come out of the cell. He was laying down on the floor. He didn't want to stand up. So that's why he brought the tie-down strap. Graner went in there and he put the strap around his neck. He was going to make him crawl out. Then Gus was crawling out of the cell. When he was about halfway out of the doorway, Graner turned around and handed me the strap and said, 'Hold this.' So I did. I just grabbed it, and he went over and he took a picture. Gus continued to crawl out. In the first picture he's half— and then the last two he's fully—out of the cell. There was three total. He was crawling, and then he kind of laid there. You can see Megan on the side, standing. I'm just kind of holding the tie-down strap. You can see the slack on it. I know people said that I dragged him, but I never did. After Graner was done taking the pictures, he put the camera back in his cargo pocket, walked over, took the strap from me, and I guess Gus wanted to cooperate then, so he took it off of his neck, and he dragged him up, and he took him to his cell. That was the end of that event."

TO ENGLAND, the event was no big deal. "At the time, in that place, it was the norm," she said. The photographs were the first Graner had shot of her with a prisoner, and the only reason she was holding the tie-down strap was so that he could shoot them—as "a souvenir," she said, "something to say he's seen this, he's seen that, he did this, he did that." *Snap, snap, snap:* the entire photo session took twenty-two seconds.

The first picture is poorly lit and shot at an odd angle so that the concrete floor of the prison corridor, littered with empty plastic baggies and scrap paper, appears to slant upward, and only the right wall, punctuated by cell doors draped with blankets, is visible. England stands just left of the center of the frame, in the middle of the corridor. She wears an Army-issue brown T-shirt, tucked into belted desert camouflage cargo pants, which are tucked into tan GI desert boots. Her stance is what soldiers call at ease, feet apart, shoulders relaxed, her right hand hanging slack at her side and the left loosely outstretched, holding the tie-down strap. The angle of her head and her expressionless gaze are aligned with that arm and the strap, creating a steady downward diagonal line to Gus. If it weren't for the strap, one might not immediately notice him: his head, arms, and shoulders are heavily obscured in shadows and partially blocked from view by a white plastic chair beside his cell door. His face, although turned to the camera, is illegible in the dark orb of his head, which hovers a few inches above the floor. His elbows and forearms bear his weight; one arm is outstretched above his head, the other is tucked beneath his chest. In military drill, this position is called low crawling—pulling with the elbows, pushing with the feet, and dragging everything from navel to knee over the ground.

In the second photograph, the frame shifts and the perspective balances: both sides of the corridor are visible and Megan Ambuhl appears at the left, dressed identically to England, with her back to the wall and her hands in her pockets. England's posture is unchanged, except that her head is now turned more sharply in profile, as she looks blankly down on Gus, who has emerged from the hole and rolled onto his right side, exposing himself fully to the camera. You can see that he is bearded, but his face remains shadowed. His body, bare except for an ID bracelet that England might have made and snapped on him, is streaked with filth. He lies with his right arm outstretched on the concrete, and his left arm crooked over his throat with the hand bearing the weight of his stiffly elevated head. His legs are splayed in an awkward sort of frog-kick position. He looks like a man writhing in pain.

The composition of the third photograph is the same, but England is in motion, taking a step toward the camera, and making eye contact with it. Gus's face is finally visible, and his eyes are eerie—rolled back in his head, flashing white. On the plastic chair by the cell door, a previously unidentifiable object can be seen to be a megaphone of the sort used for yelling at prisoners to keep them awake. This is the best-lit and the least-staged-looking of the three pictures, and therefore the most disturbing; it creates the impression that England is taking Gus for a stroll on a leash and has just run into Ambuhl on her way. But it was a crop of the second photograph, showing only England and Gus, that was first leaked to the press and seen around the world, becoming almost overnight one of the most recognizable images of our time, and making England an iconic figure of American disgrace: "leash girl."

England understood how perverse the picture looked on a TV screen or in a newspaper. But she said, "I don't see the infamous picture from the Iraq war. I just see me. It's just a picture. The first thing that comes up in my mind is just that's me, and yeah—that happened at the prison when I was in Iraq, and that was one of the pictures taken." As far as she was concerned, it wasn't a snapshot of her relationship to Gus, because she had none; it was a snapshot of her relationship with Graner. "It's showing that he has power over me, and he wanted to demonstrate that power," she said. "Anything he asked, he knew that I would do it." Beyond that, she scoffed at the idea that the photograph depicted sexual humiliation. "Just because Gus is naked?" she said. "That's standard operating procedure." Still, she allowed that Graner might have seen what he was doing when he posed her with Gus and snapped the shutter. "Maybe he wanted to show me, a ninety-five-to-one-hundred-pound female—short female at that—dominating him," she said. "Maybe it was for documentation, maybe it was for his own amusement. I don't know what was going through his head."

12.

GRANER SAID THAT WHEN HE GRABBED his camera before extracting Gus from the hole, he was thinking about what he would do as a prison guard back home. "At the Department of Corrections in Pennsylvania you document planned use of force usually by videotape," he said. The idea was that if anything went wrong, the pictures would tell the story. Graner said he had checked Gus out when he took over the tier from the day shift. "He had wounds on his side or his back, and he was laying in feces and urine," he said. Gus tried to get up, saying, "I will kill you." Graner shut the door. "I really didn't have a clue on how I was going to get him out of there," he said. "I didn't want to fight him in the cell." He went back to the office, where his cargo strap caught his eye. "I thought that if I could get the sling around his shoulder—he wasn't that big of a prisoner—I could just yank him out of the cell. That was my game plan going down." He said he asked England and Ambuhl to come along for backup because "usually Iraqis don't fight women." He found Gus as he had left him, and slipped the strap around his shoulders. When Gus started to get up, Graner gave the strap a pull. "It ended up around his neck, and he started to crawl out," he said. That hadn't been the plan, Graner said, so he handed England the strap and took the pictures.

Graner said that England didn't know he was going to give her the strap until he did, and he would have handed it to Ambuhl if she had been the one closer to him. Perhaps he would have. But the pictures of Gus on the tether are the only photographs from Abu Ghraib in which Ambuhl appears in the same frame as a prisoner. "She just happened to be in the way," England said. "She didn't like to be in pictures." Ambuhl said she didn't like the pictures of England and Gus—period. "It made it look like we were just fooling around with a detainee for our own pleasure," she said. "That wasn't the case. That was an uncooperative detainee who needed to get out of that cell—a guy with sores and stuff. You're not going to touch him. You get him out, and it may have been unorthodox, but he didn't hurt anybody and he didn't get hurt."

Ambuhl said that it was in deference to her feelings that Graner had cut her out of the notorious photograph when he showed it to some medics at the prison shortly after taking it. "They wanted to have a copy of it," Ambuhl said, "and he didn't know if I would care or not that I was in it." But, she said, what interested her about Graner's exchange with the medics was their response to the picture. The medics, she said, had approved the way he'd handled Gus under the circumstances.

It was true that Major David Auch, a physician who commanded the Abu Ghraib medical unit in the fall of 2003, later told the authors of an article in the *New England Journal of Medicine* that he had personally authorized the use of the leash on Gus before the pictures were taken. After all, there were no straitjackets at the prison, and, Auch said, "My concern was whatever it took to keep him from getting hurt." But Graner had not, in fact, discussed his approach to Gus with any medical officers until after the fact. Auch was confusing Gus with another prisoner, nicknamed Shitboy, who was brought to Tier 1B five nights later. Like Gus, he was transferred from Camp Ganci after throwing rocks at MPs; and, like Gus, he was not mollified by the move indoors.

SHITBOY WAS A MANIAC. "He was one of our worst to deal with," Ambuhl said. "We used to feed them in these little plastic containers, and
they would sometimes get a cup for chai. He would start by putting
his feces and his urine in that. Sometimes he ended up drinking it.
Then he would spit at us or masturbate while we walked by. He would
ruin his jumpsuits all the time getting feces all over it. He'd lay with
his ass in the air and stick stuff in his rectum—chicken bones, anything you can think of. And he'd fling his feces everywhere, at us or
detainees. Those kinds of things are considered a crime in an American
prison, throwing your bodily fluids at someone. And the toilet—it was
a hole in the ground, but it was actually like a toilet, porcelain—he
broke that piece out, digging the concrete out, and was eating it. Then
he's eating the paint chips off the cell door, and attacking the soldiers,
banging his head against everything."

Nobody knew what to do with Shitboy. Lynndie England said
that Graner used to wear a gas mask when he went into his cell, and
Shitboy always burst into song at the sight of it. He was constantly
being hauled off to the showers, and placed in isolation, and once,
when he smeared himself with his waste, Graner and Frederick took
him out in the rain and made him roll in the mud—a standard
punishment for soldiers in basic training, but for a man of Shitboy's
tastes hardly a discouragement. Photographs taken immediately
after his mud bath show him standing in the middle of the cell
block, lean and muscular and caked in filth, with his ankles chained
together, his arms thrown wide, and his head thrown back as if in
ecstasy. In another set of photographs Shitboy is seen naked and
hanging upside down in his cell, with his feet bound to the frame of
the upper bunk, his knees in the air, and his head dangling just
above the floor. The pictures look just like scores of others that show
prisoners at the hard site contorted in bondage. But Shitboy's pre-

dicament is more extreme than any stress position the soldiers had contrived, and the reason for this, which is not communicated by the photographs, is that Shitboy had hung himself from the bunk— of his own accord and unassisted.

Javal Davis said that Shitboy was a relentless mimic who would repeat everything that was said to him; and in his frenzies of self-abuse, too, he seemed to mock the grotesque rituals of MI's counter-resistance techniques by imitation and exaggeration. By choosing to go naked, then taking his self-exposure to extremes—soiling himself and masturbating—he inverted the prevailing order of humiliation on the cell block, inflicting himself on the soldiers, making his distress theirs. While soldiers laughed at other prisoners to redouble their shame, Shitboy laughed at the soldiers, and in his reckless pursuit of the last laugh he knew no bounds: while soldiers drove hooded prisoners into walls, Shitboy, unhooded and with his eyes open, was forever doing the same thing to himself. "I walked in one day," Hydrue Joyner said, "and he's basically taking his head and at full force slamming it against a wall—pa-pam!"

Day and night, week after week, Shitboy found new ways to challenge his keepers, and he was just one of as many as ten mentally deranged prisoners warehoused on Tier 1B at the time. Twitch was one of them; he had violent fits and, Sabrina Harman said, "he would sing every hour, on the hour. I don't know how he did it, but he knew." Twitch was another head banger. There is a series of photographs from a night when Graner had to stitch up his brow, while England stood over him, holding a shotgun. And there are more photographs of Twitch, handcuffed back-to-back to another prisoner, "a slicer—he cut himself up," Graner said; both men are naked and straining away from one another, and the slicer's face looms toward the lens like a mask of pure desolation, his eyes awash in mayhem. Swamp Thing was another handful. He had a Shitboy-like tendency to play with his stool. "He'd make little figurines like clay, but it wasn't clay," Jeffery Frost said. "He liked to play with water, and he would literally have inches of water in his cell. We'd have to constantly go and dry his mattress out. We don't know what his problem was, but he'd talk to himself, whole conversations."

Then there was Thumby's sister, a shrieker and flailer, who would tear at her own clothing. Thumby was ex-Fedayeen—it was said he'd lost four fingers when he waited too long to toss a grenade—but nobody knew why she was there. And Santa Claus, too, was a puzzle, less dramatic than the others—maybe he was just senile—but the MPs all agreed that he was crazy. "He was always beating on his chest and saying, 'Oh, I can't breathe. My heart, my heart,' " Frost said. "I'd say, 'You want a cigarette?' He'd say, 'Yes.' 'All right, well, you're not having a heart attack, now, are you?' " There was something about Santa that made the other prisoners want to pick on him. "They would try to throw things at him and get him riled up, and then he would try to attack them and stuff," Ambuhl said. When she took Santa for a shower, she would always ask Graner to come along. The other prisoners held their fire when they saw Graner, and Ambuhl said, "He didn't want to see this guy who was mental be harassed by the other detainees. Same with Shitboy—we weren't interested in seeing these people suffer."

The medics were sympathetic, but they were in over their heads, too. "All our nutcases, we were just feeding them Benadryl," Graner said. Major Auch told the *New England Journal of Medicine* that the Abu Ghraib clinic was well stocked with anti-psychotic drugs, but there was nobody on his staff qualified to dispense them. So the prisoners were left to their demons, and the guards to their own devices.

THERE IS A SET OF PHOTOGRAPHS showing Shitboy in a jumpsuit, with first one arm, then both arms, swaddled in foam rubber, as Graner constructed a sort of makeshift straitjacket. In the final picture of the sequence, Shitboy is fully trussed. His padded arms are stuffed into a sandbag and lashed around his waist with a padlocked chain, and Graner stands behind him, wearing a kaffiyeh around his neck, his mustache lifted by a proud smile. Nine hours later, in the log, Graner left a note about Shitboy: "Chewed through the restraints on left arm—re-restrained." A later photo session shows how Graner and Frederick sheathed Shitboy in heavy Styrofoam, laid him facedown on a stretcher on the floor, placed another stretcher on top of him, and used tie-down straps to bind the two stretchers together, immobilizing him. Ambuhl said that medics called this arrangement a "litter sandwich," and that they had been there to supervise its assembly. Graner posed beside Shitboy at each step of the process, and when it was done, Frederick sat for his picture on top of the flattened prisoner. Before long, Shitboy had got loose. "He was almost shot that night for trying to get out of the tier," Ambuhl said. "So it wasn't like that was a successful method."

"We called him Houdini," Javal Davis said. "Any time they tried to restrain him, he'd break out of it. He broke locks. He almost escaped. He was running down the hallway, naked, before Sergeant Snider caught him. And he started laughing. He'd laugh at everything." Davis thought Shitboy was "pretty funny" and Harman called him "entertaining," but Ambuhl was not amused. By her count, Shitboy broke at least four pairs of handcuffs and several shackles. "We showed the pictures of Shitboy to Chief Rivas, and pretty much any of the higher people that would come around, so we could say we don't have what it takes," Ambuhl said. "We were trying to let people know that we couldn't deal with this and still do the things that we were actually supposed to be doing. We were trying to get him off the block." But nobody knew where else to put him, and it didn't help, Javal Davis said, that a psychiatrist who visited the prison concluded that Shitboy was just a malingerer. "I guess he wanted to make people think he was crazy," Davis said. "He did a damn good job."

Lynndie England shared the view that Shitboy was a performance artist. "He was playing us, just like when your kid is playing you— you can tell," she said. "He just wanted to leave the prison and go to the mental ward at the combat support hospital. I guess he thought it would have been a lot better. It probably would have, because the CSH was in the safe zone, the Green Zone. Our prison got hit with mortars every day and night. Makes sense to me." To be sure, England regarded head banging and coprophagy as pretty extreme. "I don't know if I would have gone that far," she said. "But I wasn't an Iraqi prisoner, either."

It hardly mattered whether Shitboy was a madman or a con man. He could not be ignored. When the litter sandwich failed to contain him, Graner's next move was to fashion a body harness from tie-down straps, and hitch Shitboy to a cell door. This was the technique that Major Auch had approved and later mistook for the leash used on Gus, and it was not a success, either. Shitboy quickly found sufficient slack in the rigging to rock his head back and butt the solid door. Again and again, he drove his forehead against the steel until he collapsed to the floor, leaving a bloody streak to mark his fall. Graner captured the scene on camera, in three still photographs and four fifteen-second video clips. Once again, he showed the pictures to Chief Rivas. "Shortly after that," Ambuhl said, "Shitboy and the other mental detainees were transferred to a hospital."

PROOF. Like Harman, with whom he regularly swapped snapshots, Graner said he took photographs for proof. He kept his pictures on his laptop in the Tier 1A office, and in the case of Shitboy they had helped him make his point. But photographs cannot tell stories. They can only provide evidence of stories, and evidence is mute; it demands investigation and interpretation. Looked at in this way, as evidence of something beyond itself, a photograph can best be understood not as an answer or an end to inquiry, but as an invitation to look more closely, and to ask questions. Graner used his photographs to demonstrate that Shitboy could not be handled at the hard site. But the photographs by themselves proved nothing. They could as easily— perhaps more easily—have been read differently. They looked like pictures of prisoner abuse, especially the photographs that showed Graner and Frederick posing beside the prisoner as they packaged and hog-tied him.

Why does Graner smile? Why does Frederick squat on the litter sandwich? In those pictures they look like tourists, and Shitboy becomes a prop, even a souvenir, a symbol of their adventure, like the Eiffel Tower or the Sphinx—the backdrop that says: we were here, we did this. But what have they done? Is he their victim? Have they defeated him? There is nothing in the pictures to indicate that he might be defeating them.

When the soldiers aren't in the frame and Shitboy is solo, at ease or rampant, the pictures might still be souvenirs, but not Shitboy. He commands our full attention, or repels it—and, either way, we don't know what we're looking at. His image alone cannot tell us. We need an explanation. Seeing Graner and Frederick there with him is not an explanation. But their presence, like Lynndie England's in the photographs of Gus, suggests a story, and encourages us to imagine that we know what the story is, when in fact we don't. Once we learn Shitboy's story, however, the pictures of him with Graner and Frederick become relatively anodyne. With Gus and the tie-down strap, the opposite is true: even when we find out the story, the pictures of him with England remain shocking—only now the shock lies in the fact that the pictures look worse, more deliberately deviant and abusive, than the reality they depict.

What if, instead of handing England the tie-down strap as Gus crawled out of the hole, Graner had dropped it on the floor and taken a picture of Gus unaccompanied? What would we have seen? The picture would still have accomplished what Graner claimed he intended it to: the documentation of a planned use of force gone slightly awry. And it still would have shown a naked prisoner wearing what appeared to be a leash. Gus would still look abused; you would still see that something had been done to him and wonder who had done it; and the picture would still be appallingly sad, maybe even outrageous. But England's presence at the other end of the tether makes the pictures that Graner actually took sensational. She seems to answer all the questions that her absence would raise, creating a sense of direct agency—falsely, according to everyone who was there: she becomes the violator.

The fact that England is posing, aware of the camera and presenting herself to it, also implicates the photographer in the drama. He becomes the director of the scenario of violation, and suddenly the act of taking the picture can be regarded as part of the offense—so much so that the picture itself, rather than what it appears to depict, might be considered offensive. After all, Graner's posing of England, however intentional or unintentional it may have been, implicates us, too, as viewers, by putting us in his position and inviting us to think that we know what we're seeing. A picture of Gus alone, with the leash dropped on the floor, would allow us to feel like witnesses; with England there, we are put in the position of voyeurs.

For Graner, taking pictures was always, explicitly, an autobiographical project. He told Frederick and several other soldiers who served with him at Abu Ghraib the same story he told England about how his experience of being disbelieved after the Gulf War led to his idea of photography as a form of credibility insurance. So he used his camera to assert his presence. He wanted to show his hand. He also liked pranks, and he liked to shock, and as he grew accustomed to the depravity of the MI block, his standard for a scene that merited a photograph—something "unusual" or "off-the-wall"—kept rising.

13.

ON THE SAME NIGHT that Charles Graner photographed Lynndie England with Gus on the leash, Chip Frederick and Javal Davis and another MP delivered two hooded and handcuffed prisoners to Tier 1A from Davis's cell block, where they had been accused of raping another inmate, an adolescent boy. Rapes and other forms of assault, confirmed or alleged, were a constant problem at Abu Ghraib, particularly in the tent cities of Camp Ganci and Camp Vigilant, and just as there was nowhere else to isolate the mentally ill, the MI block was often the repository for prisoners suspected of such crimes against one another. Of course, boys weren't supposed to be in the general prison population, and Frederick had removed the accuser, and placed him on Tier 1B where, England said, "He gave him water and candy and all kinds of stuff to make him feel comfortable." Then Frederick joined Graner and England in roughing up the accused men, stripping them and running them through a strenuous PT regime, before locking them in separate cells and ordering them to confess. But it hardly mattered what the men said—"The boy kept identifying them as the ones that did it," England said—and the next night their ordeal continued.

By then the word had got around that there were a couple of prison rapists on the block, and some MI men had come to have a look at them—Specialist Roman Krol, an interrogator, and two analysts, Specialists Armin Cruz and Israel Rivera. They found Frederick and Graner PTing the two men, and since there was nothing else to do, Roman Krol said, "We just stayed to see what was going to happen. Just curiosity, I guess." Then another MP showed up, Specialist Matthew Smith, who worked as a convoy driver and gunner. Smith was a buddy of Graner's who would often stop in for a visit at the hard site. He got hold of a megaphone and started yelling at one of the prisoners, while the other one kept doing push-ups.

Lynndie England was upstairs, in the office with Megan Ambuhl, who was playing spider solitaire on Graner's computer, and at some point they stepped out to see what was happening. Graner shouted to England to grab his camera and get some pictures, but Krol didn't hear him. There was so much yelling going on—"random stuff that made no sense," Krol said, "just like word diarrhea"—and he soon found that he and his MI buddies were joining in: "Just yelling vulgarity," he said, "you can imagine."

The yelling was loud and relentless—six soldiers and an interpreter bearing down on two naked prisoners—yelling for yelling's sake. Even as he took part in it, Krol wondered what the idea was. People were barking, "Confess, confess," but this wasn't an interrogation; it was jailhouse justice. "Everybody knew that this was a wrong thing to do, even though the rapists deserved it," Krol said. "I think they just wanted to punish them in front of everybody so this wouldn't happen again. The other prisoners were uncomfortable seeing naked people. It was done so everybody can see it, in the corridor between the cells. It's like a theater proscenium, and detainees that were watching were making their comments, too. A lot of them were actually supporting what was being done. Well, actually, most of them said that we should have just killed them. So they were OK with them being killed, just not OK with them being naked, from what I understood."

England said that even on the upper tier, prisoners who couldn't see what was happening were cheering. Their enthusiasm was a new sound on the block, but England said, "They were always supposed to watch. That was part of being humiliated and forced to do shameful things. It's a really big issue in their culture to be naked, especially in front of females. It's part of their weakness, and in time of war, when you're trying to get information or to get them to do something, you use their weakness."

SERGEANT KEN DAVIS WASN'T IRAQI, but he thought the nakedness was a big deal, too, when he showed up on the tier that evening and found so many soldiers involved in the scene. Ken Davis was with the 372nd MPs, but he was still doing what the company was trained to do, running convoys, and he'd come looking for Specialist Smith, who was one of his soldiers. Maybe his surprise showed on his face, because he said he'd barely got in the door of 1A when Specialist Cruz asked him, "Have we crossed the line?" Davis thought so. But he wasn't sure what the line was. "It's not like they were trying to hide anything," he said. "That's what stands out to me. If you know you're doing something wrong—I mean, dead wrong—you're going to hide it. You're going to do your best to conceal it so people that know better don't see it."

Davis stayed and watched. The PT session had ended. Now Graner began handcuffing the prisoners to one another, and arranging them on the floor, entwined in various sexual positions. Davis was baffled. "I'm thinking, if something's wrong here Graner would tell me," he said. Then he noticed Lynndie England on the upper deck with a camera. He said, "I remembered Graner earlier in October telling me he's taking pictures to show what they're making him do. So it all started adding up to me—OK, she's taking pictures to help cover Graner."

Meanwhile, another prisoner was brought onto the tier, and Frederick announced that he, too, was accused of taking part in the rape. "Cruz is yelling at him, 'Get undressed, get undressed!' " Davis said. "And the guy's like, 'No, Mister, no.' So they say, 'Graner, make him get undressed.' And Graner yells—if you've ever heard a drill instructor yell, it's just that bad, it's enough to make you jump—'GET UNDRESSED!' So the guy starts getting undressed."

When the new man was naked, somebody threw water on the floor, and he was made to low-crawl through the puddle. He tried to raise himself onto all fours, but that wasn't allowed. "Cruz would go put his foot in his butt and push him down to make him drag his genitals on the concrete," Davis said. "And I'm like, what is going on here? I said, 'Is this the way y'all interrogate people?' He goes, 'There's lots of different ways we interrogate people.' So I said, 'I've had enough,' and I left. I knew I was going to report it, because this is crazy. I went to bed, and it's amazing, because when you're laying there, no matter how much music you play, no matter how loud you turn it up, you still hear the screams. You still see the pictures. You still see the vision of what was going on."

"I THOUGHT I SHOULD LEAVE," Roman Krol said. "Then I couldn't make myself leave." So he watched as the third prisoner was piled on top of the other two on the floor and handcuffed to them in a messy tangle. While they writhed there, somebody produced a Nerf Football, and the soldiers began tossing it around, playing catch. "It might seem weird," Krol said. "I wasn't really having fun. We just kept throwing the ball to each other." Then they began bouncing the ball off the prisoners on the floor. Krol threw it at them, and hit one of the men in the leg.

At that same moment, up on the balcony, Lynndie England

snapped a picture. She wasn't using a flash, and Krol said he had no idea he was on camera until he saw the pictures months later, after he had returned to the States and settled back into civilian life. The images were dingy, distant, and crowded—difficult to read—but there he was and there was the Nerf Football, airborne on the rebound from his toss. All he could think was: why? "I mean, when you do something wrong, taking pictures of that is stupid," he said. "It's kind of like providing evidence."

What's more, Krol said, "On pictures it looked so much more horrible. What I feel when I look at the picture here, and what I felt when I actually saw that incident is just a completely different perspective. When you sit in your living room, on your comfortable couch, and watch this on TV, even after seeing this in real life, it looks so much worse. On the photos it seems like it's actual real torture. The worst thing that was done to the prisoners physically was they had to crawl on the floor, and they were naked, so it was really, really uncomfortable. I can't call it torture. It was a really, really bad case of humiliation, but that's about it. Back then I didn't pay that much attention to that incident. I thought, OK, so two detainees got punished for what they should have gotten punished for. Whatever—I moved on."

The photographs took Krol back and made him want to account for himself. In his own interrogations, he said, he had only rarely felt the need for aggressive approaches to prisoners. He remembered three cases when he'd used fear up harsh to get someone to talk, but for the most part he said interrogation was "much like a journalist job." He found that ninety percent of the Iraqis who were brought to him in his booth were happy to talk, because they had nothing of value to tell him; they had been arrested en masse and were obviously innocent, and it was tiresome to see them there, one after the other, and to put through the paperwork for their release, knowing that they would continue to be held for weeks or months for no reason. When he'd gone to Iraq, Krol had been excited about the war, and thought it was the right thing for America. But he had assumed the plan was to go in, give the Iraqis their freedom, and get out. At Abu Ghraib he had come to regard the occupation as inane and demoralizing, a waste of his time and everyone else's. Maybe Krol hadn't put all these feelings together at the time, but that night on Tier 1A, his discontent found a focus.

"During the whole incident, at first I was somewhat indifferent, then I just kept feeling negative emotions toward the rapists," he said. "Abu Ghraib was mortared almost every day. Our people were dying there. So my frustration level was really high." In fact, he said, Specialist Cruz had been wounded in the September 20 mortar attack that killed Sergeants Brown and Friedrich at the MI tent, and Cruz had been close to Friedrich. "He said, when he was abusing these prisoners and making them roll and crawl on the ground, he was actually seeing the people that had killed his friend," Krol said. "I think everybody had their own motive. I have a five-year-old brother, and when I think about people raping a child, I just felt sick. That was my motive, just a hate for what they've done. And I think that's what happened to most of these MPs and MI. They just snapped. I think they were just so sick of all this stuff, dealing with prisoners, and when they heard something horrible—the rape of a fifteen-year-old boy—they all just snapped. Well, that's what happened to me, at least. I just completely went nuts on the inside. Right before I left, I was so pissed off that I had a bottle of water and I splashed some of them, just to show pretty much my hate, that I hate what they have done to the poor boy."

AGAINST THE LITANY OF TRAUMAS to which the three prisoners had been subjected for well over an hour, splashing them with bottled water might hardly seem worth mentioning. Rather, it is the feeling behind the act that makes Krol's outburst striking. None of the MPs who spent their working hours doling out affliction on the MI block spoke of such hatred for their prisoners. They regarded them as enemies, with varying degrees of fear, anger, hostility, and contempt. But the animosity the MPs projected in the course of their dark labors was essentially impersonal. At times some of them may have found satisfaction, even pleasure, in their power to treat men as sacks of meat, but that power came from being in control, not from losing it. What had felt to Krol like a crisis of passion was for the MPs simply a drill—the standard hell night chore they performed with all new arrivals on the tier. They did not have to search inside themselves to explain their behavior. "If MI didn't exist at Abu Ghraib," Megan Ambuhl said, "the detainees would have been in their cells, and we would have been in the office watching a movie or drinking coffee."

Of course, the alleged rapists were not MI prisoners, but the involvement of so many MI soldiers in their torment left Ken Davis with the impression that MI was running the show—and the fact that it was a show, unabashed and unconcealed, gave him pause the next morning, when he went looking for his platoon leader, First Lieutenant Lewis Raeder, to report what he had seen. "A lot of different things go into your thinking," he said. "For not reporting something, you can get nailed for dereliction of duty. And if it comes out that it was OK, some people might be angry that you reported it. But, oh well, at least you're covering yourself, you're covering the situation." Knowing that Lynndie England had taken pictures while he was there bolstered his resolve. "So I went in to Lieutenant Raeder. I said, 'Sir, Military Intelligence over at the hard site—they are doing some pretty weird things with naked detainees.' He told me I had no business being over there, and he also told me, 'Stay out of MI's way and let them do their job.'"

Ken Davis let it go at that, and Ambuhl said that MI did, in fact, end up questioning the accused rapists, then turning the matter over to the Iraqi police, who determined that they hadn't raped the boy after all. Two of them remained on Tier 1B, where they were deemed likable and trustworthy enough by the MPs that they were soon given the honor of performing cleaning duty. The third, who was returned to his old cell block, was scheduled for a release hearing several weeks later, but he was killed when the convoy taking him to the courthouse struck a roadside bomb. It fell to Javal Davis to collect his belongings from his cell, and to break the news of his death to the other inmates on the block. That was the one story from Abu Ghraib that always caught in his throat when he told it.

"It bothered me," he said. "It saddened me, because a lot of those guys, even though they were criminals, and a lot of them had anti-American sentiment, and they expressed it, you know, they were human beings. They were becoming casualties of war just like U.S. soldiers or Iraqi insurgents and other people that aren't in uniform. He wasn't able to protect himself. I just—I was hurt by it. Man, the guy was on the way to get ready to go home and he didn't make it. So everyone's a loser in this situation—that was my take."

14.

THERE IS A CONSTANT TEMPTATION, when rendering an account of history, to distort reality by making too much sense of it. This temptation is greatest when the history is fresh and deals with crises that are ongoing—crises that mold our understanding of our world and ourselves. Surely, if you have come this far in this sordid tale, you must crave some relief, some release, from the relentless, claustrophobic annihilation of the dungeon: a clear and cleansing note of sanity, an interlude of avenging justice or an eruption of decency, the entry of a hero. But surely you don't want to be deceived. There is no such solace or sanctuary in this story. Abu Ghraib was bedlam, and the MI block was its sick, racing heart. There was no excuse for it, and there was nothing to show for it either, no great score of useful intelligence, no ends to justify the means. Nobody has ever even bothered to pretend otherwise. The horror of Tier 1A was entirely gratuitous, and it just kept getting worse.

"You probably know this by now, too," Sergeant Ken Davis said. "Once you dig your hands into Abu Ghraib, you don't come out the same. There's a part of you that either died, or that is totally confused."

So what's the point? What's the use? Why vex your soul?

What's the choice? There is no keeping our hands clean of Abu

Ghraib. Ignoring it doesn't work, nor does denouncing it, and there is no disavowing it, never mind denying it. The stain is inescapable and irreversible, and it is ours, and if we have any hope of containing it and living it down it can only come from seeing it whole.

THE STAIN IS OURS, because whatever else the Iraq war was about, it was always, above all, about America—about the projection of America's force and America's image into the world. Iraq was the stage, and Iraqis would suffer for that, enduring some fifty deaths for every American life lost: in this, and by every other measure of devastation, it was very much their war. But, although there were Iraqis who supported the war, seeing hope and opportunity for their country or themselves, the war was not their choice. It was an American war because America's elected officials decided to wage it of their own initiative, "at a time of our choosing," as the president said, and it was a war about America because it was fought in the name of our freedom and the world's. What was at stake, for the war's advocates, skeptics, and opponents alike, was an American story—the story of America as a champion of law and liberty at home and abroad, a tough but righteous arbiter of the destiny of nations, intolerant only of intolerance, a scourge to rogue regimes and bandit dictators who usurp the innate craving of all humankind to aspire to her example.

In their most soaring pitches the authors of the war described its objective as nothing less than the extension of the American Revolution to Saddam's tyrannized subjects—and then, by sheer power of influence, or by expansion of the campaign, to the rest of the Muslim world. Because of such claims the war was often cast by its more sympathetic chroniclers as a war of ideas: liberty, democracy, and human rights versus fascism, tribalism, and tyranny. And because democratic self-rule has never been imposed upon a people by the

military invasion of a foreign power, many of the war's critics regarded the adventure as romantic and reactionary, an imperial folly.
Either way, the president and his heralds were understood to be
charged by bold ambition, and as Abraham Lincoln said of America's
Founding Fathers: "If they succeeded, they were to be immortalized;
their names were to be transferred to counties and cities, and rivers
and mountains; and to be revered and sung, and toasted through all
time. If they failed, they were to be called knaves and fools, and fanat-
ics for a fleeting hour; then to sink and be forgotten." Only, by now,
the Founding Fathers' ambition had succeeded too well for an American failure on the scale and scope of the Iraq war to be so readily
consigned to oblivion.

One of the signal successes of Lincoln's great hero, General George
Washington, in the War of Independence was his insistence on the
civilized treatment of enemy prisoners. British policy allowed the
slaughter of Continental soldiers who were captured or surrendered,
and a great many of those who were not killed on the spot soon died
of savage abuse, disease, or starvation. But when the Americans took
hundreds of Hessian mercenaries prisoner after the battle of Prince-
ton, Washington ordered, "Let them have no reason to Complain of
our Copying the brutal example of the British army in their Treatment of our unfortunate brethren." And, just as the redcoats' atroci-
ties hardened anticolonial sentiment, this unilateral expression of
humanity gave Washington an advantage. Not only did it win over
the Hessians, scores of whom chose to settle in America after the war,
it also helped win international support for the American rebellion.

In Iraq, it had been obvious, long before the fighting began, that
with such a politically loaded war of choice it would never be enough
to win by overwhelming force; victory had to be secured equally in
the theater of global public opinion, where the war had been joined
in the immediate aftermath of September 11. Even in those fevered
times, with the wound fresh and the thirst for avenging justice run-

ning high, the cause was a hard sell; and in the wilderness of rhetoric that surrounded Iraq in the run-up to the invasion, it was impossible to be sure of the war's purpose. Yet amid the murky warnings of weapons of mass destruction being passed out to terrorists or aimed at London, and of smoking guns turning into mushroom clouds, a promise to replace Saddam's Stalinist prison system with the just and humane rule of law stood out as one of the clearest, most unobjectionable notes of the call to arms: no more nocturnal knocks on the door, no more disappearances, no more arbitrary arrests, no more torture and extermination of prisoners.

The whole of Iraq was portrayed, with some accuracy, as a giant penal colony, where even the unimprisoned were held hostage and shackled by fear of the state. And when we took the place over, and the dreaded arsenal proved to be a mirage, the claim that our presence was essentially humanitarian only grew louder and more insistent. Even as the president called an end to the conventional war in Iraq, and cast the occupation as the new front in the war on terror, he ended his May Day "mission accomplished" speech to the troops aboard the USS *Abraham Lincoln* with the rallying cry: "And wherever you go, you carry a message of hope—a message that is ancient and ever new. In the words of the prophet Isaiah, 'To the captives, "Come out," and to those in darkness, "Be free." ' "

Actually, Isaiah attributes those lines to God:

This is what the Lord says:
"In the time of my favor I will answer you,
and in the day of salvation I will help you;
I will keep you and will make you
to be a covenant for the people,
to restore the land
and to reassign its desolate inheritances,

> to say to the captives, 'Come out,'
> and to those in darkness, 'Be free!' ''

The Lord, the prophet, the president—whoever was speaking, the words seemed to suggest a greater favor than the simple reassignment of the desolate inheritances of Abu Ghraib. Did he really think nobody would notice? Did he even care? Perhaps he thought he could get away with it. And he has. But we can't.

OF COURSE, America has always run nasty clandestine operations in the name of freedom. In the past, however, such work was undertaken with the understanding that crimes committed in the name of national security were still crimes. That's why the vice president called it the "dark side," and spoke of the need to put "some very unsavory characters" on the payroll. But that was before his lawyers and the president's decided that in the war on terror it was more expeditious to replace the law with the theory that torture is a phantom crime, defined by an unprovable intention to impose an unattainable level of pain. With that nagging problem dispatched, and in the face of a deadly and determined insurgency that nobody involved with launching America's biggest military operation since Vietnam had anticipated, much less prepared for, the "mean, nasty, dangerous, dirty business" of rounding up Iraqis, imprisoning them without charges, insulting, abusing, and, yes, torturing them, was assigned to the sort of people the vice president presumably meant when he spoke dismissively of "officially approved, certified good guys": ordinary American soldiers who could not see themselves as thugs even when they photographed themselves engaged in thuggery.

It is much easier to understand the vice president's attraction to the dark side than the abject incompetence and amateurism with which it was brought to bear in the bright glare of the flashbulbs at Abu Ghraib. It is almost as much a cause for national pride as it is for despair that some American soldiers didn't seem to understand, or to care, that they were supposed to be keeping their diabolical assignment a secret, that they never fully accepted the guilty code of *omertà* that comes naturally to those who are truly and self-consciously corrupt. They never entirely lost sight of the absurdity and insanity of their position. Even as they sank into a routine of depravity, they showed by their picture taking that they did not accept it as normal. They never fully got with the program. Is it not to their credit that they were profoundly demoralized by their service in the netherworld?

Inexperienced, untrained, under attack, and under orders to do wrong, the low-ranking reservist MPs who implemented the nefarious policy of the war on terror on the MI block of the Abu Ghraib hard site knew that what they were doing was immoral, and they knew that if it wasn't illegal, it ought to be. They knew that they had the right, and that it was their duty, to disobey an unlawful order and to report it to their immediate superior; and if that failed—or if that superior was the source of the order—to keep reporting it on up the chain of command until they found satisfaction.

"You're taught from the very beginning that you have to follow your orders, and if you don't you're going to get in trouble," Megan Ambuhl said. "And if you do, obviously you'll end up in trouble if someone finds out and they didn't like the orders that you were given. It's easy for retired colonels and generals and majors or whatever to stand there and say, 'Well, these people should have known illegal orders, and they should have stood up to these lieutenant colonels and majors. They should have stood up to them at the time, in a war zone where lives were at stake.' It's just kind of unrealistic to think that would happen." Besides, Ambuhl said, "At the time, everyone in our chain of command said that was OK. The questions were asked and answered. So after that, what do you do?"

"I don't know what I could have done different," Sabrina Harman said. "I could have said, 'Screw you, I'm not working here,' and just gone to jail for disobeying an order. I guess. But I don't know. I'm sure everybody can do something different. I just don't know what I would do different, put in the same situation."

Do these soldiers sound like they're just making excuses? Didn't some of them take liberties, and go to extremes—didn't they treat suggestions as orders, and then interpret them as they pleased—when they might instead have shown compassion? Yes. But what happened to command responsibility? There would have been no liberties to be taken, and no extremes to go to, if anybody had wanted to keep the MPs in check. Nobody wanted to because at Abu Ghraib lawlessness was the law.

ONE AFTERNOON, IN MID-NOVEMBER, Charles Graner reported for the night shift on Tier 1A, and found six new prisoners, hooded and waiting. Sergeant Joyner explained that they had just been brought from Camp Vigilant, where they had allegedly tried to start a riot. Joyner passed on a request from Lieutenant Colonel Jordan that Graner should PT them—"which was assumed at this point that it was, you know, naked and ups and downs with the sandbags on their head," Graner said. He took charge of them, and began strip-searching them, an inevitable procedure for new arrivals to the tier, but the prisoner he started with was resistant. "I bashed him against the wall," Graner said. The prisoner collapsed to the floor, and in the log Graner wrote, "Blood began to come from under the sand bag. When I checked it

looked as if his nose was bleeding and the sandbag was placed back
on his head. Someone notified medical and a corpsman checked and
found a 1½ inch laceration on the right side of his chin."

The prisoner required eight stitches, and Graner helped sew him
up. He also made sure the situation was photographed in step-by-step
detail: the prisoner lying on the floor with blood running under his
chin, as if his throat had been slit, and more blood smeared over his
face; Graner crouched over him, wearing surgical gloves, focused in-
tently on his forceps and thread; the blood-streaked wall where the
prisoner had been bashed; the prisoner's blood-soaked shirt, laid out
with care on the floor, like a holy relic. Graner then passed out the
evening meal on the tier, and while he was at it Captain Brinson and
First Sergeant Lipinski came to see what was up with the wounded
man. When Graner turned his attention back to the other new arrivals, one of them was not following his instructions, so he hit him, too.
"You know," he said, "I tell you what to do in Arabic, and you didn't
understand what I'm saying—smacked him across the face just like I
did everybody else."

Graner began stripping the prisoners for PT, as he understood
Jordan wanted him to, but Brinson told him to keep them clothed
and put them in their cells. So Graner put them in jumpsuits, and,
he said, "As each prisoner was finished, except for the man with
stitches, who I had walked to the cell, the others with sandbags were
made to crawl to their cells while First Sergeant Lipinski and Captain
Brinson watched me." Graner also said that Captain Avery, a Marine
lawyer with the Judge Advocate General's Corps, was on the tier that
night, as he was "almost on a daily basis." Avery and another JAG
officer, Captain Fitch, who was Colonel Pappas's legal adviser, were
familiar with the sight of naked inmates, "people out on the floor
getting PT'd, prisoners hanging from the doors," Graner said. Sometimes, one of them would see something happening with a prisoner,
and say, "Hey, this is wrong," or, "Operationally, we can't do this."

But when they said nothing, Graner took their silence as "implied consent—that this was all OK because here's a JAG person, and he doesn't seem to see that there's anything wrong with this."

Apparently Avery was not so comfortable with the sight of the prisoner with the gashed chin, and he mentioned it to another JAG officer, who was less familiar with the tier. "A red flag had gone up," Graner said, and Brinson, who was his platoon leader, felt compelled to leave a paper trail about the incident. Two days later he presented Graner with a Developmental Counseling Form, a standard Army document by which an officer can formally communicate his concerns to a soldier whom he considers to be in need of guidance. Under the heading Key Points of Discussion, Brinson had written:

> CPL Graner, you are doing a fine job in Tier 1 of the BCF [Baghdad Correctional Facility]. As the NCOIC of the "MI Hold" area, you have received many accolades from the MI units here and specifically from LTC Jordan. Continue to perform at this level and it will help us succeed at our overall mission.

> I am concerned about two matters related to your performance. First, SFC Snider has spoken to you about your appearance while on duty. I require all soldiers to maintain the Army's uniform and appearance standards at all times and encourage them to exceed them when possible. I want to reinforce this issue with you now.

> Second, due to the higher level of stress associated with working in Tier 1, I am concerned that it does not affect your performance. Many times you have to deal with security detainees that are of the highest intelligence value. These detainees often try to incite our soldiers to aggressive acts by taunting them or not responding to commands. In addition, Tier 1 houses the isolation cells for the hard site prison. These cells are filled with detainees whose non-

compliant and/or aggressive behavior has placed them in isolation. Also, Tier 1 holds detainees with mental health issues. These detainees add to the stress of working in Tier 1.

There was an incident on 14 NOV 03 involving a security detainee whose actions in your words required you to use force to regain control of the situation. The detainee received abrasions and cuts on his face from the incident. Let me state first and foremost, you have an inherent right to self-defense that cannot be taken away from you. I one hundred percent support your decision when you believe you must defend yourself. You stated that you escalated your actions through the approved levels of force. You stated you used the appropriate level of force up through the continuum of the use of force to contain the situation. Then you stated that you ceased all use of force and sought medical attention for the detainee. Statements from the other MP working that evening do not shed any light on the incident. Unless other evidence presents itself, I accept your version of events.

That was the first page, and on the second, under the heading Plan of Action, Brinson advised Graner that he would be provided again with the MPs' rules of engagement—the sheet that laid out the shout, shove, show, shoot approach to the escalation of force—as well as a JAG officer to answer any questions he had about it. Brinson also told Graner that his work assignment would be adjusted to allow him time away from the tier, and that he would be given access to the chaplain and "other counseling options for stress management." If Graner ever sought or received counseling, there is no record of it, and he remained on the MI block for another month before being reassigned for a month to work on prisoner transport convoys, which was what he said he'd wanted all along. Technically, the counseling form was a warning. But Brinson had a political mind; in civilian life, he worked as the legislative director and homeland security liaison for Congressman Mike Rogers, an Alabama Republican on the Armed Services Committee. If he had found fault with Graner, he would have had to account for it, and for himself, to his own commanders. By heaping his soldier with praise, he covered himself in both directions, and Graner and his colleagues took his write-up at its word, as a commendation and a green light.

"He got a that-a-boy," Javal Davis said.

THE RED CROSS, TOO, WAS POLITIC—albeit in the name of remaining apolitical. Less than a week after the 372nd had assumed duty at the hard site, the ICRC had returned to Abu Ghraib to complete its suspended assessment of the MI block. This time, after testy negotiations, the delegates were able to see the prisoners they asked to see, albeit briefly, during the day shift, and under the watch of military minders who prohibited them from inquiring about anything but the inmates' identity and health. "That was a whole bad situation," Sergeant Jeffery Frost said. "They wanted us to just open up all the cells and let them walk around and interview all the detainees. We understood that it's their right, but this is our prison—you do have to go by our rules."

Never mind that the Army's rules were officially the same as the ICRC's—the Geneva Conventions; Frost said that even when General Janis Karpinski toured the prison, the word would come down in advance to clean up the tier: the floors would be scrubbed; the prisoners would be bathed and made presentable. "We'd have a dog and pony show," he said. "Everybody would get their mattress back. Everybody would get their clothes back. And then, as soon as the people left, whoever was deprived of certain things got deprived of it again." Karpinski's visits were rare, but Frost said the charade was a nuisance.

The Red Cross delegates, however, were not so readily diverted and, based on their two visits, they reported—in person, at the time, to the prison command, and several weeks later, in writing, to Karpinski herself—that Tier 1A was the scene of gross and systematic violations of the Geneva Conventions. The ICRC's written report described prisoners kept naked and sleepless, in stress positions, in lightless cells, with wrists raw and scarred from improper handcuffing, and minds rattled by psychological trauma—"incoherent speech, acute anxiety reactions . . . suicidal ideas"—and the ICRC ultimately concluded that the "ill treatment" of these prisoners "in some cases was tantamount to torture."

The findings were damning, a sharp cry of alarm—especially as the report made it clear that the brutality on the MI block was known and condoned by the top officers in charge at Abu Ghraib. But the ICRC is run out of headquarters in Geneva with the same tight-lipped ethic of client confidentiality as a Swiss bank, sharing its assessments of prison conditions only with the governments and armies responsible for them. This closed-circuit system of monitoring and accountability, which relies on mutual good faith and rectitude, leaves the Red Cross toothless, and effectively an accomplice to cover-ups, when the abuse of prisoners is the result of policy, as it was at the hard site. So when Red Cross delegates visited Nazi concentration camps during World War II, they told nobody about what they saw and heard except the Nazis. In such compromised circumstances, Red Cross reports cannot serve their legal or humanitarian purposes unless they are leaked to the public, as the report on Abu Ghraib was—six months later. At the time, however, it had no effect.

Karpinski, who understood Tier 1A to be MI's turf, not hers, passed the report on to Colonel Marc Warren, the legal adviser to General Sanchez, who had written the interrogation rules for the prison. "I couldn't believe it," Warren said. So he made inquiries: "I spoke to Judge Advocates and MI officers who were familiar with the conditions at Abu Ghraib, and the uniform reaction was that these reports could not be credible." In particular Warren spoke to Colonel Pappas's deputy and his chief legal adviser, and, he said, "I remember a conversation in which the statement was made that the allegations were crazy." With these reassurances, Warren set about drafting a letter for Karpinski to sign that dismissed the ICRC's findings as a misguided and hostile fantasy.

It would have been outrageous, of course, if the overseers of America's biggest MI operation in Iraq didn't know what was happening with their most valued prisoners. But the complicity, the blind eye and the cover-up, the buck passing and the butt covering, the self-deception and the cowardice, the indiscipline and the incompetence infected every link in the chain of command that ran from the MI block to the Pentagon and the White House—a military bureaucracy that had been politically cowed and corrupted from the top down by civilian masters who had no experience of combat. Later, when the photographs from the MI block were made public, and America's disgrace was the talk of the world, there would be no end of speculation as to whether a direct link could be found—a document or a trail of documents, some undeniable evidence—tying the scenes in those pictures directly to those top civilians, the president, the vice president, the secretary of defense. This supposedly missing link was spoken of as the "smoking gun." But it wasn't missing; it was there right in front of us. Abu Ghraib was the smoking gun.

15.

<hr/>

A LITTLE AFTER FOUR IN THE MORNING on November 4, 2003, a new prisoner was brought to Abu Ghraib and driven straight to the hard site. The day shift had just begun, and Sergeant Tony Diaz was filling in for Hydrue Joyner as the MP in charge of the MI block. Jeffery Frost was there, too. The Americans who appeared with the new prisoner, an interrogator and his translator, were clad in black, and identified themselves as OGA men. "CIA guys," Frost said. The prisoner had a sandbag over his head. His hands were cuffed at his back, and he was wearing only a T-shirt—no pants, no underwear, no shoes or socks. "He was pretty banged up. They said that he was resisting being arrested," Frost said, and Diaz said, "He was breathing very hard. You could hear his heart, too. It was a very loud beat. I mean, everything was OK—he was talking while he was coming in. They were interrogating him."

The MPs asked no questions. "Who this guy was, what he did, that wasn't our business," Diaz said. "All we did was process him." There was no paperwork, of course, with a ghost prisoner. Processing him meant taking away his shirt, searching him, zipping him into a jumpsuit, and marching him to the shower on Tier 1B, where the CIA interrogator instructed the MPs to shackle his handcuffed hands to a window behind him in a Palestinian hanging position. Then the MPs were dismissed. They locked the barred shower-room doors behind them, draped them with bedsheets for privacy, and got on with their morning rounds.

An hour later—or perhaps it was an hour and a half—Diaz and Frost were having coffee, when the interrogator emerged from the shower and asked for their help. The prisoner wasn't responding to questions, and the interrogator wanted his hands bound higher on the bars to increase his discomfort. The MPs went in, and Diaz hoisted the man up while Frost raised the shackle. Then Diaz let go, and the prisoner sagged forward on his arms. "I was like, 'Wow, this guy is strong,' " Diaz said. "I mean you could see the handcuff—it's like all his weight was resting on his wrists."

The interrogator, who had taken a seat, kept asking questions steadily while he watched the MPs maneuver his silent prisoner. Now he asked them to raise the man's hands higher still. This time, Frost did the hoisting. "I'm just holding him by the jumpsuit," he said. "I'm not holding him under the arms or anything, and his jumpsuit is riding up his crotch. I said, 'Damn this guy is pretty good at playing possum, because I know I'd be howling like whatever.' Everybody just kind of laughed and nobody really thought anything of it."

When the handcuffs were readjusted, Frost let go. "I remember how far back his arms were going," he said. "It was just a really awkward position, and I again was like, 'This guy's pretty damn good, because his arms are almost about to break, or I'm surprised they haven't broken. I'm waiting for the pop.' "

Diaz said the interrogator kept on with his questions. "We were like, 'Whoa, this is just not right,' " Diaz said. "I kind of came close, trying to hear his heart. I didn't hear anything." He sent an MP for cold water, and when the bucket came he splashed the prisoner. The man didn't flinch. "That's when I raised the hood," Diaz said, "and that's the first time I saw his face. His face was totally messed up— huge black eyes, and bruises everywhere." One eye was swollen shut, and the other was open. Diaz couldn't make out what that open eye was looking at. He wiggled a finger close to the prisoner's nose, but the eye stared right past it, and it occurred to Diaz: "This guy is not even alive."

He said he told the interrogator, "Sir, this guy is dead," and the interrogator said, "Really? He can't be dead."

"I don't know if he actually knew that he was dead, and he was trying to cover it up," Diaz said. "But to me, he pretended like he didn't know that he was dead. I said, 'Yes sir, he's dead.' And that's when he picked up his cell phone, and started calling people. He walked out of the shower."

When Diaz and Frost uncuffed the prisoner and lowered him to the floor, blood spilled from his nose and mouth. Diaz told the interrogator, "Hey, listen, this is on you guys." Then he got on his own radio and called for help, too.

During his time at Abu Ghraib, Diaz had devoted many evenings to the video game Max Pain, whose eponymous hero is an ex-cop seeking revenge for the murder of his wife and son. "He goes after the bad guys," Diaz explained. "He goes on his own, takes everything into his own hands, trying to find out the guys that actually killed his family. He succeeds at the end. He kills them all." Diaz had mastered the game; when he became Max Pain he, too, killed all the bad guys. "That was a way to entertain yourself," he said. But he had never before had anything to do with a real dead person—"cemeteries, that's all I seen, tombs," he said—and he couldn't get his mind around the idea that he'd seen the corpse at his feet walk in the door an hour and a half earlier.

"This whole time we were messing with this guy, carrying him and lifting him—this entire time the guy was dead," Diaz said. "I even got some blood on my uniform because he was dripping. And it kind of felt bad, because I know I'm not part of this, but it kind of makes you feel like you are."

AS WORD OF THE DEATH SPREAD through the Abu Ghraib chain of
command, a parade of senior officers filed through the Tier 1B shower.
The CIA men refused to take their destroyed prisoner with them
when they left, and nobody knew how to handle the corpse of someone who had been officially nonexistent when he was alive. What do
you call a dead ghost? Nobody even knew his name.

When Colonel Pappas showed up, he said, "I'm not going down
alone for this." It wasn't clear if he was threatening anybody in particular, but nothing more needed to be said to ensure that the collective interest in deniability was keenly felt. So medics were called in
to clean the dead man up, bandage his open wounds, and pack him
in ice in a body bag. Then the shower was scrubbed down with bleach,
the body bag was zipped shut and placed in a corner, the room was
locked, and a note was made in the cell block log: "1B shower not to
be used until OGA is moved out."

That afternoon, when the night-shift MPs reported for duty at the
hard site, Captain Brinson called them to a meeting. "He said there
was a prisoner who had died in the shower, and he died of a heart attack," Sabrina Harman said. She and Graner were on duty that night,
and they were curious, of course—everyone was—but they got on
with their work.

The night before, a CID agent named Ricardo Romero, who was
a regular on the MI block, had brought in a new prisoner who was
suspected of involvement in the killing of one of Romero's fellow CID
agents. The story was that the prisoner kept giving a false name, and
insisting that he was not who the CID said he was. "They thought he
was lying," Graner said. "If they could figure out he was lying about
his name, they had him on the other thing, so I had instructions from
Chief Romero . . . His words were 'Make his life a living hell for the
next three days and find out his name.' " Graner had given the pris-

oner the nickname Gilligan, and subjected him to the standard treatment: the yelling, the PT, the MRE box to hold or stand on. He kept Gilligan hooded, and normally he would have had him naked, too; only, he said, "It was ungodly cold those couple nights." So Graner had cut a hole in a prison blanket and draped it over the prisoner like a poncho. But that was it for pity. Now, for a second night, Gilligan was standing on his box, this time in the shower on Tier 1A, and Graner was yelling at him in his best Marine drill instructor's voice—"just yelling at him the whole night," he said, "you know, more or less repeating the first half of *Full Metal Jacket,* loud as you could to him, and then asking him what his name was."

For a while that night, Graner's friend, Specialist Matthew Smith, stopped by and joined in the yelling, and Javal Davis, too, paid a visit and loaned his voice to the chorus. So did Sergeant Frederick. Frederick said that when he came through the block on his nightly security rounds, he found Agent Romero on Tier 1B flirting with a female prisoner through her cell bars—chatting with her and blowing kisses. Frederick said that he asked Romero about Gilligan, and that Romero said, "I don't give a fuck what you do to him, just don't kill him."

Frederick said he took Romero's words "like an order, but not a specific order," and he explained, "To me, Agent Romero was like an authority figure, and when he said he needed the detainee stressed out, I wanted to make sure the detainee was stressed out." So Frederick went to the shower and surveyed the scene. Graner was taking a break, and Gilligan was perched on his box. Frederick noticed some loose electrical wires hanging from the wall behind Gilligan. "I grabbed them and touched them together to make sure they weren't live wires," he said. "When I did that and got nothing, I tied a loop knot on the end, put it on, I believe, his index finger, and left it there." Frederick said that Javal Davis and Harman came into the shower while he was doing this, and somebody then tied a wire to Gilligan's other hand, and draped another below his throat. "I recall

Davis saying something about, where is the switch—or something like that," Frederick said. But Harman said, "I told him that. I told him not to fall off, that he would be electrocuted if he did."

Harman had been busy for much of the night, keeping the prisoner they called the Claw awake, and attending to Shitboy, who had soiled himself again. She was taking a break when she joined the others in the shower, and although Gilligan understood English, she wasn't sure if he believed her threat or not.

"I knew he wouldn't be electrocuted," she said. "So it really didn't bother me. I mean, it was just words. There was really no action in it. It would have been meaner if there really was electricity coming out, and he really could be electrocuted. No physical harm was ever done to him." In fact, she said, "He was laughing at us towards the end of the night, maybe because he knew we couldn't break him." The whole mock-electrocution business had lasted no more than ten or fifteen minutes, just long enough for a photo session. As soon as the wires were attached to Gilligan, Frederick had stepped back, instructed Gilligan to hold his arms out straight from his sides like wings, and taken a picture. Then he took another, identical to the first: the hooded man, in his poncho cape, barefoot atop his box, arms outstretched, wires trailing from his fingers. *Snap, snap*—two seconds—and three minutes later, Harman took a similar shot, but from a few steps back so that Frederick appears in the foreground at the edge of the frame, studying the picture he's just taken on the display screen of his camera, the picture that would become the best known, most recognized, and most widely reproduced image of the war.

These were not the first photographs taken on the block that night, nor were they the last. Shortly after the session with Gilligan, somebody noticed water trickling out from under the door to the shower on Tier 1B. Graner got the key, and Harman accompanied him to see what was going on. "The guy who got killed—he started to melt," she said. "He was there for hours, and all the ice that was on top of him was just draining out." As she entered the shower, Harman snapped a picture of the black rubber body bag lying along the far wall. Graner shot it, too. Then, with their hands sheathed in turquoise-colored latex surgical gloves, they went over and unzipped the bag.

"We just checked him out and took photos of him," Harman said. "Kind of realized right away that there was no way he died of a heart attack, because of all the cuts and blood coming out of his nose. You don't think your commander's going to lie to you about something. It made my trust go down, that's for sure. Well, you can't trust your commander now."

TRANSLUCENT PLASTIC ICE BAGS blanketed the dead prisoner from the neck down, but his battered, bandaged face was exposed—mouth agape as if in midspeech. Harman, the aspiring forensic photographer, shot him from a variety of angles, zooming in and out, while Graner swabbed the floor. When he was done he took a photograph of her, posing with the corpse, bending low into the frame, flashing her Kodak smile and giving the thumbs-up with one gloved hand. She used his camera to take a similar shot of him, and with that, after about six minutes in the shower, she zipped the body bag shut, and they left.

"I guess we weren't really thinking, Hey, this guy has family, or, Hey, this guy was just murdered," Harman said of those parting happy snaps. "It was just—Hey, it's a dead guy, it'd be cool to get a photo next to a dead person. I know it looks bad. I mean, even when I look at them, I go, Oh Jesus, that does look pretty bad. But when we were in that situation, it wasn't as bad as it looks coming out on the media, I guess, because people have photos of all kinds of things. Like, if a soldier sees somebody dead, normally they'll take photos of it."

Harman might have more accurately said that it's not unusual to take such pictures. Soldiers have always swapped crazy war stories—whether to boast or confess, to moralize or titillate—and the uncritical response of other soldiers at Abu Ghraib to the photographs from the MI block night shift suggests that they were seen as belonging to this comradely tradition. Javal Davis took no photographs at the hard site, and he appeared in none, but he said, "Everyone in theater had a digital camera. Everyone was taking pictures of everything, from detainees to death. Like in Vietnam, where guys were taking pictures of the dead guy with a cigarette in his mouth. Like, 'Hey, Mom, look.' It sounds sick, but over there that was commonplace, it was nothing. The mind-set over there, I'd say, would be numb. I mean, when you're surrounded by death and carnage and violence twenty-four hours a day, seven days a week, it absorbs you. You walk down the street and you see a dead body on the road, whereas a couple months ago, you would have been like, 'Oh my God, a dead body,' today you're like, 'Damn, he got messed up, let's go get something to eat.' You could watch someone running down the street burning on fire, as long as it's not an American soldier, it's, 'Somebody needs to go put that guy out.' "

But there's a big difference between photographing the outrages of war and using them as the backdrop for staged trophy shots. Seeing Harman and Graner mugging over the dead prisoner, there is no escaping the impression that these soldiers were celebrating his death, and the suggestion that perhaps they had some hand in it. The pictures may have been taken as a gag—"for personal use," as Frederick said of his photos of Gilligan—but they seem starkly at odds with Harman's claim to a larger documentary purpose in taking pictures at Abu Ghraib. By contrast, her grisly, intimate portraits of the corpse by itself convey her experience of shock at discovering its wreckage.

Later that evening, Harman returned to the shower with Frederick to examine the body more carefully. This time, she looked beneath the ice bags and peeled back the bandages, and she stayed out of the pictures. "I just started taking photos of everything I saw that was wrong, every little bruise and cut," she said. "His knees were bruised, his thighs were bruised by his genitals. He had restraint marks on his wrists. He just had bruises everywhere. You had to look close. I mean, they did a really good job cleaning him up. The gauze on his eye was put there after he died to make it look like he had medical treatment, because he didn't when he came into the prison. There were so many things around the bandage, like the blood coming out of his nose and his ears. And his tooth was chipped—I didn't know if that happened there or before—his lip was split open. And it looked like somebody had either butt-stocked him or hit him against the wall. It was a pretty good-sized gash. I took a photo of that as well. I just wanted to document everything I saw. That was the reason I took photos. It was to prove to pretty much anybody who looked at this guy, Hey, I was just lied to. This guy did not die of a heart attack. Look at all these other existing injuries that they tried to cover up."

Graner had a different idea of what the photos proved. The next time some OGA men asked him to take a prisoner who'd collapsed during an interrogation back to his cell, he said, "I didn't worry about it. You know these guys can kill people. Somebody unconscious—I'll drag him back to his cell."

AFTER NEARLY THIRTY HOURS in the shower, the corpse was removed from the tier disguised as a sick prisoner—in order, Lieutenant Colonel Jordan said, not to spark a "general uprising" in the prison. Jordan described the procedure like this: "They put the body on a gurney, rolled down the body bag that he'd been in, put a blanket over, taped a used IV inside his arm like he was receiving IV, and put an oxygen mask on, and moved him out." Hydrue Joyner, who was back on duty that day, was reminded of the slapstick Hollywood farce *Weekend at Bernie's,* in which two buffoonish corporate climbers treat their murdered boss as a puppet, pretending he's alive to avoid suspicion in his death.

"Un-freaking-believable," Joyner said of the charade with the IV bag. "But this came from on high. They didn't want any of the prisoners thinking we were in there killing folks." In the log, Joyner referred to the dead man as Bernie, but Army investigators soon identified him as a suspected insurgent named Manadel al-Jamadi, who was alleged to have provided explosives for the bombing that blew up the Red Cross headquarters in Baghdad a week before his arrest. Within the week that followed, an autopsy concluded that al-Jamadi had succumbed to "blunt force injuries" and "compromised respiration," and his death was classified as a homicide.

Around the same time, the CID determined that Gilligan was not, after all, who he was suspected of being during his ordeal in the shower. "So all of that, and the poor guy was innocent," Harman said. He remained on Tier 1A, and soon became one of the MPs' favorite prisoners. Like the men on 1B who had been accused of rape, put through hell, then exonerated, Gilligan was given the privileged status of a block worker, and regularly let out of his cell to help with the cleaning. Megan Ambuhl called him "pretty decent," and said she had a picture of him sharing a meal and a smoke with Charles Graner. Gilligan, she said, "didn't seem to be suffering any ill effects" from his earlier treatment; and Sabrina Harman said, "He was just a funny, funny guy. If you were going to take someone home, I definitely would have taken him."

Under the circumstances, Harman was baffled that the figure of

Gilligan, as Frederick had photographed him—hooded, caped, and wired on his box—had eventually become the icon of Abu Ghraib, and probably the most recognized emblem of the war on terror after the World Trade Center towers. The image had proliferated around the globe in uncountable reproductions and representations, in the press, of course, but also in murals and placards, T-shirts and billboards, on mosque walls and in art galleries. Years later, Harman herself had even acquired a Gilligan tattoo on one arm, but she considered that a private matter. It was the public's fascination with the photograph of Gilligan—of all the images from Abu Ghraib—that she couldn't fathom. "I think they thought he was being tortured, which he wasn't," she said. "There's so many worse photos out there. I mean, nothing negative happened to him, really."

Why Gilligan, when al-Jamadi had been lying dead in the adjacent shower? Harman's pictures, taken fifteen minutes after the Gilligan session, were the only evidence outside of secret Army and CIA and Justice Department investigations that the man had been killed during an interrogation. And never mind murder. "Look at Taxi Driver," Harman said. "That was pretty bad." Her first photograph of a prisoner still haunted her, the image of her moment of initiation into the horror of Abu Ghraib. Taxi Driver had been hung from his back-stretched arms—naked and hooded with underpants—in exactly the same agonizing position that al-Jamadi had been in when he died. "I thought that was worse than Gilligan just standing there, being kept awake," she said.

Harman was right: those pictures were worse. But, leaving aside the fact that photographs of death and nudity, however newsworthy, don't get much play in the press, the power of an image does not necessarily reside in what it depicts. A photograph of a mangled cadaver, or of a naked man trussed in torment, can shock and outrage, provoke protest and investigation, but it leaves little to the imagination. It may be rich in practical information while being devoid of

any broader meaning. To the extent that it represents any circumstances or conditions beyond itself, it does so generically. Such photographs are repellent in large part because they have a terrible,
reductive sameness. Except from a forensic point of view, they are
unambiguous, and have the quality of pornography. They are what
they show, nothing more. They communicate no vision and, shorn of
context, they offer little, if anything, to think about, no occasion for
wonder. They have no value as symbols.

Of course, the dominant symbol of Western civilization is the
figure of a nearly naked man being tortured to death—or, more simply, the torture implement itself, the cross. But our pictures of Christ's
savage death are the product of religious imagination and idealiza-
tion. In reality, with his battered flesh scabbed and bleeding and
bloated and discolored beneath the pitiless Judean desert sun, he must
have been ghastly to behold. Had there been cameras at Calvary,
would twenty centuries of believers have been moved to hang photographs of the scene on their altarpieces and in their homes, or to wear
an icon of a man being executed around their necks as an emblem of
peace and hope and human fellowship?

Photography is too frank to allow for the notion of suffering as
noble or ennobling. Frederick's photograph of Gilligan achieves its
power from the fact that it does not show the human form laid bare
and reduced to raw matter, but rather because it creates an original
image of inhumanity that admits no immediately self-evident reading. Its fascination resides, in large part, in its mystery and inscruta-
bility—in all that is concealed by all that is revealed. It is an image
of carnival weirdness: this upright body shrouded from head to foot;
those wires; that pose that recalls, of course, the crucifixion; and the
peaked hood that carries so many vague and ghoulish associations.
The pose is obviously contrived and theatrical, a deliberate invention
that appears to belong to some dark ritual, a primal scene of martyr-
dom. The picture fixates us because it looks like the truth, but, look-

ing at it, we can only imagine what that truth is: torture, execution, a scene staged for the camera? So we seize on the figure of Gilligan as a symbol that stands for all that we know was wrong at Abu Ghraib and all that we cannot—or do not want to—understand about how it came to this.

16.

────

BRUTALITY IS BORING. Over and over, hell night after hell night, the same old dumb, tedious, bestial routine: making men crawl; making men groan, hanging men from the bars; shoving men; slapping men; freezing men in the showers; running men into walls; displaying shackled fathers to their sons and sons to their fathers. And if it turned out that you'd been given the wrong man, when you were done making his life unforgettably small and nasty, you allowed him to be your janitor and pick up the other prisoners' trash.

There was always another prisoner, and another. Faceless men under hoods: you stripped them of their clothes, you stripped them of their pride. There wasn't much more you could take away from them, but people are inventive: one night some soldiers took a razor to one of Saddam's former generals on Tier 1A and shaved off his eyebrows. He was an old man. "He looked like a grandfather and seemed like a nice guy," Sabrina Harman said, and she had tried to console him, telling him he looked younger, and slipping him a few cigarettes. Then she had to make him stand at attention facing a boom box blasting the rapper Eminem, singing about raping his mother, or committing arson, or sneering at suicides, something like that—these were some of the best-selling songs in American history.

"Eminem is pretty much torture all in himself, and if one person's getting tortured, everybody is, because that music's horrible," Harman said. The general maintained his bearing against the onslaught of noise. "He looked so sad," Harman said. "I felt so bad for the guy." In fact, she said, "Out of everything I saw, that's the worst." This seems implausible, or at least illogical, until you think about it. The MI block was a place where a dead guy was just a dead guy. And a guy hanging from a window frame or a guy forced to drag his nakedness over a wet concrete floor—well, how could you relate to that, except maybe to take a picture? But a man who kept his chin up while you blasted him with rape anthems, an old man shorn of his eyebrows whose very presence made you think of his grandkids—you could let that get to you, especially if you had to share in his punishment: "Slut, you think I won't choke no whore / til the vocal cords don't work in her throat no more! . . ." or whatever the song was.

The one good thing Harman could say for the incessant din on the tier was that it helped her ignore the screams of prisoners undergoing interrogation in the showers, or under the back stairs. Lynndie England wished she could say the same. There was a night when she thought she was listening to a man being killed. "OGA was in there, doing the interrogation," she said. "We didn't see what they did to him, but we heard it. I was only in there for about five to ten minutes, and I couldn't take the screaming, so I left. It was that bad."

The others couldn't leave, but they could still be shocked. For Megan Ambuhl there was the night when she was having a cigarette, and an OGA guy—she was pretty sure he was FBI—emerged from the shower and told her she could take the prisoner in there back to his cell. "I went to get him," she said. "He was handcuffed to the window in the manner the guy died in, so I uncuffed him, and I was bringing him back to his cell, and the FBI guy said something about it would be funny if I burn him with the cigarette. That one—I just kind of let the guy leave—and I took the detainee and put him in his cell."

The MPs could even shock themselves. On November 7, two days after al-Jamadi's corpse was fitted with an IV and an oxygen mask and rolled out of the hard site, there was a riot at Camp Ganci. Protests over conditions in the overcrowded tent city were a regular occurrence, and it hadn't taken long for the prisoners to discover that they were sleeping on landfill; with a little scraping and digging they could unearth bits of scrap metal and bottles and other debris that made handy projectiles, and they all seemed to know how to use a scrap of cloth as a slingshot. That afternoon, as guards scrambled to control the angry captives, something hard and rough, a brick or a chunk of concrete, flew over the wire and struck a female MP in the face. The Quick Reaction Force and three additional MP teams were called in, Ganci was surrounded by Humvees mounted with SAWs—squad automatic weapons—for laying down suppressive fire, and order was restored without further injury. That night, under a near full moon, seven men who had been identified as the instigators of the melee were delivered to the hard site for isolation and possible interrogation on the MI block. They arrived on Tier 1A around ten, and by the time they were shown to their cells three and a half hours later, they had been thrown in a pile, jumped on, punched, stripped, written on with a magic marker, stacked atop one another in a human pyramid, posed to simulate oral sex, lined up against a wall, and made to masturbate—and none of the MPs who took part in this unhinged variety show could come up with an excuse for it.

"IT REALLY STARTED OUT as a very normal night," Specialist Jeremy Sivits said. "I finished my day in the motor pool, and I had generator detail that night in the company tactical operations center. Just sitting there at night, it gets very boring. I was trying to get on the computer—we had just gotten e-mail established, and it would take

STANDARD OPERATING PROCEDURE

like a half hour sometimes to load up—and Sergeant Frederick walked in. We started talking, and he got a call on the radio that he had some individuals he had to in-process. He said, 'Hey, if you ain't got nothing to do, you want to go down to the hard site with me?' I was like, 'Yeah, anything to make the time go by quicker.' "

The seven prisoners from Camp Ganci were in a holding area at the front of the hard site, with sandbags on their heads and their hands bound behind them with zip-tie flex cuffs. As a mechanic, Sivits never dealt with prisoners at Abu Ghraib, but he considered Frederick a good buddy, and he was always happy to help his comrades out, so he offered to escort one of the prisoners to Tier 1A. Javal Davis was also there to lend a hand, along with Sergeant First Class Snider, Frederick's overseer at the hard site, and Specialist Matthew Wisdom, an MP who worked the night shift on one of the CPA cell blocks. Sivits took his place toward the end of the procession of guards, and as they came onto the tier, Graner instructed them to dump the prisoners in a pile on the floor. Sivits gave his man a push, and he fell on top of the others. Graner stood over them, yelling in Arabic and English. He appeared to Sivits to be genuinely enraged. Then Davis took a few steps and hurled himself on top of the tangled heap of bodies, crushing them to the concrete.

Sivits had visited Frederick a few times on the MI block, so he had a sense of the scene there, but he was not prepared for what he was seeing. "Javal is like six foot two," he said. "I don't know why he did it. I have no idea. I don't know why a lot of people did things that night. I wish I did. Anger, fatigue, boredom, stress, I think, just a lot of everything combined, and it's like a cabinet—you can fill it, you can shove stuff in there for so long, but it's going to hit a certain point you ain't going to be able to put anything else in it. It's just going to explode open. I almost think that's what happened that night. It just got to the point they just couldn't take anymore, and just started exploding open."

Or, as Davis put it himself: "It got down to everyone was pissed. You know, soldiers got hurt—it was a real heated moment." Davis understood why the prisoners would riot. They were pissed off too, he said. Corrupt Iraqi contractors were serving them inedible food— "bringing dirty rice, bugs in it, you know, rotten food, leftover food, or whatever wasn't eaten from the restaurant that day or that night, put it in buckets, put it on the back of a feed truck, bring it out, and serve it to the prisoners and get paid." And that was just the beginning of the prisoners' grievances. "Their port-a-johns were disgusting—they were overflowing," Davis said. "They were living in the most rank conditions, on top of a garbage dump, surrounded by razor wire, and during the daytime, the sun beating down on them, sweating, bad hygiene—people stinking and disease and open sores and things like that. And a bunch of them were there for no reason, just because they got swept up in a raid. Like they were in a concentration camp, you know. I mean, I'd riot too. I wished I could riot down at Camp Victory, go jump on some commander's desk who's eating steak and shrimp every night in air-conditioning while I'm out in the suck, humping it out with the detainees that outnumber me like two hundred to one."

When he jumped on the prisoners instead, Davis's attitude was, "We're here sucking it up just like you." Feeling powerless, he made what power he had felt. "I lost it," he said. "I'm like, 'You hurt one of our soldiers, so that's it.'" And when he got up from the body pile, he began walking around it, stomping on the prisoners' hands and feet. "He was stomping pretty hard, and the detainees were crying out in pain," Specialist Wisdom said.

Davis said that he was actually restraining himself. "Luckily, thank God, I didn't snap fully," he said. "I had a soldier die that I knew, got killed by an insurgent. We were getting bombed every night. All those things balling up into a ball in your mind, and you just want to take it out on that guy, right there. He wants to take your life, or wants to see you hurt, when you're there to try to protect him from being hurt. I wanted to hurt him, the gentleman who hit the female MP in the face with the brick. I wanted to hurt him really bad, because I felt that he deserved it. I felt that they all deserved it. So I stepped on the guy's finger. I stepped on the guy's toe. At the time, of course, I was like, 'Wow, I think we're crossing the line.' But the answer to that was the contrary: We're at war. They blew up New York, and anything goes. So it was like we were crossing the line, but we should have crossed the line. That's what the mentality was. That's what the atmosphere was like. It was, They blew up our buildings, they're killing us out there, you know, kick the crap out of them."

Sivits was all for self-defense. He was descended from a long line of military men, including several who had died in battle or its aftermath, and on his combat helmet, he had written "Freedom Isn't Free." But the prisoners Davis was stomping were totally under control, and posed no threat. "They were scared. You could look at them and tell they were scared," Sivits said, and he was as relieved as he was startled when the sternest voice he'd ever heard suddenly barked Davis's name from overhead. Davis froze. It was Sergeant Snider looking down from the balcony of the upper tier. He drew a finger across his throat, and told Davis to knock it off. Davis obeyed: "I left," he said, "and that was the end of my participation."

Snider left too. He went to bed. Before long, Lynndie England and Megan Ambuhl had taken his place as observers on the balcony. England had Graner's camera, and she snapped a picture as he crouched among the prisoners, grinning up at her and giving the thumbs-up. Meanwhile, Sabrina Harman, who was working as a runner at the hard site that night, had come onto the tier, looking for Ambuhl. Phones had just been installed at Abu Ghraib, and Harman had finally been granted a home leave—she was to depart in thirty-six hours—and she wanted Ambuhl to accompany her while she went to call Kelly with the good news. But when she saw the prisoners on the floor, she too stopped to take some pictures. As she did, Graner cradled one prisoner's head in his left arm, drew back his right arm in a cocked fist, posed as if to strike, and asked Sivits to take a picture of him. It was obvious to everyone that Graner was staging the situation for the camera, and Sivits obliged, using Frederick's camera. Harman, too, snapped the scene.

Then Graner began punching the prisoners for real, and nobody took pictures. "It was like a monster got released," Sivits said. "I hate to say it, but that's what it seemed like. It just didn't seem like the Graner that I had got to know." Wisdom said he saw Graner strike the first man he went for in the jaw, and others in the head or chest. "I don't know if he hit every single one, but pretty close," Wisdom said. Sivits and Frederick remember seeing Graner deal a particularly hard blow to one man's temple. "The detainee fell motionless, but he was still breathing. He made like a moan when Graner hit him," Frederick said, and Sivits said, "After he punched him, he kind of shook his hand, and he said, 'Ouch, damn, that hurt.' "

SO IT WENT, the mood swinging between angry violence, and clowning jocularity. Graner summoned England to come down and take some pictures at close range. He and Frederick started stripping the detainees, and removing their flex cuffs. One naked man was made to sit on the floor bent forward with his head against the wall. Harman photographed him there. Moments later another naked man was brought over and seated on the first man's shoulders. Harman photographed that pose, too. Then she was given the paperwork that had come with the prisoners from Camp Ganci, and she discovered that one of them had originally been arrested for rape. Graner grabbed the leg of that man's jumpsuit and tore it open with his hands. Harman took a Magic Marker and wrote "RAPEIST" on his thigh. She wasn't sure why she did it—"for identification, or to single him out"—but at Abu Ghraib, she said, "It wasn't uncommon to write on people."

Sivits was still preoccupied with the prisoner Graner had punched in the temple. He thought the man was lying awfully still. "I walked over and I lifted the sandbag up to where I could see his eyes," he said. "The guy was unconscious. I said, 'Graner, you knocked that dude out.' He didn't seem too concerned about it. Then I walked back over by Freddy. We were standing there. And Freddy looks at me, and he says, 'Hey, watch this.' He goes over, gets the guy that I escorted down, lifts the guy up, marks an X on his chest, punches the guy right square in the chest. I'm like, 'What? Who are you, and what did you do with Freddy?' Because I've never seen Freddy do something like that. I mean, when we were in Al Hillah, this is the guy that would take like a five-pound bag of candy and just hand it out to the kids, and actually go up to the individuals and talk to them, and have a good time. And as soon as he hit the guy, the guy dropped. He walked over to me, and he said, 'I think I put him in cardiac arrest.' "

Wisdom didn't hear that remark, but he saw Frederick punch the prisoner in the chest, and he said, "Frederick told me, 'You have to get some of this.' " Wisdom, who had just returned to Iraq from a home leave, had never spent time on the MI block before, and it was only his second or third night at the hard site. He didn't know why MPs were assaulting prisoners, but he said, "I thought it was weird that they would do it in front of me as they didn't know me at all. They seemed like they thought it was cool to hit the prisoners." After maybe five minutes on Tier 1A, he said, "I was so disgusted with what I saw, so I left and went to my regular assigned cell area. I never hit anyone and never would."

The prisoner Graner had knocked out had begun moving again,

but the man Frederick had decked was still lying as he fell, and hyperventilating. While somebody called a medic, and Ambuhl was summoned to fetch an inhaler from an asthmatic prisoner on the block, Sivits crouched over the prone prisoner. "I pointed to my eyes, and pointed to him, and I'm like, 'Look at me. Look at me,' " Sivits said. "I showed him how to take deep breaths, and try to get himself calmed down, and I finally got his breathing slowed down." The inhaler helped too, and when the medic arrived, she saw no cause for alarm. "As she was leaving, it was really weird," Sivits said. "They looked at her and they said, 'Hey, you want to get yourself a couple shots in? You want to get some?' She's like, 'No.' And she just turned around and walked out."

After that, it seemed to Sivits, the guards became more relaxed. Graner and Frederick continued to terrorize the prisoners, but they left off battering them, and resumed stripping them naked, and placing them against the wall, seated atop one another; and as Harman resumed taking pictures, England got into the act, posing with the naked men, pointing at them, laughing, and giving the thumbs-up to the camera. Graner said he had used the women on the tier in this capacity so regularly that England did it "automatically" that night.

As Sivits surveyed the scene, he noticed that the hands of a prisoner who was still on the floor had turned purple. His flex cuffs were too tight and wouldn't come off. He told Graner, "This guy is going to lose his hands." So Graner and Frederick helped him stand the man up and hold him, while Sivits worked at the tourniquet-tight cuffs with his knife, and Harman photographed the procedure. Cutting through the hard plastic cuffs without cutting the prisoner took a while, but Sivits managed, and he felt good about that. It made him glad he was there. "As far as I know, the guy kept his hands," he said. "Maybe he wouldn't have if I wouldn't have got them in time. I don't know. I've never been in the situation to see how long something like that takes."

A short PT session followed, before Graner began leading the prisoners one by one to the middle of the tier, and arranging them on all fours, shoulder to shoulder and hip to hip. When he had four men in a row, he made the next two climb on top of them. "We didn't know what he was doing," England said. "He didn't say anything. And then he told us that he was piling them in a pyramid. We're like, 'OK, why?' He's like, 'To control them, so they're all in one area.' " Of course, the prisoners were already entirely at Graner's mercy, naked and hooded and unresisting, and he kept them in the pyramid—with the seventh man on top—for less than ten minutes. As far as Sivits could tell the objective was humiliation, and he said, "I think it was also for the camera, just another picture to add to his collection."

It wasn't much of a pyramid; it was more of a dog pile, toppling this way and that, as the prisoners, unable to see, scrambled for balance. Harman photographed them from behind, a mess of buttocks, legs, and feet, as they assumed their positions. England stood on the other side of the heap, and photographed Harman working her camera, with a blur of sandbagged heads in jagged motion in the foreground. Then Harman turned on her smile for a photograph with Graner standing behind her, beaming, with his arms crossed over his chest, muscles flexed. And finally, another photograph full of buttocks: England and Graner posed at the head of the pyramid, with their arms around each other, and their free hands giving the thumbs-up. That picture was taken a few minutes before midnight, and at midnight it was England's birthday. She was twenty-one.

"I HAD HEARD GRANER SAYING, 'Well, this is your birthday present,' or something," England said. "I don't know why he would have said it, because I wouldn't have really wanted that." But in the photographs she appeared to be in high spirits, and that is how Frederick remembered it. "She was laughing and having a good time," he said. "She didn't show any signs that she wasn't enjoying it or wanted to leave or anything like that." In fact, Frederick said, they were all having fun. He described Graner's mood that night as "pretty normal, laughing," and he said that he, too, thought that the goings-on were, for the most part, "kind of funny."

Graner was more cautious about describing England's state of mind. "She smiled in a lot of photographs," he said, "but I can't say if she enjoyed what she was doing." He didn't remember having laughed much that night, but he allowed that it was possible. "As far as the laughing and joking," he said, "you know, we had seen some horrendous things happen, and we did some horrendous things—not horrendous but outside the box, outside the norm. And a lot of times we dealt with it by joking around."

Even Sivits, who spent much of his time on the tier that night attending to the health of the prisoners, said, "There were some things that was being done that I laughed about. To see them start the pyramid, it was a little funny. But then it clicked. It's like, How would I feel? Man, them guys probably feel like crap. And to make it worse, we were taking photographs of them. Yeah, just what I want, somebody to take pictures of me while I was naked with seven other naked guys. No, that ain't right. No, this ain't a joke anymore. This ain't fun." Still, Sivits stuck around. "Graner outranked me," he said. "Freddy outranked me. So I didn't question their authority. I never asked any questions. I didn't need to know stuff. It wasn't my business. I wasn't working in that area. Yes, you know a difference between right and wrong, but you also are taught to follow orders when they're handed down, and Graner told me that they were doing what they were told. So I figured, OK. That's why you do it. You follow orders in the military. That's all you can do."

Of course, as Sivits recognized, the pyramid had been staged in order to take photographs. In fact, pretty much everything that was done to the prisoners that night, once they were naked, was done for the cameras. This made that night different from other nights on the tier, although Sivits had no way to know it. Yes, the sexual humiliation of prisoners was routine, and taking pictures of it had become normal too. But the photography had always been a response to what was going on, not the occasion for it. And yes, the photograph of Gilligan, wired up on his box, was posed, just as the pictures Harman and Graner took of one another with al-Jamadi's corpse were. But those were one-offs, tableaux conceived of an instant, by way of a diversion, in the midst of the action. The human pyramid and the scenes that preceded and followed it were something new.

From the moment that Graner squatted among the newly arrived prisoners with his fist cocked and asked for his picture to be taken, the documentary impulse that had prevailed among the MPs on the night shift had given way to the old urge to produce happy snaps; and, as the night progressed, that urge gave way to a spirit of high theater. The tier became a photo studio, where the grim work of the MPs was enacted as a bawdy farce for the cameras, while their raw, angry violence—the stomping and punching—went unrecorded. So much for photography as simple "proof" of reality.

There had never been an episode before when work and play and picture taking were so comprehensively, so consciously, and so indistinguishably mixed up on the MI block, and it never happened again. As Graner and Frederick strove to outdo one another in choreographing the naked bodies of their prisoners in ever more outrageous compositions, it was as if they felt that the only way to create an image that would do justice to the sheer lunacy of their experience at Abu Ghraib was by exaggeration and artifice. No doubt they were also showing off for England and Harman, who did just what conventional men are supposed to want conventional women to do when they swagger: point, laugh, snap pictures, and strike poses.

Megan Ambuhl, as usual, kept at a sensible remove from the

cameras. To Ambuhl "it was just another crazy night," and, she said, "there were some mistakes made all along the way, and it probably wasn't a good idea to smile or take pictures, but that's what people do." She had remained upstairs and uninvolved, except when she delivered the asthma inhaler. Then, as the pyramid was being disassembled, Harman went to get her, and when they came back down on their way to use the phones at last, they found the prisoners rearranged in oral sex positions. "Frederick was standing there with two detainees," Harman said. "One was kneeling, and one was standing. I took a photo. And I believe he took the sandbag off of the one kneeling, and I took another photo."

Harman said, "That was kind of odd," and Ambuhl was equally reserved in her judgment. "That was kind of bizarre, and something that I would have thought was a little too much," she said. "At that point, Sabrina and I just got out of the situation."

"We left," Harman said. "I told Frederick we were going to use the phones, and that was it. I mean, if I was there for the masturbation, I probably would have taken a photo of that, too. But I wasn't there for that."

As Harman and Ambuhl walked away, Sivits said, "Freddy walked over and said, 'Watch this,' and actually took the Iraqi's hand and had him start masturbating. And when that started, I said, 'Yeah, I'm leaving too.' It was getting a little too far out of hand." Describing that moment of decision, Sivits seemed to relive it. "I was like, Uh-uh, no, good-bye, I ain't being involved in this, not anymore. That was just out-and-out wrong. No, come on. Why? Why make somebody do something like that? I mean, they were scared. They didn't know what was really going on. They were naked in front of men and women, without their own free will. I mean, we were there to show them that we were good people, and we were there to help them. We were just going against what we were there to do. And as I was leaving the tier that night, I was told, 'Hey, you didn't see shit.' And me being the person that I am—I try to be friends with everybody—I said, 'See what? I didn't see nothing.' "

Sivits regretted being so easily silenced. "I wanted to say something to somebody," he said, "but I promised them that I wouldn't. Because, like my dad told me, if you couldn't trust somebody for something small, how do you know when the stuff really hits the fan that you can trust somebody? And Graner and Freddy were two individuals that, if we were in a firefight, and a bunch of fire was coming from a building, and they would have told me, 'Hey, we're going to take that building. We're going to charge it and take it,' I'd have went with them. I trusted them that much. I trusted both of them with my life."

MINUTES AFTER SIVITS quit the tier, Matthew Wisdom returned. Frederick was his shift commander, and Wisdom needed to ask him a question. "When I arrived," he said, "I saw one prisoner on his knees with his mouth open, and another prisoner masturbating with his penis in the prisoner on his knees' face. Both of the prisoners were entirely naked. The only person I saw near these two prisoners was Staff Sergeant Frederick. I called out for Sergeant Frederick, and he turned towards me and said, 'See what these animals do when we leave them alone for two seconds.' "

Wisdom asked Frederick his question, and left. Then he walked off the hard site, and across the prison grounds to the watchtower, where his team leader, Sergeant Robert Jones, was on duty. Wisdom told Jones everything he'd seen that night on Tier 1A, and said that he didn't want to work at the hard site anymore. Jones told him that he would talk to Frederick about it.

Several hours later, when Harman and Ambuhl returned to their living area at the end of the shift, Jones was there, and Harman overheard him say something about masturbation on Tier 1A. Harman couldn't make out the details, but Jones sounded irate, so she told Ambuhl, and they decided they'd better tell Sergeant Snider about what had gone on after he left the tier and went to bed. "We went to his room where he was sleeping," Harman said. "I'm afraid of the dark, so I didn't go in there. But Megan talked to him. I heard him say he'd take care of it."

"That was the end of that," Ambuhl said. "I don't know what he did. I didn't really have the drive to follow through with it. I mean, he's several levels above me, so we made him aware of it, and if he says he's going to take care if it, then that's it."

"Nothing really happened," Harman said, "except for Wisdom got taken out of the hard site. He moved to the towers with Sergeant Jones."

Lynndie England didn't see what the fuss was about. "The stuff that we did was common," she said. "It was standard operating procedure." Graner wasn't so sure. "Not the masturbation," he said. "Everything else that happened on the tier were what my instructions were." The masturbation bothered him. He said that Frederick told him MI had wanted the prisoners to do it, but he was skeptical—and he knew that Snider and Jones had talked to Frederick about it. So Graner, too, reported it the next day, when he saw Lieutenant Colonel Jordan. "It seemed like he took it in stride," Graner said. As he remembered it, all Jordan said was, "OK."

Graner also showed the photographs from that night to Snider, and to Lieutenant Raeder and other officers; and although he didn't mention it, Frederick, Ambuhl, Harman, and England all said that he changed the screen saver on his laptop to a picture of the human pyramid—the one shot from behind, while he and England embraced on the far side—so anyone who entered the Tier 1A office could see it. The extent to which Graner's exhibition of the photographs was showing off, and the extent to which it was his way of saying that it was no big deal, was anybody's guess. In either case, he said, "It wasn't a secret, but nothing was done about it."

Still, the reckless abandon of the night of the human pyramid, the perverse glee with which the guards involved presented themselves to the cameras and made a sport of violating their prisoners, and the haste with which so many of them then confessed to their chain of command makes it seem as if they almost wanted to be caught—or, like Javal Davis, to be told to knock it off. And the ease with which absolution came instead, the reflexive, blasé manner with which their superiors shared complicity, was only partly reassuring. Was it really desirable to have dominion in a place where right and wrong were inconsequential? Was it even possible?

On the morning after, Sabrina Harman wrote:

Kelly,
I haven't slept all night. I just can't sleep. Six prisoners escaped last night. We did a sweep but no luck in finding them. They're smart. That's eight we've lost in three nights. Something bad is going to happen here. I'm leaving to come home in about 3 1/2 hours. I'm not sure how to feel. I have a lot of anxiety. I think something is going to happen either me not making it or you doing something wrong. I think too much. I hope I'm wrong but if not know that I love you and you are and always will be my wife. I hate to be so scared. I hate anxiety. I hate the unknown.

A soldier in her unit had advised Harman to delete any photographs she had taken at the prison. She didn't know what to make of that, and she told Kelly,

We might be under investigation. I'm not sure, there's talk about it. Yes they do beat the prisoners up and ive written

this to you before. I just don't think its right and never have
that's why I take the pictures to prove the story I tell people.
No one would ever believe the shit that goes on. No one.
The dead guy didn't bother me, I even took a picture with
him doing the thumbs up . . . they said the autopsy came
back "heart attack." It's a lie. The whole military is nothing
but lies. They cover up too much. This guy was never in our
prison. That's the story. . . . If I want to keep taking pictures
of those events—I even have short films—I have to fake a
smile every time. I hope I don't get in trouble for something
I haven't done. Im going to try to burn those pictures and
send them out to you while Im in Kuwait—Just in case.

I love you and I hope to see you in the next day—

Your wife—

Sabrina

17.

IN THE ACRONYMIC SLANG derived from the military's phonetic alphabet—Alpha, Bravo, Charlie, Delta—Charlie Foxtrot means cluster fuck, a hopeless entanglement of rudderless forces, and Tim Dugan, a civilian interrogator who arrived at Abu Ghraib on a CACI corporation contract in early November, said, "It was Charlie Foxtrot without a doubt—without a doubt. I've never seen anything like that, and I never thought that I would see American soldiers so depressed and morale so low. A bunch of unprofessional schmucks that didn't know their damn jobs, all thrown together, mixed up with a big-ass stick. Pisses me off, because the whole time we're screwing around, Americans are dying. Our kids are dying and the Iraqi kids are dying—everybody's dying. And we don't have any intelligence."

Most interrogators won't talk about their work. Dugan wouldn't stop. He sketched the general atmosphere: "We got no force protection. You can't trust the 'terps'"—the interpreters. "You can't trust the MPs. There's a pissing contest between MI and MPs. You can't trust MI. They're throwing everybody under the bus. You've got mortars coming in every night. You got prisoner escapes—the Iraqi police take bribes and let them go all the time. It was insanity."

Then he got specific: "Captain Wood and Sergeant First Class Johnson gave us our orientation about what we could do, what approaches were authorized, what approaches weren't. I was assigned to an antiterrorism section on Sunday morning, and I pissed off the section sergeant and the interrogator. I says, 'What about pocket litter?' Pocket litter is whatever the guy was arrested with, whatever he had in his pockets, on his person. Did he have a gun? Did he have a bloody rag? If he says he wasn't shooting mortars, and he has a mortar table in his pocket litter, then he was probably shooting frickin' mortars. That's evidence. When I got there, they've got an evidence locker, but they didn't know what I was talking about.

"I was transferred to force protection about an hour after that. There was two female specialists, one was an interrogator, one's an analyst. I was doing the left-seat, right-seat with them. We went to do an interrogation on this guy, the Wolf. Abu G had been hit by a mortar barrage on September 20, killed two Americans and wounded like sixteen, and this Wolf was the cell leader of that, supposedly. They took him in the stairwell at the hard site, took all of his clothes off and got him totally naked, which we weren't supposed to do from my briefing. When we got done, my section sergeant, he's like, 'Yeah, we're not really supposed to do that, but we let the females do some things like that to get over the Arab culture thing.' And I'm like, 'You just said we weren't supposed to be doing that,' and he's like, 'They're allowed to do it, but you can't do it. I wouldn't recommend it if you did it.'

"So, my first interrogation on my own, I bring this guy in and his ankle is just almost like elephantiasis—huge and mangled looking. He tells me all this stuff, and then I try to get his ankle fixed. Our doctors won't see him because he's a fuckin' Iraqi. They say, 'Kiss off.' I'm like, 'Nobody can help him?' And they're like, 'Well, what the fuck you want me to do?' That's a quote. I'm not adding my own 'fuck.' I got a guy giving me info, and we won't even help fix his fucking ankle.

"And they're having me interrogate a frickin' barber. This is November. He got arrested in April. Do you know why we arrested him? Because he lived about five hundred yards from a target house, and nobody was home. I put in a letter of release for the son of a bitch. He was still there when I left in February. Do you call that winning the hearts and minds?

"The thought of abusing detainees—I don't have to abuse the detainees. I'm an interrogator. That's what I frickin' do. For years, I found out what my Christmas presents were before Christmas just by asking open-ended, leading questions. Eighty percent of the population, you can walk up and talk to them, and they'll tell you everything. One of the things an interrogator does every time is evaluate the truthfulness and reliability of the information given. That's the very last paragraph of every report you ever write. So, if I get information through torture, I have no way to verify anything, because I would just assume that you're going to tell me whatever the hell you want so the pain stops.

"I just thought it was a bunch of schmuck MPs acting like idiots from the little bit I heard when I was there, you know? I don't think so anymore, not at all. When I got to Abu G, they had a group of these tiger teams that were classified as the breaker teams, and they worked from 8 P.M. to 8 A.M. when the vast majority of us worked from 8 A.M. to 8 P.M. The breaker teams did their interrogations in the hard site and, dang, then all the abuse happened at the hard site at nights. The breaker teams weren't allowed to talk about anything they were doing. So you tell me what the hell was going on in the hard site at nights. I don't think those kids came up with that BS by themselves, but I don't know who the hell authorized what.

"In the military, if somebody that's higher ranked than you says, 'Jump,' then in the middle of the air you say, 'How high?' because you've already jumped. Common sense is unfortunately not a common virtue. From what I've heard, Steve Stefanowicz told them to soften them up and do those kind of things. He was working on the breaker teams, and Steve came to me and told me that I ought to get with the MPs and use them—they could help soften up your detainees. I told him I thought he was out of control, I thought the MPs were out of control, and I told him he could kiss my ass.

"And he's like, 'Why do you think our orders are from the Department of the Interior?' I didn't even know it. I mean, it looked just like the orders that I've always had from the Department of Defense, but it says 'The Department of the Interior.' And he's like, 'Why do you think that is?' He's like, 'Because we can do anything over here and we can't get in trouble for it.' There's ramifications for people at Department of Defense who do things. But if you're Department of the Interior, nobody has any jurisdiction over anything you do."

IN PREPARATION FOR HIS TIME IN IRAQ, Dugan had read a number of books. He read about Iraqi history, and he read the Quran, and he also reread the life story of Hanns Scharff, the man who was known as the master interrogator of the Luftwaffe during World War II. Scharff, who had been raised in aristocratic affluence—his family owned a big textile mill—settled in South Africa as a young man and married an Englishwoman who was, it so happened, the daughter of a pilot who had been shot down during World War I by Baron Manfred Albrecht Freiherr von Richthofen, the German fighter ace, better known as the Red Baron. According to the family story, when the Baron saw the British plane falling from the sky, he followed it, landed beside it, extricated the severely wounded pilot, conveyed him to a field hospital, provided him with chocolate, cigarettes, and champagne, and remained at his bedside until he died. In 1939, Scharff was visiting home when the Nazis invaded Poland; he was soon drafted into military service, and when he became an interrogator, he adopted the Baron's chivalric code as his own.

Unlike his colleagues in the Gestapo, Scharff was never known to raise his voice at his "guests," much less to abuse them physically. He simply chatted them up in his elegant English and charmed them with his suave, ingratiating manners, employing what the army field manual now calls a "we know all" approach, to fill in the blanks in his ever-expanding knowledge of Allied war plans. In the process, he forged enduring friendships with the captured American airmen he interrogated. After the war he emigrated to America, where he established a second career as a mosaic artist, creating, among other monumental works, the three-hundred-thousand-tile mural of Cinderella's life in the Cinderella Castle at Walt Disney World.

By Scharff's account, his work as an interrogator was as easy as it was genteel. "Barbarism is not necessary," he wrote, and explained, "The strongest character, the most unyielding soldier, is exposed to violent psychological strains by the fact of captivity. It exerts powerful pressures upon the mind and spirit of a man who knows he is innocent of any wrongdoing. . . . This unfathomable 'barbed-wire psychosis' does things to a man which have nothing at all to do with fear or discomfort or anger. The POW's core, or soul, is eroded by this psychosis which distorts his conception of the world and the humans that share it with him."

Happily, Scharff's insights weren't enough to help win the Nazis the war, but he emerged from it a hero to both sides by adhering to a creed he attributed to his chief, Horst Barth: "An interrogator, to my mind, should be a man who fights without words, fences without a sword, fights only with his brain. He must be a very curious man . . . a gregarious man." This flattering self-image had obvious appeal to subsequent generations of American inquisitors, many of whom studied Scharff's methods at the U.S. Army Intelligence School at Fort Huachuca. One officer who taught them there was Colonel Stuart

Herrington, and one of his students had been Barbara Fast, who was now the MI chief in Iraq. In the first week of December 2003, Herrington visited Abu Ghraib at General Fast's behest. She told him she was not comfortable with the quality of intelligence that was coming to her from throughout her command, and Herrington's mission was to have a look around and see if opportunities were being missed.

Herrington had a storied career. He was a veteran of the CIA-run Phoenix Program in Vietnam, a counterinsurgency operation that took credit for having "neutralized" more than eighty-one thousand Viet Cong operatives by capturing them or, in more than twenty-seven thousand cases, killing them. He was one of the last Americans airlifted off the roof of the U.S. Embassy in Saigon in April 1975, and he went on to make his name as a connoisseur of espionage, spy catching, and interrogation, first as the head of the Asia/Pacific Division of the Defense Intelligence Agency, then as the chief of the U.S. Army Counterintelligence Unit. During the U.S. invasion of Panama, in 1989, he ran the interrogation center for captured members of General Manuel Noriega's inner circle, and in the Gulf War he was in charge of a similar operation for high-ranking officers of Saddam's army. Herrington had retired from the military shortly before the Iraq war, and gone to work for a manufacturer of golf clubs, tracking down counterfeiters in China. His itinerary in Iraq allowed for only one day at Abu Ghraib, but that was enough for him to see that the operation was at odds not only with the Geneva Conventions but also with the aim of collecting intelligence.

"You couldn't have picked a worse place," Herrington said. "When you try to run a sophisticated detainee exploitation facility, and you're getting mortared at night, the Iraqi police they've given you to help you are not vetted, and the higher chain of command is not wild about coming and visiting you—nobody wants to drive down that road—it's a very bad situation from the get-go." That was his first impression; and after touring Camp Vigilant and the MI block, talking to Colonel Pappas, Lieutenant Colonel Phillabaum, and Lieutenant Colonel Jordan, and hosting "a long, private bitch session" with interrogators, he said: "We had a pretty good picture of a beleaguered, undermanned team in a really, really bad situation—three hundred sixty degrees bad."

A month before Herrington's visit, the U.S. Provost Marshal, Donald Ryder—the country's top Military Police officer—had presented General Sanchez with a report on prison operations in Iraq. "Generally," Ryder wrote, "conditions in existing prisons, detention facilities and jails meet minimal standards of health, sanitation, security, and human rights established by the Geneva Conventions." But Ryder expressed concern about overcrowding, inadequate tents, and poor sanitation at Abu Ghraib, as well as the lack of standard operating procedures for MPs at the prison. Although he stated that his team "did not identify any military police units purposely applying inappropriate confinement practices," Ryder objected to what he described as "the template" for military prisons in Iraq, whereby MPs were subordinated to MI and made to "actively set favorable conditions" for interrogators. "Such actions, generally run counter to the smooth operation of a detention facility, attempting to maintain its population in a compliant and docile state," Ryder wrote, and he urged that the military should establish prison procedures "clearly separating the actions of the guards from those of the military intelligence personnel."

General Sanchez, however, ignored Ryder's advice, and in mid-November he named Colonel Pappas the overall commander of Abu Ghraib. Placing an entire prison—an entire forward operating base, for that matter—under MI command was an unprecedented move. Pappas was known not as a soldiers' soldier but rather as a remote and anxious man who had been on edge and suffering from shell shock since the September 20 mortar attack that killed his driver, Specialist

Brown. His installation as the top man at Abu Ghraib was taken as an insult by the MP chain of command, which responded by instructing its soldiers to refuse MI's requests to escort prisoners to and from interrogations. "They said they're not going to transfer the prisoners, they're not going to search the prisoners, and we can't use their handcuffs," Tim Dugan said. "They're pissed that Pappas is in command, but you know, it's insane. Part of the thing you do as an interrogator is you sit in a booth and you wait for those guys to be brought in to you and you're seeming omnipotent to the detainee that comes in. I mean, basically, in my interrogation booth, I'm God, OK? I say what happens, I say anybody that can talk—everything in there, I'm in control. It usurps my authority to be walking through the mud and fetching a detainee and walking him around like I'm a schmuck and just like anybody else."

Herrington agreed. In direct contrast to Ryder, he regarded MPs' service to MI as essential to the sort of interrogation center he liked to run, which he described as "a very controlled environment with the right number of guests to landlords, under control of the MI guy—a total and complete, mature, Red-Cross-can-come-any-day-they-want-because-we're-proud-of-what-we-do-here type of thing." At Abu Ghraib, he found "the opposite." He called it "a mess," "clearly a nightmare," "overcrowded and seething with discontent," "absolutely how not to," "a perfect storm of everything that can go wrong," and he said, "This perfect storm consists of insecure, poisonous location, inexperienced MP unit poorly led, inexperienced MI unit, hardworking interrogators trying to do the right thing, hamstrung by the language, mortared, huge pressure to produce results from on high, very few resources, at the far end of the support chain." At one point, a soldier opened a supply drawer and said, "Look, sir, two reams of paper. We've been asking for paper for a week."

Meanwhile prisoners kept arriving by the truckload, arrested en masse, without supporting evidence; and when evidence was collected,

Herrington found that it was often rounded up in an equally arbitrary and chaotic fashion. He said, "One of the officers told me that one division brought up five hundred pounds of documents that they'd accumulated from various operations and just dumped them off, with no idea of where they come from, when they were seized, what headquarters they were in, what persons are attached or associated with them. That's kind of called 'cut your own schwantz off' if it comes to really productively using that stuff. Plus it's all in Arabic—oh, by the way."

There was no way to handle such a swamp of people and information. Colonel Pappas told Herrington that there were three thousand eight hundred prisoners—more than half the security detainees at Abu Ghraib—whom he had no intention of interrogating, but General Fast's review-and-release board at headquarters wouldn't let him let them go. Herrington would not discuss the specifics of his written report to General Fast, but the report had been leaked and in it he had told Fast about Pappas's complaint.

While he was in Iraq, Herrington also visited an interrogation center at the airport, which was run by the Iraq Survey Group—a team organized by the Pentagon and the CIA to hunt for weapons of mass destruction—and he learned that a number of prisoners there had been beaten when they were captured by members of Task Force 121 (the successor to the special forces Task Force 20 that killed Saddam's sons). Herrington was unable to gain access to a Task Force 121 interrogation center, but he said that a CIA representative told him that "practices there were in contravention to his agency's guidance on what was and what was not permissible in interrogating detainees." By contrast, Herrington saw no evidence at Abu Ghraib that detainees were "illegally or improperly treated," but he warned that the prison was nearly out of control. In his final report to General Fast, he wrote: "Even one year ago, we would have salivated at the prospect of being able to talk to people like the hundreds now in our custody. Now that we have them, we have failed to devote the planning and resources to optimize this mission . . . History may show that we had a twelve-month opportunity to accomplish this task, and at best managed a C-minus in the effort."

A WEEK AFTER HERRINGTON'S VISIT to Abu Ghraib, Saddam Hussein was captured, hiding in a hole in the ground on a sheep farm near his hometown of Tikrit. A number of his associates, who were taken prisoner at the same time, were delivered to Abu Ghraib, and the next night, Tim Dugan was summoned to join a meeting with Colonel Pappas to discuss the interrogation of this fresh crop of Saddam cronies. Pappas explained that he'd just got off a conference call with General Sanchez and the secretary of defense. "He said, 'We're starting a special projects team, and we're going to break the back of the resistance. Anybody who doesn't want to volunteer for this has to leave the room. And if you volunteer, you can't talk about this to anybody,'" Dugan said. "We all volunteered and he said all approach techniques were authorized. Someone asked, 'Even dogs?' And he says, 'Yep, even dogs.' He's like, 'We got a chance to break this unlawful insurgency, and the people in an unlawful insurgency have no protection under the Geneva Conventions.'"

Dugan thought that was pretty definitive. "If the fuckin' secretary of defense designates the motherfucker an unlawful insurgency, I mean, what the fuck am I supposed to say? It's an unlawful insurgency, wouldn't you think? He's the second-highest motherfucker in the country during the war." But, he said, "I was never told that I could physically abuse somebody. You weren't even allowed to threaten the use of physical violence."

Despite his admiration for Hanns Scharff, Dugan did like shouting in the interrogation booth. "Cussing is a big deal to an Arab," he said. "And I cussed my ass off to get their frickin' attention. I'm yelling at 'em or smackin' the table, 'Goddamn it, listen to me!' They can't stand it. They don't do it. They don't like it. And you press at 'em and you call 'em things. And it scared the shit out of 'em and made me more of an infidel. I told a lot of them, 'Listen, I want to make sure you understand one thing, OK? If you were on fire right now, I wouldn't piss on you. That's how much I care about you, OK? But who I do care about is the Americans. And if you can tell me about somebody that's trying to kill Americans, I'll take care of you.'"

Sometimes Dugan would bolster his shouting by putting his fist through a plastic table. But when it came to members of Saddam's Sunni entourage, he said, "The greatest thing to get them to talk was the elections. You know, 'Who's going to win the election?' 'The Shiites.' And I says, 'How's the Shiites going to treat you compared to the way Americans treat you?' 'They're going to kill me.' I said, 'Really? Sounds like you've got a problem there, Hoss. I got no problem writing on the bottom of this form: 'Transfer to the Iraqi sovereign government.' And it's like, 'What do you want to know?' "

Still, Dugan said, "Nobody really got any intelligence there, very few of us. Most of our interrogators were eighteen-year-old kids that were reservists. Think about it. You got a forty-five- to a sixty-five-year-old one-, two-, or three- or four-star general you're going to be talking to, and you're eighteen years old, just got out of high school, joined the Army, and went to interrogator school. These kids are intimidated as hell, and the generals and the colonels and these older guys know it. And it's like they laugh at them."

He said, "I love the Army. I always wanted to be in the military. And the big thing about being in the military is that, in my opinion, it could be the most honorable profession on the planet. You do the right goddamn thing all the time. At Abu Ghraib, there was no professionalism. There was no honor. There was no standards. There was no discipline. It's like some third-world fuckin' army that I was deal-ing with. I couldn't believe it. I still can't believe it. I mean they're just sending our kids into a meat grinder."

And he said, "I'll tell you what. My father died when I was eight years old. I was raised on Social Security. Got a job when I was nine, been working ever since. I felt my whole life that I owed the country something. There's not many places we could have lived the way we did, with me working at a gas station. I was on Social Security. My little sister didn't know how bad everything was until she was sixteen or seventeen. It was positive in that regard. I just always felt like I owed something because everybody in the country helped us out. That's what Social Security is. That's how I looked at it. And I'm a history and political science major. I studied all about the history of the world. And we're fucked up, but this country is the best goddamn thing going on on the planet, and I know that for a fact. The whole thing that makes us different and makes people come over to our side is that we're not torturing, lying, thieving bastards like everybody else in the world.

"Don't get me wrong, I'm not naive enough to think that the Army was pure. But it was a pure ideal. I know our founding fathers were human. I know George Washington wasn't any frickin' saint. But they put down on some papers some incredibly high moral standards, values, and ideas. Right afterwards got corrupted, slavery in the South, all kinds of things. But that's the shit we need to try to live up to. And I'll tell you what, nine times out of ten you can't. But as long as you try things are going to be all right. It's just really hard to deal with it when what you think is the right thing and always stood up for is turned into a piece of shit. It sucks being a history major."

18.

EVERY MORNING AT ABU GHRAIB, Sergeant Ken Davis would go up to the roof of his building and talk to God. "God," he'd say, "do me a favor today. Make sure my soldiers make it home alive. Make sure that I don't have to kill anybody here. And just make sure my family gets to see me again. That's all I ask." It was a lot to ask, and every evening, Sergeant Ken Davis would go back to his rooftop and say, "Thank you, God, for answering my prayer today, even though I don't deserve it."

Some soldiers at Abu Ghraib called Davis the Preacher Man, and some called him the Rev, because he wrote scripture on the walls of his cell. There was Psalm 91, the one about God the strong tower, God the fortress, God who takes you under his wing if you're faithful, so that you need not fear the arrow by day, nor the pestilence of night, nor the plague at noon, and though a thousand may fall at your side, ten thousand at your right hand, no disaster will come to your tent. And there was Chronicles 4:10, in which Jabez calls on the God of Israel to bless him and to enlarge his territory and to shield him from harm, and God grants him all he asks. That is the story of Jabez in its entirety, just one line, and Davis understood it to mean, "If you bless me with something, I will bless other people." He said, "If we live like that, if we live to the extreme that we would give everything we could to better someone else, we wouldn't be in the state of affairs we're in right now." Given that state of affairs, however, Davis's scriptural graffiti also included Psalm 23: the Lord is my shepherd et cetera—from the green pastures and the still waters even into the valley of the shadow of death.

Davis was a road MP, a transport man. He spent his days on the MSRs, the main supply routes, running convoys. Out there, hurtling down the tarmac pocked from IED explosions and littered with the charred remains of vehicles just like the ones he traveled in, it was the valley of the shadow for sure—no metaphor. Davis didn't mind. After his foray onto the MI block on the night of the torment of the three accused rapists, he considered himself lucky to have the kind of old-fashioned soldier's job the 372nd was supposed to do. He got the VIPs where they needed to go—if a colonel had to catch a flight at Baghdad International Airport, say, or attend a meeting at Camp Victory—but mostly he moved prisoners, the ones held in the CPA blocks of the hard site and in Camp Ganci, who had been arrested for civilian crimes and had been recognized by the Iraqi criminal justice system. There weren't too many of them, and the work was routine—every week, certain days, the same drill: sign them out, take them to court, wait for their hearings or trials, bring them back to Abu Ghraib, sign them in. When he was killing time around the court-houses, Davis liked to show his goodwill to Iraqis, chatting with them and handing out gifts: candy, Bibles, teddy bears. The worst part of the job was having to tell the prisoners who got acquitted or released that they were going back to Abu Ghraib until the Americans saw fit to let them go—that, and knowing insurgents were watching your every movement outside the prison.

You would see them out there, people checking their watches to time your convoys' comings and goings, people filming you, memorizing your routes and routines. After each detail, Davis and his men reported their sightings of these spies to their commanders, and

begged to change their patterns, so as to become surprising. Sometimes it seemed nobody heard their warnings, and sometimes it
seemed everybody heard, but the brush-off was the same: just do like
we told you. Davis always knew he might die at Abu Ghraib—"we
were on borrowed time," he said, "it was a war zone that had been
classified as mission accomplished"—but if the higher-ups weren't
watching your back, you could feel like you were supposed to get
killed.

Davis said that a lot of soldiers took the view that they were walking dead people, still breathing but dead all the same; it was just a
matter of time, and no sense thinking about it, because that slowed
you down and made you vulnerable. Davis understood the feeling,
but he didn't like it; with an attitude like that, anything goes. He
figured we all have an appointment, but while he didn't want to be
early for his, he didn't want to fear death either. That's where the
writing on his cell walls came in: it gave him an anchor, he said, a
positive place to come back to if he started to drift or lose focus. That's
how his grandmother raised him.

Still, things could get out of hand. On the morning of November
8, Davis was trying to call home on his satellite phone when his
driver, Matthew Smith, learned he'd been passed over for a promotion
on account of a paperwork error, and announced, "I quit." Davis told
him, "You can't quit—you're in Iraq, man." Fourteen prisoners, with
their hands cuffed behind their backs, were being loaded into a deuce,
a two-ton truck, to carry them to their court date. But Smith was
clearly in no shape to drive. Davis told him to ride in the turret and
man the gun until his head cleared, which was fine with the regular
gunner, because he was supposed to go home on R&R the next day,
and was happy to keep his head down. The problem was, the gunner
was a terrible driver, so Davis decided he had to drive his Humvee
himself. He was still trying to call home, and it was to time to roll—

everything was off-kilter—and it was only as he was pulling out onto MSR Sword on the tail of the deuce that it occurred to him: I forgot to pray, I didn't pray, I've got to pray.

NORMALLY DAVIS CLOSED HIS EYES when he prayed, but he was driving, so he kept watching the road, and hoped God would hear him anyway. "I said, 'God I need you to keep my soldiers safe today,' " he said. "It was an expedited prayer, and as I'm saying it a white Caprice passes me at a high speed, flashing his lights. My lead Humvee is about a hundred yards up, and I see him try to run the car off the road. They were trying to slow him down, just in case there was a car bomb. As I'm paying attention to that, I say, 'Amen.' " And, as Davis said Amen, an explosion ripped up from somewhere off his right fender, and the day went black.

Davis remembered his training: in an ambush, gun the engine, keep driving, get past it, then engage. You do not want to stop where you're being attacked. As he emerged from the smoke, the deuce with the prisoners veered to a halt on the left shoulder, and he cut his Humvee in behind it, broadside to the road to form a protective wall. He saw the truck's passenger door swing open. An M-16 rifle and a grenade launcher fell out and bounced on the road. Then Sergeant Cook fell out, clutching at his ears, which were bleeding—and there was much more blood in the back of the deuce: the prisoners there were soaked in it.

Davis could hear Smith firing overhead—so he was OK—but he didn't want to get in a fire fight. He got on the radio and mustered the convoy to head for an MP outpost a couple of miles up the road. Somehow Sergeant Cook had got back in the deuce, but the truck's rear tires were flat; it was bumping along on its rims, much slower than Davis wanted to be going. Smith was firing at a taxicab that he thought might have been involved in the attack, and Davis told him to shoot anybody else who got close, just in case.

At the outpost, the guard shouted to slow down and observe the speed limit, and Davis's adrenalin was suddenly channeled into a feeling of unaccustomed rage. He was not a curser or a shouter, but the smoke flume of the explosion still stood black against the sky behind them, and he hollered back, "Screw you, we've got dead and wounded." It troubled him, though, that he didn't know if anyone had died. As soon as the deuce stopped he went to check. The Iraqi prisoners were all in a heap there, unable to untangle themselves from one another on account of their handcuffs. Some had taken shrapnel in their backs, and a few had shrapnel coming out of their chests. As the MPs pulled them apart, one of the prisoners pleaded, "Help my friend, help him." His friend was lying under him on the floor with part of his head gone.

The dead man was heaved into a body bag, and stashed in a tent. Davis went in after him to free him of his handcuffs, and to say that he was sorry. "Because we were responsible for his safety," he said. "And I remember, I walked away from the group, and I put my sunglasses on, and just started bawling. I told God he had the wrong guy for the job, because I was getting tired of watching people die, innocent people to me. You know, if you wanted to hit me, the answer is, you should hit me, not him." Hearing himself cry to God like this, and asking to die, it struck Davis that he was being selfish. "Being hit and living probably hurts worse than being hit and dying, because you have to live with it," he said. "You have to live not only with survivor's guilt, but you have to live with the fact that there's nothing I can do. I'm here to help these people, and now they're trying to kill me."

As Davis's mood darkened, he found no end of fodder for despair. First, the Apache helicopters and M1 Abrams tanks that were mobilized in immediate response to the attack on his convoy were sent to the wrong coordinates—nearly three miles off the mark. Then he got back to Abu Ghraib and learned that a finance team, which had arrived from Baghdad shortly before he left that morning, had observed suspicious activity by the roadside where he was hit but only reported it after the attack. Then he waited for his commander to ask him if his soldiers were OK, and the commander never asked. And to top it off, he heard that the prisoner who'd died was one of the accused rapists he'd seen being abused on the MI block two weeks earlier. This was the prisoner whose death left Javal Davis feeling "everyone's a loser in this situation now." Ken Davis agreed, and it pained him to think of the last time he'd seen the man alive, crawling naked on the floor. "That might be the only way he remembered us before he died," he said. "As people that weren't promoting peace, but were promoting torture and abuse."

IN THE DAYS AFTER his convoy was blown up, Ken Davis was overwhelmed by an uncontrollable surge of violent emotions. "I was in this black, black place," he said. "I wanted to kill. I wanted so bad to pay back. I wanted freedom from what I was feeling. I was going through a period of hate for the first time in my life. Hating everything, hating everyone, hating anything, because I was just bitter over that morning, because I went over there with the right intentions—to help, not hurt—and the Iraqis didn't know me that way. They knew me as an American soldier."

On the third morning of his wild temper, Davis begged off his normal assignment to transport prisoners to court, and volunteered instead to go to Camp Anaconda at Balad Air Base, north of Baghdad, to pick up a high-value prisoner for transfer to Abu Ghraib. When he got there the prisoner, an insurgent suspected of killing Americans, refused to be handcuffed. "I remember my corporal saying, 'I'm going to handcuff you,' " Davis said, "and I snapped around on the guy and drew my 9-mil, and said, 'You either put your f'n' hands behind your back, or I will blow your head off.' And in my head I did it, but fortunately for me, I didn't do it." The prisoner put his hands behind his back and took the cuffs, but Davis's team was studying him with concern. "I said, 'I'm fine,' " he said, "and I walked out."

Back at Abu Ghraib that afternoon, Davis found everyone from his regular convoy team in a somber mood. "You haven't heard?" somebody asked. "Another team was hit today with an IED." This time there were no casualties, but Davis went off in a rage. "I took my paperwork and threw it at the captain, and I started yelling, 'Why don't you just write the letters now and send them home, that you're going to kill my soldiers. Because no one is listening to us here. You stay here behind the wire. You stay here in this containment area. We go out there and we risk our lives every day, and you're going to get us killed.' " The Captain told him to calm down. "Sergeant, we know you're upset," he said, and Davis told him, "No, you don't know anything."

Davis knew what had triggered him—the attacks—but he couldn't understand his fury. He considered himself good-natured, even-keeled, a pretty sunny guy. "And the hardest part of it is, I didn't know who I hated," he said. "Did I hate the Iraqis? Did I hate the Americans? Did I hate our government? I didn't know. I just hated. And it hurt." A session with the captain of a combat stress team brought no relief. "I'm dying here," Davis told him. "But there's no help for this." The captain offered to pull him out of Abu Ghraib for a few days, to unwind in the relative sanctuary of Baghdad International Airport, but Davis couldn't see leaving his soldiers behind.

Feeling as he did, Davis found himself thinking about Charles Graner and the other MPs who worked at the hard site. Sometimes, when Graner couldn't sleep after the night shift, he'd ask to ride along with Davis on his missions, just to decompress. Davis knew that Graner was "riled up" from his work on the MI block, and he remembered an encounter they had after Graner's first days at the hard site: "He was really hoarse, and I said, 'You getting sick?' And he goes, 'Uh, no. I'm having to yell at detainees.' And he says, 'I've got a question for you. They're making me do some things that I feel are morally and ethically wrong. What should I do?' I said, 'Don't do it.' He goes, 'I don't have a choice.' And I said, 'Sure, you do.' He goes, 'You don't understand. Every time a bomb goes off outside the wire, Big Steve comes running in, saying, "See that's another American losing their life out there. And unless you help us get this information, their blood's on your hands as well." '

"So you take a person like Graner," Davis said. "His marriage had ended. He knows what life he goes back to when he goes back to the United States. Maybe he doesn't like the choices he's made. Now he's in Iraq at Abu Ghraib, where high-profile detainees are, a war on terrorism, and you've got OGA, CIA, MI coming in saying, 'You're our go-to guy. Help us get this information.' He's the man of the hour. And he's going to do what they ask him to do, especially when he takes it to different people in his chain of command, and they tell him, shut up and keep doing his job, quit complaining. When you reach out for the lifeline and people keep pulling it back from you, you're just going to drown. So no one's helping this guy, and I don't condone abuse, but I understand how it escalated to such a level, because no one was willing to do anything about it, because policies were set in motion that were unclear, that were accepted."

Davis, too, felt that he was drowning, and he said, "If me, knowing how I am, can in one instant change, and hate so bad that I wanted to kill somebody, I can only imagine what it was like to work in that environment all the time, and know that they're bringing the killers of Americans and putting them right there in your face. A soldier's mentality is to fight." But the question that plagued Davis was: what was he fighting for? "Before I went over there I was always concerned with who would I be killing," he said. "Am I going to kill a father, a son, a cousin that's only protecting his family from what they deem infidels." And now, as he found himself hankering to kill, he wondered, "How do we know if they're not people that were housed at Abu Ghraib, and they're pretty bitter about their experience?"

Davis felt no need to prove his patriotism. He was an Air Force veteran, and in 1994, while visiting Washington as a tourist, he was one of three civilians who tackled and subdued an aspiring assassin from Colorado, Francisco Martin Duran, who fired twenty-nine rounds from a semi-automatic rifle through a fence overlooking the north lawn of the White House. When Davis enlisted as an MP in the Reserves after September 11, his wife "had a fit," but his attitude was, "You struck my home country. I'll fight you for that." Only, he said, "My problem was with the terrorists. I would have loved to have gone to Afghanistan, because that's where I felt the war was." In Iraq he felt that he was engaged in a "kind of parody" of the war on terror, and as he grappled with the unfamiliar demon of vengeance, it seemed to Davis that what made him want to kill was the same thing that made Iraqis want to kill him: the fact that he was there.

So Davis's days of wrath carried him to the brink of an understanding that he could not accept. It wasn't just his convoy that had been blown up; it wasn't just the life of a prisoner entrusted to his care that had been lost; it was also his belief that he had put his life at stake for a just and worthy war. That belief—already under duress since he'd seen his fellow soldiers doing "weird things with naked detainees" at the hard site—had given the idea of his death meaning. Davis wasn't prepared to die in defense of those weird things. He thought he was there to fight against them, and while he didn't question the rightness of his intentions in serving the occupation, he could no longer muster the conviction that the occupation served his country, much less the Iraqis who had become the enemy.

Davis's crisis had no solution. It only abated when he picked up the thread he'd dropped on the morning when he forgot to pray. "On the seventh day," he said, "another guy that would write scriptures on his wall pulled me into his jail cell, and sat me down. He said, 'Where you going with this, man?' I broke. I said, 'I don't know.' And he read a few scriptures to me. He read different passages about peace and about loving your enemies, and Psalm 23. And that snapped me back to my anchor point. I regained my focus then. I said, 'I can't be angry at the Iraqi people.' "

ON NOVEMBER 24, nine days after he rediscovered his equilibrium in his friend's cell, Davis was returning from a mission, rolling into Abu Ghraib in his Humvee with the windows down, when he heard shotgun blasts echoing across the prison yard. A riot was in progress at Camp Ganci, and over his radio he heard a voice trying to raise Shadow Main, the MPs' tactical operations center: "Ganci Shadow Main, Ganci Shadow Main, we're out of nonlethal rounds. What do we do?"

Shadow Main said, "We're in a combat zone, go to lethal rounds."

Davis was stunned. The prisoners in Ganci were ordinary Iraqis—not insurgents, not terrorists, just the herds picked up by infantry sweeps with some more-or-less properly arrested criminal suspects mixed in, and they were too densely packed in their concertina-wire enclosed yards to target them with any precision. There were more than five thousand prisoners in the camp, which was built to house no more than four thousand, and better suited to twenty-five hundred. Now soldiers were running toward the riot, and as Davis grabbed his gun to join them, Ganci came back on the radio: "We copy. Lethal rounds. Shadow Main confirmed."

Why shoot to kill? The only reason Davis could imagine was that the prisoners were on a rampage, storming the wire, overwhelming the guards. That was a constant fear of the MPs. Riots were sometimes staged to create a distraction during escapes, and riots had a way of spreading from camp to camp, and even to the CPA tiers of the hard site. "If every prisoner at Abu Ghraib would have rioted at one time, they would have had a very good chance of taking over the facility," Major David DiNenna said. "They could take blankets, they could take each other, throw them on the wire, and jump over. It would be extremely easy. If they wanted to come over the wire in masses, they could. Obviously, I think what held them back was the tower guards with automatic weapons."

When the firing began, Davis said, "The only way to describe it would have been 'Hell was unleashed upon them. The fury of God.' The eeriest sound was the SAWs just opening up on those yards. So I'm running up, expecting to see people breaching the wire of the containment area. I jumped up on a box of MREs, and I had my M4, my carbine rifle, pointed in, thinking, 'I'm ready.' But I don't see anybody coming out. They're all by their tents. Then I start seeing the dead and the wounded. And they pull a dead person out that's still twitching and throw him at my feet. I look down at him. He's still fully clothed. And I broke. I looked at the chaplain's aide—I hung out with the chaplain a lot, I would escort her into Babylon— and I started to cry. I said, 'What are we doing here? Is this what we resort to? Because these people were throwing rocks? Because they were angry because glass is in their food? They're angry because when I take them to court and the judge says 'you're innocent' we keep them here another three months? Is this what we have resorted to? Because if it is, I'm done. I'm finished.' "

Davis said he broke again that night, when he called home to tell his wife what had happened. Then he called his father, and said, "Dad, I can't take this. I can't take innocent lives being destroyed by American bullets. I can't do it." But he knew he had to take it. "Being done, being finished in a combat zone's totally different than being done here," he said. "We just can't quit. You've got to keep going."

19

BY THE TIME THE SHOOTING ENDED at Camp Ganci, four prisoners were dead, and seven were wounded severely enough to require a medevac. Lynndie England was at her post in administration during the riot. "They started bringing the dead bodies over to where we were," she said. "The first guy they brought in to us, they had his face covered with his own jacket. They laid him on the floor, and went for the other bodies. So we're sitting there talking, and this guy starts moaning and his arms start moving. We go and take the coat off, and this guy had got hit in his eye—he took three rounds—so it took half his head off. I mean, he was dead, but it was just his nervous system, his post-death moans and groans, I guess. One medic kept going over and checking the guy's pulse. He was definitely dead. It was just crazy. And we had to go on alert again after night fell. All their buddies on the outside started hitting us with mortars and rounds and stuff, because they felt like it again. It was a long night."

On the MI block too the night was long and heavy with menace. Graner had the shift off, and Sergeant William Cathcart was in charge of the tiers. Around six o'clock, Megan Ambuhl told him that a mentally ill prisoner on 1B was acting deranged. Cathcart went to get a medic, and left Ambuhl to keep an eye on one of the favored prisoners, who was on cleaning duty that evening. She watched him go from cell to cell, collecting the trash. As he came out of Taxi Driver's cell, he said, "Missus," and beckoned her. Ambuhl approached, and found that Taxi Driver wanted to tell her something. She couldn't make it out exactly, but he seemed to be saying that there was a prisoner on the tier who had got hold of a gun or a grenade or some knives—or maybe it was all three: a gun and a grenade and knives.

Ambuhl got Cathcart and they marched Taxi Driver out of his cell, hustling him down the corridor as if he was causing trouble so the other prisoners wouldn't know he was an informant. They took him to the showers and, with the help of an interpreter, got the story: a gun, a grenade, knives—somehow, one of the Iraqi guards from the CPA cell blocks had smuggled them into the hard site and got them to a Syrian prisoner on the upper level of 1A. The weapons had been on the tier for a couple of days already, and had been passed around between several prisoners for safekeeping at different times. Taxi Driver said he knew because he'd briefly been in possession of them. The Syrian trusted him that much.

Taxi Driver had given the MPs useful information about other prisoners before. They had no reason to doubt his claims about the Syrian's deadly arsenal. The question was how to disarm him as safely and swiftly as possible; and the MPs also had to wonder: who else had weapons? Sergeant Frederick was summoned to help formulate a plan of action, and Staff Sergeant Robert Elliot, another MP on duty at the hard site, joined the discussion. Then Lieutenant Colonel Jordan showed up, bearing sweets.

"I had fudge or cookies or some kind of pogie bait that somebody had got in a package," he said. "When you got extra, you shared, so I said, 'I'll take some of this stuff by the folks at the hard site.' " Jordan knew that the soldiers were on edge after the riot and the killing in Camp Ganci, but he was taken aback when Frederick told him, "I could care less about your fudge." When Frederick filled him in about the prisoner and the gun, all Jordan could think was, "No way." But the MPs were strapping on their body armor and getting weapons from their office, and it occurred to Jordan that things could get out of control. Taxi Driver had said the gun had migrated around the tier. The MPs could be walking into an ambush: they'd go for the Syrian and another prisoner across the corridor would open fire. And if there was a grenade?

"There was—I like to call it 'rumored intelligence,' " Jordan said, "that, on the outside, there was going to be attacks on the gate and some of the towers, while possibly some of the Iraqi security police and detainees attacked from the inside. That was a very big concern, a coordinated attack, where you have maybe thousands of detainees coming at you, trying to escape or overpower you, taking weapons, and things of this nature. And you always felt that if something did go woefully wrong there could be some intense, intense soldier deaths."

Jordan said he told everybody to slow down and call the Quick Reaction Force. But the MPs didn't want such a high-profile raid, which would immediately raise the alarm on the tier, and would draw the attention of the Iraqi guards at the hard site as well. If they were smuggling weapons to prisoners, it was best not to find out which side they'd take if all hell broke loose. Better to keep it simple, the MPs said: make it look like they were conducting a routine, cell-by-cell search for contraband. Jordan was persuaded, and he volunteered to join the posse.

Meanwhile, on 1B, Shitboy had tripped into his nightly mania, trying to eat everything in his cell and making a mess of himself. Ambuhl had got him in the shower, but just as the operation was getting underway to neutralize the Syrian, Shitboy bolted past her and took off down the corridor, wet and naked and possessed. It was one of those days, Ambuhl said: if she'd had a gun in her hands, she believed she'd have shot him. He ducked into the MPs' supply cell, cornering himself, and was recaptured and locked down. But Ambuhl was rattled as she suited up in her Kevlar and joined the men on 1A for the search.

THE SOLDIERS MOVED OUT single file, with Cathcart in the lead, and Ambuhl, who was the lowest in rank, at the rear. They stayed close to the wall, so the Syrian couldn't get a bead on them before they got to him. As they progressed, cell by cell, they had the prisoners come forward and stick their hands through the bars to be cuffed. It was a familiar drill, except that this time there were a couple of medics standing by in case they were needed. That was as unnerving as it was reassuring. Ambuhl kept expecting a signal to go out among the prisoners for a general uprising and attack.

As Cathcart approached the Syrian's cell, Sergeant Elliot, who had circled around the tier, came at it from the other side, carrying a twelve-gauge shotgun. The Syrian spoke English, and Jordan heard Elliot say, "Step forward." The Syrian said, "No."

"Step forward. Put your hands through," Elliot said.

"I don't have a gun," the Syrian said.

Nobody had said anything about a gun. Jordan couldn't see into the cell. He had his back to the corridor wall, keeping watch on the facing balcony of the upper tier for any alarming movement in the cells there. When the shooting started, it was deafening, and Jordan had no idea what was happening. Several guns were going at once; bullets were ringing off metal rails.

What happened was that the Syrian had dived onto his bunk, reached under his pillow, and come up firing a Soviet-era Makarov nine-millimeter pistol. Cathcart stepped in front of the bars, and a bullet ricocheted off his protective vest. Elliot returned the Syrian's fire with several nonlethal rounds from his shotgun. The Syrian was hit in the chest, but he kept firing, crawling around in his cell, trying to get an angle on the soldiers. He got off five or six more shots, while Elliot reloaded, this time with lethal rounds—double-ought buckshot—took aim, and fired into the cell. The blast tore into the Syrian's legs. By then he'd run out of ammunition, and he slid his pistol out into the corridor as a sign of surrender.

Soldiers entered the cell and dragged the bloody gunman out. While the medics attended to his wounds, and called in a medevac to take him to the combat support hospital at Baghdad International Airport, the MPs searched under his mattress and found two bayonets. But even when they stripped the cell, they found no grenade.

"We had to continue going around the cells, to get all the prisoners up and secured," Ambuhl said. "And a couple of them didn't seem to understand, or were freaked out by all the noise of all the guns going off. So it was pretty stressful. You didn't know if they were just scared, or if they had a gun, too. Downstairs, there was a guy in the second cell, and he didn't want to put his arms through the doors. The detainees across the tier from him were telling him in Arabic to do it—and he wouldn't do it. We were just, like, inches away from shooting this guy because he was acting so strange. But he finally put his arms through, so we didn't have to hurt him. So we locked them all to their doors, and that's when the canine MPs came through."

The military working dogs that Major DiNenna had first requested as a force multiplier in June had only arrived at Abu Ghraib a few days earlier, after DiNenna sent an impatient e-mail blast up his chain of command: "Last night we had a significant riot in Camp Vigilant. MWDs are a must and we need them asap. We currently have 4500 prisoners in three different locations. We need the dogs." The Army sent two dogs and their handlers, trained in narcotics operations, and the Navy sent a three-dog team trained in explosives detection. Neither team had prison experience, nor had the dogs been on the MI block before the Navy team was summoned to help in the search for munitions. None were found—if there had ever been a grenade it had been disposed of—but the dogs were kept around to bark and snarl at the prisoners, as soldiers descended on the tier, frantic for information and control.

"It was total chaos," Frederick said. "It was civilian and MI interrogators running everywhere. The dogs were going crazy." Jordan and several other officers were rounding up all the Iraqi police and corrections officers at the hard site, searching them and ransacking their belongings to determine who had smuggled in the weapons. "Some of them were discovered to have notes that were being passed from the inmates back to family members," Jordan said. "One or two were found to have some sort of narcotics on them. A couple others had razor blades that could be made into a knife or a shank." By the end of the night more than half of the Iraqi guard force had been identified as having ties to Saddam's old security apparatus. They were led off to prison cells for further questioning, and the Americans at the hard site went to bed feeling more embattled than ever.

"They would bring terrorists in to be prison guards," Javal Davis said. "It's like, come on. The decision makers way up the chain did not have things worked out. So not only did you have to risk your life from the shelling on the outside, you was risking your life dealing with the unscreened Iraqi corrections guards. There were more of them than us, and not all of them were bad, but a vast majority were bad. The guy who smuggled in the pistol I thought was a good guard. He turned out to be Fedayeen. Smile on your face, stab you in the back."

During the panic on the tier that night, Graner had showed up and photographed the bullet-scarred walls of the Syrian's cell, the blood-painted floor, and the bloody tracks left by his legs as he was dragged away. The place looked like a slaughterhouse, gleaming with gore, and the pictures troubled Megan Ambuhl—especially later, when they were made public, and anyone could see them. To Ambuhl, the photographs represented a moment when American soldiers spared the life of someone who had sought to kill them, then rushed to care for him as they would have cared for one of their own. "But it doesn't appear when you see a picture that that's what happened," she said. "Your imagination can run wild when you just see blood, and you don't have a story behind it. The pictures only show you a fraction of a second. You don't see forward and you don't see backward. You don't see outside the frame."

A DAY OR TWO AFTER the shoot-out with the Syrian, Specialist Joe Darby returned to Abu Ghraib from a home leave. He was sorry he'd missed the action. "I heard that it was just blood everywhere," he said. "So naturally I wanted to see it. And I knew somebody's got pictures of it. They always got pictures of it. So I asked Graner. I was asking a bunch of people who worked in the prison. Graner was the only one who said yeah. And he reaches into his bag and pulls out two CDs, and hands them to me. I'm honestly guessing he gave me the wrong pictures, because the pictures that I wanted weren't there."

The photographs on the first disc Darby checked out were all from Al Hillah: tourist shots of ancient Babylon, and happy snaps from the date factory. Darby was glad to have them. When he switched to the second disc, and the first photo popped up, he started laughing. His screen was full of men's buttocks. "It was a pyramid, from behind," he said. "I've been in the Army for eight years, and I've seen soldiers do some very strange things. So at first, I didn't even realize it was Iraqis."

Darby had a reputation in the unit as an aficionado of smut. During an earlier deployment he'd been known as the porn king of Bosnia, a title he enjoyed. "We had a huge footlocker of porn," he said. "It weighed a couple hundred pounds. It was in my room. And everybody from the unit would come over and borrow the porn all the time." That's how soldiers are, Darby said. "I had an NCO one time who had a philosophy which I kind of agree with. You give American soldiers three things, they'll take over the world—porn, alcohol, tobacco. Anywhere you go, even if you're not allowed to have it, you'll have it. Soldiers find a way. After the first Gulf War, they stopped allowing alcohol in combat zones. So naturally we want it, because it's not allowed. You can buy alcohol on the streets of Iraq—vodka by the can—and porn. Because American soldiers are away from their loved ones, their wives, their girlfriends, they're always going to have porn."

So Darby was neither squeamish nor a moralist, and he had thought nothing of the photograph Graner showed him in October of a naked prisoner hung by his wrists and hooded in panties. He knew that uncooperative prisoners were kept nude on the MI block. So that didn't bother him, and he said, "The panties were there when we got there. That was something that the unit before us had instituted." But he said that as he flipped through Graner's photos, and realized that they were shot on Tier 1A, he focused on the images of "sexual stuff" from the night of the pyramid, and it occurred to him that what he was looking at was evidence of prisoner abuse. "And then the next thought is, 'What do I do?' " he said. " 'Do I turn these in? Do I look the other way?' "

Darby didn't do anything in a hurry. "I'd been in the military and around a lot of these guys long enough to know we take care of our own," he said. He anticipated what would be said if he reported the pictures: "That I was turning in my friends, that I was a traitor, that I was a stool pigeon." He decided to sound out his roommate, and a sergeant he regarded as his mentor and role model. But he said, "I was very vague when I talked to people. I said, 'What would you do if'—and I wouldn't ask them a direct question. Or I'd invent something, a story to go around it, because I didn't want them to know that I had the pictures." So Darby kept his options open. Even as his friends told him he should always do the right thing, he said, he kept wondering, "Is it going to be worth possible retaliation?" He was particularly concerned about Graner.

"I got along with Graner," Darby said. "He wasn't a friend, he wasn't an enemy. Earlier in the deployment, when we were in Al Hillah, I'd had some problems, and I wasn't sleeping well at night. Graner was working the gate out in front of the date factory. I had nothing to do but smoke cigarettes, so I just walked over and started talking to him. He asked me what was wrong, and I told him. And he said he had had a similar problem." The problem, Darby said, was "an unfaithful spouse." He said, "I had the problem when I first got to Iraq, and he had went through it before he came to Iraq. But the way he told me he handled the problem was the completely wrong way to handle it. It was a very dark way to handle it. He told me that when it happened to him, he had sat across the street from his wife's house with a rifle, waiting on her to come out."

Graner had not shot his wife. According to the story he'd given up his vigil before she appeared. But, as Darby thought about Graner's photographs from the MI block, he remembered that evening in Al Hillah; and he remembered the early morning at Abu Ghraib when Graner told him, "The Christian in me knows it's wrong, but the corrections officer in me can't help but love to make a grown man piss himself"; and he began to see Graner as a truly diabolical figure. "He is the most charismatic, most manipulative person you will meet," Darby said. "You want to like him when you talk to him. But he has a very dark side, a very, very dark side."

Darby saw Frederick and England and Harman and Jeremy Sivits, too, in the pictures, but he was fixated on Graner. To Darby, it was obvious that Graner was the source of the abuse, and that the others, while culpable as well, were simply under his sway. And Darby found comfort in this idea, as he brooded about how to handle the photographs. He said he did not feel that he had to act quickly to try to stop further harm from being done to the prisoners on the MI block, because shortly after he got the pictures, Graner had finally been rotated out of the hard site, as his counseling statement had promised, and assigned to work with Ken Davis on convoys. "The abuse wasn't happening at that time frame," Darby said, "because Graner wasn't working in the prison."

In fact, Graner continued working on Tier 1A until mid-December, three weeks after the gunfight with the Syrian, and he said, "After the shooting it was a very violent place." He and Frederick were repeatedly called upon by interrogators to beat prisoners up, and several incidents ended with Graner fetching the surgical needle and thread to repair the resulting damage. Although fewer photographs were taken in December than in the preceding months, they make it clear that the abuse of prisoners continued apace in Graner's absence. None of the pictures from December were staged; many were bloody, and many were blurry with commotion, and these include the scenes of purest terror ever recorded at the hard site—images of prisoners, naked and clothed, beset by dogs.

SABRINA HARMAN HAD RETURNED to Abu Ghraib from her leave at the end of November. She, too, had missed the shoot-out with the Syrian, but she didn't mind. If she could have stayed away from the prison without facing a court-martial as a deserter, she said, she would have. On one of her first nights at home, she said, she had tried confessing to a complete stranger: "I went to a bar in D.C., and I got really drunk, and I just started talking. Some girl said she worked for CNN, and I was like, 'Oh, I got a story for you—even got photos.' There's no way I didn't tell her everything. She gave me her business card, but I don't even know if she believed me. I don't know what happened to that card. I was so trashed, I lost it."

Of course, Harman showed Kelly all the Abu Ghraib pictures. Kelly might have known from Harman's letters what to expect, but Harman said, "She seemed kind of in shock." That made an impression on Harman. "I guess reality hit," she said. "What was going on wasn't right, which of course you know from the beginning. But I didn't want to take any more photos. I don't think that taking photos helped me cope. It didn't relieve any stress. I had had enough."

Besides, as Harman had written to Kelly, she'd heard a rumor just before she left Abu Ghraib that the MPs were under investigation. Harman thought it was best to play it safe. She had left a complete set of her photos with Kelly and erased them from her computer before flying back to Iraq. When she returned to work at the hard site, she no longer took her camera. "I didn't want to see anymore," she said.

But she couldn't stop looking. On the night of December 12, Harman saw something new on Tier 1A, and a few nights later she wrote about it to Kelly:

> The other day an inmate was in his cell. They did a cell
> check and found he had busted out the board on the
> window and had a rope he made out of the blanket he was
> given. The rest of the shredded blanket was in a oval ball
> shape. He said he didn't knock the window out and he has a
> baby, that he was making a baby doll out of the shredded
> blanket to remind him of his baby. They didn't buy it so
> they brought him out of the cell, stripped him down and
> called K9. This is the first time ive seen military police dogs
> here. Two dogs w/two owners come in and go to the man
> against the wall. The guy is scared out of his mind. Iraqis

are afraid of dogs, not sure why. So the dogs are barking
and hes getting more and more nervous.

So Graner tells the guy to lay down and he starts to but the
dogs get closer so he stands back up they start yelling at him
the Iraqi starts screaming and runs straight to Graner and
the interpreter. It looked like he was going to jump in his
arms. Graner and the interp move and one of the guys lets
his dog lose enough to bite him on the leg—for no reason—
so the guy is hysterical and he started to run towards me.
The guy couldn't control the dog by this time the dog got in
another bite on his other leg—blood was everywhere. . . .

The guys tackled him from behind. He wasn't trying to
escape anything but those dogs. Now the floor is covered
with blood—I run up and get the medic bag + water and of
course they took pictures—I stopped taking pictures I'm
not getting in this mess anymore than I already have. So I
start to clean him up and the first bite isn't that bad took a
few layers off but not too bad to need anything more than a
gauze pad. It was teethmarks. But the other one a tooth had
punctured his skin and that's where all the blood was
coming from. One of our medics came and he taught me
how to give stitches. He put one in, I put one in. . . . I felt
horrible for this guy. The dog should have never been there.

Graner said it was true: there had been no need for the dogs. The
prisoner had been making no trouble until the dogs arrived, barking
and straining at the end of their leashes. Ambuhl took the pictures
that night—Lynndie England had gone home on leave—and in them
the prisoner's panic in the moments before he bolted toward Graner

is palpable: he stands naked and cowering, clutching his head with both hands, and as the dogs converge on him, he bends over at the waist, backing away, but with a wall at his back there is nowhere to go. "I don't know where Shout, Shove, Show, Shoot, Bark comes in," Graner said. "We had no instruction on how to use the dogs."

But the dogs kept coming back. The next day Saddam was captured, and the day after that, when the secretary of defense authorized the special projects team, it seemed that the dogs were everywhere, whining hungrily outside interrogation booths or barking and snapping at prisoners hanging from their cages in stress positions. Frederick said that Big Steve encouraged the MPs to make prisoners do "the doggy dance," and that the dog handlers who became the regulars on the block, Sergeant Santos Cardona and Specialist Michael Smith, had an ongoing contest to see which one of them could make the most prisoners piss in fear. The soldiers at the prison were all in awe of the dogs, and when they came around there was always an audience. The doggy dance was what passed for a Roman entertainment on the MI block.

Frederick remembered a night when Smith and Cardona showed up with Special Agent Tyler Pieron of CID. "One of the K-9 handlers asked me if I had any detainees that was being a problem that night 'cause Pieron wanted to see what happened when the dogs were at the detainees," Frederick said. He had seen Pieron and the dog handlers hanging out together on and off duty—they were clearly good buddies—and he said, "I told them I did have one or two detainees that had been acting up. So we went down to 1B where the Ba'ath general was. We took the general out of his cell and put him in the middle of the floor and the dogs started barking at him. He just sat there and didn't move, really no reaction at all. So we moved the dogs and put the general back in his cell. Then, as we were walking out, the Iraqi police had another one handcuffed to the iron bars outside in the hallway. So Smith went behind the gate and let his dog bark at the detainee from behind, and the detainee was jumping around a little bit. The dog kind of nipped the detainee on the wrist, nothing serious though, to barely break the skin."

It was hard to capture the doggy dance on camera: the men and the dogs, jigging about, kept getting in the way of the shot. But on December 30, Ambuhl did it, with a set of pictures of Smith and his dog confronting a prisoner who was known as AQ, because he was believed to be an Al Qaeda operative. AQ was considered the prize prisoner on the block at that time. The secretary of defense was said to have a particular interest in him, and to check in with Colonel Pappas several times a week by phone or videoconference for updates on his interrogation. Big Steve was AQ's handler, and according to Frederick, "He said put the dogs on AQ every chance we got—to use the dogs to bark at him, scare him, intimidate him. He just basically wanted us to use the dogs on him to treat him like shit. He would tell us to put AQ in this position or that position, then put the dogs on him. Then he would tell them to pull the dogs off, then he would go in the cell, shut the door, and I guess interrogate him."

On the night of the photographs, AQ was laid on his side on the floor, with his hands tied behind his back, and Smith let his dog bark in his face from no more than a foot or two away. Then AQ was hoisted into a kneeling position with his back to a wall, and a sandbag was placed over his bowed head. Once again Smith moved in with the animal. In one picture you see it lunging, ears back, a black blur of muscle and jaw, aimed straight at the top of the sandbag. In the next picture you see AQ bareheaded; the dog has nipped the sandbag off, and the prisoner is trying to flatten himself against the wall, which is difficult to do when you're on your knees with your hands tied over your tailbone. The movement thrusts your chest toward the avid dog, barking just inches from your throat, and this time Smith is in the picture, crouching over the dog, restraining him and urging him on at the same time.

It does not seem possible to amplify the drama of this moment, but the look on AQ's face does just that. He has the horrified, drawn-back, and quivering expression of a thoroughly blasted soul. It is all there in his eyes, moist and mad with fear, fixed on a mouthful of fangs. What secrets does he have that we want so badly, but are so precious to him that he endures this day after day? The answer in AQ's case was none. Once again at Abu Ghraib they had the wrong guy, or they had the guy wrong, and when they realized this after several months of dogs and bondage and hooding and noise and sleep-lessness and heat and cold and who knows just what other robust counter-resistance techniques, they told him to scram, and closed his case. The pictures of AQ on that night before New Year's Eve are the last known photographs of our prisoners on the MI block at Abu Ghraib, which seems fitting, because these pictures don't leave much to the viewer's imagination, except the obvious question: if you fight terror with terror, how can you tell which is which?

20.

LYNNDIE ENGLAND HAD GONE home on R&R in early December, and when she landed back at Baghdad International Airport just before Christmas, there was nobody from her unit there to pick her up. She spent the holiday at the airport, eating MREs and sleeping in her uniform, in a cold, rat-infested tent. "All I had was this little Kentucky blanket that I got for Christmas from my parents to wrap myself in," she said. Finally, another MP outfit at Abu Ghraib sent a vehicle to fetch her. The delay had turned her two-week leave into a three-week absence from Abu Ghraib. She was eager to see Graner, excited about their reunion, but he was out on the convoys by day, and at night he avoided her.

"He was spreading a rumor around that he had broken up with me," England said. "People would tell me, 'Oh, he's been messing around on you with Megan.' And I'm like, 'No he ain't.' But I could never catch him to talk to him about it. He wouldn't say anything to me. He would ignore me. So I got pretty pissed. I wanted to know what was going on. He says he wants to marry me and have a family with me one minute, and he hadn't said anything to me about us breaking up—it's just strange. I didn't believe it. Then, when I confronted him, we got in this big argument, and he went out of his way to come back and find me and sit down to tell me that, 'No, it's all a lie, they're just trying to get you riled up,' and blah, blah, blah—'I still love you,' da, da, da. He said all that. And then he's still messing around with Megan, and obviously he's telling her that we're still broke up, because she's believing it."

England wanted to believe Graner, too, and she did—at least when she was with him. The rest of the time, which was most of the time, she was shattered: suspicious, angry, wounded, disoriented, scared. She loved Graner and trusted him; she had given him her heart—while on leave she had finalized her divorce—and she wanted him back. The story of her love for him was the story of the war to her; she had served him with a devotion that would make any commander of troops envious, and now he had gone AWOL, and she could not accept that her service had been misplaced and misguided; that she had served an illusion. She wanted him to reclaim her; she wanted to be restored. She could imagine no other consolation. But it was only in stolen moments that he would allow her to forgive him.

"She would sit in her office, which was next to mine, and cry every day," Joe Darby said. Darby wasn't surprised. "I mean, it was a regular soap opera in my unit," he said. "Everybody was seeing everybody. It's the way most military units go—when you have females in the unit mixed with males, they pair off for the deployment." Besides, he had been watching Graner with more than usual interest in December, while he considered what to do with the photographs, and he said, "I suspected that he was cheating with Megan Ambuhl, because he was always with her, but I didn't know until after Lynndie got back. Then the pieces fell in. One of Graner's friends had dated Ambuhl while he was dating Lynndie, and then Graner's friend broke up with Ambuhl while Lynndie was on leave— OK, he's with Ambuhl now."

Darby didn't blame Ambuhl. He said, "She was a good person." But he identified with England. She, too, was a good person, he said, but there was more to his sympathy than that. "I mean, she would strive her hardest to do what she had to do," he said. "And, yeah—I liked Lynndie." When he heard her crying, Darby went to her. He asked her what was wrong, and she told him. During his home leave, a month earlier, he had patched up his own broken marriage, but he had not forgotten the feelings England was discovering. When he heard her crying again, he went to her again, and she told him more. England's despair reinforced Darby's image of Graner as a force of darkness, and he said, "Probably about three to five days after she got back, I turned the pictures in."

ENGLAND DIDN'T DOUBT that her romantic distress might have spurred Darby on, but she said, "I came back from leave on December 27. He turned the photos in on January 13. Doesn't sound like three days to me." It was true. Darby had a habit, in recounting his story, of muddling dates and shifting time frames to draw attention away from the fact that he had had Graner's pictures for six weeks without doing anything about them. Darby preferred to create the impression that he had acted swiftly—within two weeks, he said, or at most three. This was striking, because the dates were not in dispute, and because, in the intervening years, Darby had come to be regarded as the hero of Abu Ghraib.

Darby had accounted for himself to one team of military investigators after another; he had testified in numerous courts-martial; he had given countless interviews to admiring reporters; and he had been honored with the John F. Kennedy Profile in Courage Award. He always said that he had merely done his duty when others failed, and in accepting his award he described his decision as tough but clear: "On one hand, I had my morals and the morals of my country. On the other, I had my comrades, my brothers in arms." Having placed morality above fraternity, he appeared to be the one soldier from Abu Ghraib who had nothing to hide. So why couldn't Joe Darby get his story straight?

The explanations of the soldiers who got in trouble when Darby finally did act have to be treated with skepticism. But while most of them allowed that he had been correct to report the photographs, none of them accepted that he had done it out of simple righteousness. "Joe Darby—there's an ulterior motive to everything he does," Javal Davis said. Davis thought Darby might have been getting even with people who mocked him for being conspicuously overweight. He said that Frederick and Graner used to taunt Darby, calling him Fat Bastard, and Darby would seethe while everyone else laughed.

England and Sivits also saw Darby's size as a motive for his decision to give up the photos, but as they understood it he wasn't trying to get even; he was trying to get ahead. "He's been a specialist for, like, ever," England said. "He's trying to get promoted, but he's too fat to pass the PT test. So he figures if he does this good deed they will promote him, which they did." Sabrina Harman told a different story, in which Darby heard other soldiers discussing plans to report the abuse on the MI block, and decided to beat them to it. "Either he was like, 'Oh, shit, I'm going to get caught with these photos,' or 'Hey, you know what? I want the credit for it,' " Harman said.

But who cares if Darby was fat or calculating, vengeful or self-seeking? He didn't commit any crimes; he tried to stop some. He should have done it sooner, and by his evasions, his elisions, and his confabulations he showed that he knew it. So what does it matter why Darby did what he did, if he did the right thing? It matters for the same reason that it matters why the people whom he reported did what they did, and in what context.

To Darby, however, the evidence was self-evident: he was the soldier who chose morality and duty, they were the soldiers who chose depravity and crime; he had acted alone, and they had acted alone—

a band of rogue MPs under the thrall of the mesmeric ringleader, Charles Graner—and any attempt to place the story in a larger context was merely "political" spin. "It had nothing to do with intelligence," he said. "These soldiers were bored. They did it because they had nothing better to do. And one of them had a very sick and twisted way of doing things."

So, just as he sought to represent himself as a tidy, self-contained package of coherent motives and actions, Darby rejected any suggestion that there might be more to the story of the MPs in the photographs than what the photographs showed. "When I gave CID those photos, their investigation was almost over," he said. "They had all the evidence. They could have probably charged them that night, without talking to anybody. I mean, the photographs said everything. There was no way to misinterpret those photos. There was no way to think that they were something else that they weren't."

He said, "My proof was the pictures. The truth was the pictures. The truth was sitting on my computer in front of me." He said, "I knew before I turned the pictures in that someone was going to get prison time. I thought that they would be tried for war crimes." He said, "My desire was for them to be punished." And he said it again and again: "They needed to be punished"; "I just wanted these people to be punished"; "My intention was to see them punished"; "I would have been very, very happy if these people would have been arrested, they would have been punished, and it would have ended there."

WHEN DARBY PRESENTED THE PHOTOGRAPHS to Special Agent Tyler Pieron of the CID on January 13, he explained that he was doing so because Graner was scheduled to return to work at the hard site the next day. Apparently Darby was unaware that Pieron was familiar with the MI block, and that other CID agents had been regular visi-

tors to Tier 1A throughout the preceding months, seeing much of
what went on there without objection, and at times expressing their
approval and encouragement. Pieron and his colleagues did not let
on. They promptly rounded up Ambuhl, England, Harman, Frederick, and Graner, and before long they brought in Javal Davis and
Sivits for questioning as well. These were the seven night-shift MPs
who had been involved with the seven rioters from Camp Ganci on
the night of the human pyramid. They were suspended from duty but
allowed to return to their quarters, unsupervised and unsegregated.
Harman wasted no time reporting the news to Kelly. In all her previous letters from Abu Ghraib, she had never sounded so cheerful:

> Well sweetie you married a criminal. Yup, the pictures are
> out and I am under investigation as of 10:00am this
> morning. So much for turning those pictures in when I come
> home cause they're already out. I just didn't want to be
> envolved with it. I knew I'd get in trouble just by being there
> but how else would you let people know the shit the Army
> does. I don't know whats going to happen, what charges are
> to be for me—I was only there, not once did I touch anyone
> or even yell at them, of course you've heard it all before in
> the letters I sent you. Ive blocked a lot out—and a lot more
> than I know has happened. They have pictures I didn't even
> know about. Fucked up. I'm kind of glad it happened, it
> needed to. Ambuhl got an attorney, I waved my right to
> have one—I wasn't there enough to need one. I have no idea
> about what the others have desided. I was photographed
> and fingerprinted. You'd think I'd be scared but Im not. Its
> more of a glad they got them photos. I knew Id go down
> with them. Wrong place wrong time. What sucks is almost
> the entire company knows what happened, has seen
> pictures and have done nothing—so we could all be charged.

Ill let you know what happens, ill try calling you tonight
but we keep getting mortared today chances of more
tonight—don't know. I love you and I hope to be home soon.

Sabrina

"I didn't think I was going to be in trouble at all," Harman said.
"I didn't think I did anything wrong. Like, I took photos, and I was
in a photo. But I didn't really think I was really a part of what went
on, and it really didn't matter, because it was allowed." The others
were not so sanguine, but they were all surprised when, two days later
on January 16, Colonel Pappas issued a three-page memorandum to
all military personnel at the prison with the subject line: "Reiteration
of Standards of Conduct at Baghdad Central Correctional Facility,
Forward Operating Base Abu Ghraib, Amnesty Period, and Health
and Welfare Inspection." The memo had the flat, generic tone of a
routine bureaucratic reminder. The idea was: we have rules here, you
know them, and just in case, here they are again; now you will follow
them or else you will be held to account. "Specifically," Pappas wrote,
"the following prohibited activities are punishable":

a. Purchase, possession, use or sale of privately owned firearms,
   ammunition, or explosives . . .
b. Introduction, purchase, possession, sale, transfer, manufacture
   or consumption of any alcoholic beverage.
c. Introduction, purchase, possession, use, sale, transfer, manufacture or consumption of any controlled substances, or drug
   paraphernalia . . .
d. Introduction, possession, transfer, sale, creation or display of any
   pornographic or sexually explicit photographs, videotapes, movies, drawings, books, magazines, or similar representations . . .
e. Pursuant to Geneva Convention directives, personnel will nei-

ther create nor possess photographs, videotapes, digital videos, CD/DVDs, computer files/folders, movies or any other medium containing images of any criminal or security detainee currently or formerly interned at Baghdad Central Correctional Facility, located at FOB Abu Ghraib, Iraq. . . .

f. Gambling of any kind, including sports pools, lotteries and raffles . . .

g. Removing, possessing, selling, defacing or destroying archeological artifacts or national treasures.

h. Selling, bartering or exchanging any currency other than at the official host-nation exchange rate.

i. Adopting as pets or mascots, caring for, or feeding any type of domestic or wild animal.

j. Proselytizing of any religion, faith or practice.

k. Taking or retaining individual souvenirs or trophies . . . seized during exercises or operations.

The memo went on to define prohibited items as "contraband," and to invite anyone in possession of them to get rid of them "without penalty or legal consequence" by depositing them in one of several "amnesty boxes" that would be made available at soldiers' living areas for forty-eight hours, beginning on January 18 at one minute after midnight. At the end of the amnesty period, punitive regulations would again be in force, and there would be periodic inspections of the living areas and belongings of all soldiers at Abu Ghraib "in order to ensure the health, welfare, safety, security, military fitness, good order and discipline of our personnel." These inspections, Colonel Pappas explained, "will not be used as a pretext for discovering contraband," but if contraband were found, it would be bagged and tagged, and the soldiers in possession of it would be read their rights before questioning.

Pappas offered no explanation of his sudden concern for standards, and although he called his memo a "*re*-iteration," nobody at the prison could remember seeing anything quite like it before—particularly the bit about the photographs. The rest was boilerplate, the old catechism of vice laws out of the Uniform Code of Military Justice and General Order Number One. But the photos? That was slipped in to look like nothing special between the booze and porn and personal weapons, the gambling and looting and pets, only it jumped right out at you, starting with that unfamiliar phrase, "Pursuant to Geneva Convention directives." All the other descriptions of contraband in the memo were simple declarations, but with the photos it was a commandment, and it got local: thou shalt not at Abu Ghraib.

Sabrina Harman was perplexed. The investigation of the photographs had just begun. So why was the base commander issuing a battalion-wide order to dispose of them? Pappas's offer of clemency sounded to her like some kind of threat. Then the amnesty boxes appeared, right on schedule. They looked like mail boxes made of bare wood, and they were set up between the living areas, out in the open where you couldn't miss them. So much for anonymity; Harman never saw anybody go near one. Megan Ambuhl didn't either, and it occurred to her that the forbidding placement of the amnesty boxes was a deliberate scare tactic. "It was kind of a 'read between the lines,' " Ambuhl said, and the message was: get rid of your contraband, but do it some other way.

"There was a big fire going on that night," Sabrina Harman said. "There was a lot of porn being burned and alcohol being thrown out or buried." At the same time soldiers were scrubbing their computers' photo folders. The CID was handing out questionnaires to all the soldiers at Abu Ghraib, asking if they knew about abuse, had photos of it, or had seen such photos. "And they were wiping their disks clean," England said, "erasing everything so there was no evidence against them. And they were like, 'No, I don't know. I don't know what you're talking about.' "

"It was messed up," Harman said. "That's destroying evidence."

Javal Davis agreed. He read Pappas's amnesty memo, and felt the noose tightening. "Basically, he's wiped out in one day every last defense witness, every last single person that would have been available to come forward and say, 'Hey look, this is what I know,'" Davis said. "After the amnesty period, who's going to want to come forward? No one."

Ambuhl put the question differently. "What if somebody had actually wanted to know what was going on?" she said. "Why would they start an investigation and not want to know?"

ON THE SAME DAY that Colonel Pappas issued his amnesty memorandum, U.S. Central Command put out a press release, datelined Baghdad, which said: "An investigation has been initiated into reported incidents of detainee abuse at a Coalition Forces detention facility. The release of specific information concerning the incidents could hinder the investigation, which is in its early stages. The investigation will be conducted in a thorough and professional manner. The Coalition is committed to treating all persons under its control with dignity, respect and humanity. Lt. Gen. Ricardo S. Sanchez, the Commanding General, has reiterated this requirement to all members." A brief item toward the back of the international news pages in the *New York Times* identified the facility as Abu Ghraib, and noted that "a senior Pentagon official said authorities had been alerted to the possible abuse of detainees in the past few days and were taking the allegations 'very seriously.'" The press paid no further attention.

The next day, General Sanchez sent General Karpinski a letter of reprimand, rebuking her for her lack of oversight of her soldiers; and, at the same time, Colonel Phillabaum and Captain Reese were suspended from duty. Two days later, on January 19, Sanchez requested that Central Command initiate an administrative investigation of the 800th MP Brigade, Karpinski's command, focusing on its conduct of detention and internment operations since November 1, 2003. This mandate, which was soon passed on to Major General Antonio Taguba, was striking: less than a week after Darby gave Pieron the photographs, Sanchez had set the parameters for the Army's inquiry to exclude Military Intelligence, and even to exclude the one incident from the preceding fall in which MI soldiers were clearly identifiable in photographs, the abuse of the three alleged rapists on the night of October 25. The retrospective cutoff date of November 1 also preempted any scrutiny of the practices of the 72nd MPs, the 372nd's predecessor company on the MI block. What's more, the scope of the Taguba investigation, which covered operations all over Iraq, insured that it would take several months.

Although the 800th MP Brigade was deployed in Iraq, Karpinski's headquarters were at Camp Doha, in Kuwait, and it was there that an Army public affairs officer, Lieutenant Colonel Vic Harris, first saw the Abu Ghraib photographs not long after Darby gave them to the CID. "They had them downloaded and printed out in our legal section," Harris said, "and being a PAO, I obviously had to see them." Harris was shocked by what he saw, but what shocked him even more was the Army's response to the pictures. "I heard the discussions of the staff and our commanders, and there was no intention of doing anything other than to try to contain them," he said. "They weren't even looking to prosecute in any way. The only intent was to hide it and try to prevent the images from getting out to the media, to make it go away and not let the public know about it. I was very disappointed. I had the exact opposite attitude. I was looking at it from the perspective of—Hey, these guys ought to be brought to justice."

At one point, Harris said, Army lawyers at Camp Doha called on CID agents back in the States to try to hunt down all the friends and family members of Abu Ghraib soldiers whom they believed might

have received copies of the photographs by e-mail. Harris thought
that was "pretty insidious," since civilians were under no obligation
to turn over their computer files to Army investigators. He also
thought the exercise was impractical in the digital age. "It's ridicu-
lous to even think that you would run them all down," he said. But
the order was given—in fact, Sabrina Harman's wife, Kelly, soon had
agents at her door—and to Harris the effort confirmed that a cover-up
was under way.

"There was no intent of trying to bring the people to justice that
were obviously committing crimes, in some cases war crimes, in those
images," he said. "The Army, if they could have gotten away with not
letting the public know this happened, that's exactly what they would
have done. I'm one hundred percent sure of that—even to the point
where they would have done nothing to punish the soldiers that were
responsible for what happened, because that would probably at some
point require those photos be made public. They would have let it
slide by completely."

Harris knew a lot of people in television. He had worked on stories with 60 Minutes in the past, and been impressed with the results.
"So I called a friend of mine who was one of Dan Rather's producers
at the time, Dana Roberson," he said. "I remember exactly where I
was. I was at the Japanese Embassy at some social event in Kuwait
City." Harris told Roberson that a number of soldiers had abused
prisoners at Abu Ghraib, and that there were photos; Roberson passed
the word on to her boss, Mary Mapes, and together they began making inquiries. Eventually they made contact with Sergeant Frederick,
who gave them Joe Darby's name. So Mapes found a home phone
number for Darby, and dialed it.

Darby's wife answered. "She did not want to talk to me," Mapes
said. "She didn't want to talk about the story. She was upset at what
her husband had done. It was viewed as a major screwup early on.

And, as much as in mainstream media we like to look for villains and victims and heroes, I got the feeling from his wife that this wasn't really a simple story of a kid who saw something very bad happening and wanted to stop it, and wanted the world to know. It was somewhat darker than that. His wife indicated that what he'd done was a source of shame for the family. It had made it very hard for them."

While they were on the phone, Darby's wife stepped outside, and Mapes could hear the neighbors having a fistfight in the background. The noise gave her a picture of Darby's world—a small, tough town with strong military ties, where your family and the unit you fought with were deeply intertwined, and you broke ranks at your own peril, which was Darby's wife's point. "It was Darby who was seen as having caused this whole problem," Mapes said, "not the soldiers who engaged in this stuff at Abu Ghraib. And it had made her life very difficult. Everyone was angry at Darby and, by extension, angry at her. I think his wife started getting massive amounts of shit from her friends within the military community."

Mapes had a nine-year-old son, and she said, "Sometimes he says something that's hurtful to people, and he hasn't intended it to be. It's inadvertent. Or he'll reveal some family secret inadvertently." With Darby, she said, "It was almost like that, like he had set off this chain of events inadvertently. He had done something, but he didn't know it would be this big a deal. I've never spoken with him. But I just never got the feeling this was a story of a kid who had very simply done the right thing. I thought it was something else, and I wasn't sure exactly what it was." Mapes wasn't any closer to having the pictures, but she wanted them more than ever, and it occurred to her that the best way to get them might be to reach out to the soldiers who took and appeared in them—the soldiers whom the photographs purportedly vilified, who were now facing a heap of trouble and had never been heard from.

———

IN THE MEANTIME, the prisoner population at Abu Ghraib kept growing, and conditions kept deteriorating as the prison came under increasingly regular and intensive attack. The day that Taguba first
visited Abu Ghraib, February 2, happened to be Tim Dugan's last day
there, and he said, "We'd got attacked all night. The day before, I
think it was, we killed the main sheik for the town of Abu Ghraib.
The guys in the helicopter gunship were watching him with infrared,
and he went to two different mortar crews, two different times, and
they followed that son of a bitch all the way home. When he pulled
in his driveway, they put like several hundred rounds in his car. I
mean, it's a blood puddle. Well, when you kill the sheik, who takes
over? The fuckin' sheik's oldest son. We got hammered with thirty-
six mortars that Saturday night. I've never seen anything like it, and
I've been in some shit storms before. When I left that morning, we
were out of ammo."

That evening, Sabrina Harman wrote to Kelly:

So last night I had a dream that I was shown these cards
and reached for one and pulled one out with peoples
obituaries. I can't spell that, what goes in the paper when
people die—I open it and theres random pictures and
different meanings all having to do with a way someone
could die. So all day I've been scared something happened
to you. Right now, I just got back from an attack in our
compound. The mortar sounded like it hit my wall. Rod
jumped on me and we ran out of the building. It had hit a
truck/ gas point right behind our building. Huge flames,
kind of neat but my stress level is <u>HIGH</u>. My eyes are
starting to burn and every little noise Im scared of.

This investigation is killing me—its taking to long, I gave in
and gave them the notes I wrote down for my lawyer. . . .
So—I told them everything. I know it wont help me even if
they say it will. Im not in this for me—this is to help the
1000's more that end up being prisoners here—This will not
happen again. No regrets! Stay Safe Sweetie—I love you!

Sabrina

This was Harman's last letter from Abu Ghraib. A few days later, the
seven night-shift MPs on whom the CID investigation had focused
from the start were removed from the prison and transferred to Camp
Victory, to await their fate.

PART 3

AFTER

Happy are those who died without ever having had to ask themselves: "If they tear out my fingernails, will I talk?" But even happier are others, barely out of their childhood, who have not had to ask themselves that *other* question: "If my friends, fellow soldiers, and leaders tear out an enemy's fingernails in my presence, what will I do?"

—JEAN-PAUL SARTRE

21.

IN OTHELLO, Shakespeare's melodrama of humiliation and revenge in the Venetian high command, an exceptionally intricate plot, rife with conspiratorial machinations and deceit, hinges on a single instant of grotesque misperception. When Othello's most trusted counselor, the conniving and duplicitous Iago, tells Othello that his wife, Desdemona, is having an affair with Cassio, who happens to be Iago's rival for power, Othello demands irrefutable evidence. "Villain," he says, "be sure thou prove my love a whore, be sure of it; give me the ocular proof." Iago obliges by means of an elaborate scheme. He gets hold of an embroidered handkerchief that was Othello's first gift to Desdemona, a precious fetish object, which symbolizes their love and bond, and he plants it in Cassio's bedroom. Then he has Othello hide and watch as Cassio's wife appears and flings the handkerchief at Cassio, accusing him of having received it from another lover. Othello gets the picture—he believes what he sees without realizing that he is only seeing what he has been led to believe—and a bloodbath ensues.

The ocular proof: more than three hundred years before the invention of photography, Shakespeare described precisely the power of a snapshot to convey a sense of perfect evidentiary knowledge, and its simultaneous power to be taken out of context, or to be used as an instrument of deliberate misdirection.

IN THE LAST WEEK OF APRIL 2004, a handful of the Abu Ghraib photographs were broadcast on *60 Minutes* and published in *The New
Yorker,* and within a couple of days they had been rebroadcast and
republished pretty much everywhere on earth. Overnight, the human
pyramid, the hooded man on the box, the young woman soldier with
a prisoner on a leash, and the corpse packed in ice had become the
defining images of the Iraq war, and the president of the United
States would later say that the day of their release was the worst day
of the war.

Never before had such primal dungeon scenes been so baldly captured on camera. Had a photojournalist shot the pictures, there would
have been prizes and museum exhibitions for the incomparable scoop.
But no outsider with a camera could have gained access to the action
on the MI block, and the fact that taking the pictures was part of the
action gives them a heightened sense of raw exposé, as stolen glimpses
of something we were otherwise forbidden to see, something that had
to be leaked to the press. Visually, too, the photographs drew power
from their amateurism. The low grade of the equipment used, the
haze of digital noise, the crude glare of the flash against the dingy
yellow-green gloom of the prison lighting, the odd angles and hap-
hazard framing of many of the shots—these technical properties of
the pictures echo the bleakness and misery of the medieval tableaux
they confront us with.

But above all, it was the posing soldiers, mugging for their buddies' cameras while dominating the prisoners in trophy stances, that
gave the photographs the sense of unruly and unmediated reality. The
staging was part of the reality they documented. And the grins, the
thumbs-up, the arms crossed over puffed-out chests—all this un-
seemly swagger and self-regard was the height of amateurism. These
soldier-photographers stood, at once, inside and outside the events

they recorded, watching themselves take part in the spectacle, and
their decision not to conceal but to reveal what they were doing indicated that they were not just amateur photographers, but amateur
torturers.

So the amateurism was not merely a formal dimension of the Abu
Ghraib pictures. It was part of their content, part of what we saw in
them, and it corresponded to an aspect of the Iraq war that troubled
and baffled nearly everyone: the reckless and slapdash ineptitude with
which it had been prosecuted. It was an amateur-run war, a murky
and incoherent war. It was not clear why it was waged; too many
reasons were given, none had held up, and the stories we invented to
explain it to ourselves hardly seemed to matter, since once it was
started the war had become its own engine—not a means to an end
but an end in itself. What had been billed as a war of ideas and ideals
had been exposed as a war of poses and posturing. It was our image
versus the enemy's, a standard, in this case, by which it was easy to
stoop appallingly low before being caught out. The Abu Ghraib photographs caught us out.

That was clear at first glance. And in *The New Yorker,* the photographs accompanied an article by Seymour Hersh, who had obtained
a copy of General Taguba's classified report on what he described as
the "sadistic, blatant, and wanton criminal abuses" committed against
prisoners at the hard site. In keeping with his mandate to focus on
the 800th MP Battalion, Taguba placed the bulk of the blame on the
MPs who appeared in the photographs, and the burden of command
responsibility on General Karpinski. As a result of his investigation,
she was relieved of her command, formally reprimanded, and given a
reduction in rank to colonel. In her place, Major General Geoffrey
Miller, formerly of Guantánamo Bay, was placed in command of Abu
Ghraib. Miller's critical role in making Abu Ghraib over in Gitmo's
image nine months earlier was not yet publicly known, so some of the
irony of his appointment was lost on the press to whom he opened

the prison gates in early May 2004, and issued an apology "for my nation, and for the military, for the small number of leaders and soldiers who have committed unauthorized and possibly criminal acts on the detainees in Abu Ghraib."

In his report, Taguba had made a point of noting that MI, CIA, and civilian interrogators shared in the responsibility for brutalizing prisoners at Abu Ghraib, and he urged disciplinary action against Colonel Pappas, Lieutenant Colonel Jordan, and Big Steve Stefanowicz, among others. In the days and weeks and months that followed, a further flood of investigative reports and leaked documents kept confirming and enlarging the scope of the story for anyone who wanted to bother to follow it and piece it together tidbit by tidbit. But while the story was scandalous, the photographs were sensational, and the fact that the most obviously sensational images amounted to a group self-portrait compounded and confused their disturbing power as documents of a broader, systemic corruption. Without the photographs there would have been no scandal. Without them we might never have known, or fully have grasped, that young American volunteer soldiers who had been sent to Iraq as liberators had been put to work as criminals in the shadow of Saddam's old death house. In this respect the photographs performed a profound public service; or they would have, if they didn't make it so easy to think that they were the whole story.

A WEEK AFTER the Abu Ghraib photographs were made public, the president said that he was "sorry for the humiliation suffered by the Iraqi prisoners and the humiliation suffered by their families" and "equally sorry that people seeing these pictures didn't understand the true nature and heart of America"; and, he said, "the wrongdoers will be brought to justice."

Shortly afterward Special Agent Brent Pack, the lead forensic examiner of the computer crime unit of the U.S. Army Criminal Investigative Division, was summoned to CID headquarters at Fort Belvoir, Virginia, handed twelve compact discs, and told: These contain pictures from Abu Ghraib—thousands of pictures. We want you to find the ones that depict possible prisoner abuse, or people that were in the area at the times abuse was occurring. And we want to know exactly when the pictures were taken. Put them on a time line so that a jury can see when each incident began and when it ended; how much time elapsed in between these photographs; how much effort went into what these people were doing to the prisoners; and who else was there when these things occurred.

"The pictures spoke a thousand words, but unless you know what day and time they're talking, you wouldn't know what the story was," Pack said. "It isn't until you look at the individual acts that are documented that you can say with any certainty what they actually depict. That doesn't serve a political purpose, but it does serve a criminal justice purpose."

So Pack set about culling the files. He eliminated duplicates and a great many pictures that had nothing to do with abuse, or even with Abu Ghraib, and he was left with some two hundred eighty photographs, nearly all of them from the cameras of Graner, Harman, and Frederick. The problem was that although the cameras had left a time and date stamp on each photograph, none of them corresponded to the times or dates of the night shifts in question. Pack knew that the MPs came from the East Coast, which seemed to explain the time discrepancy with Iraq for two of the cameras, Graner's and Frederick's. But it wasn't until he grouped pictures of what looked like the same incidents, and noticed that there were eight occasions when all three cameras were shooting the same thing at the same time, that he was able to say, "This camera thought it was this time, this camera thought it was that time," and to synchronize Harman's camera with the others by adding to its time stamp a year, nine months, eleven hours, and twenty-nine minutes.

"Once I was able to make that happen, all the pictures just seemed to line up," Pack said. On his computer, he created the largest Power Point slide possible—two feet by nearly five feet—and spent the next two months building his time line in two-hour increments, moving tiny thumbnails of the photographs into place. He grouped them by incident, established their sequence within each incident, and identified them with color-coded labels according to the camera they came from. The task was akin to assembling a picture from a scramble of pixels. Toward the end of his labors Pack was given a copy of the MPs' log from the MI block, and when he cross-referenced their notes with his chart, day by day and prisoner number by prisoner number, it checked out.

Now he could say, "There's about twelve separate days that they took pictures that were pertinent to this investigation. There's twenty-six separate incidents of possible abuse. Each one of these incidents, somebody was responsible for what occurred. So you have to figure it out. Who was here for this one? Who was here for that one? And does this one actually constitute a crime or is it standard operating procedure? You have to look at exactly what the pictures depict and take the emotion and the politics out of it, because you are dealing with people that are basically going to be on trial for their freedom. It was important to separate those that were criminal acts and those things that were not criminal acts. And that's what the prosecution would have to focus on. If somebody was actually physically injured, you know you have a criminal act. Putting somebody into sexually humiliating positions, you have a criminal act. Making them abuse themselves sexually, you have a criminal act. Standing by and watching somebody hit their head on the wall and taking photographs at the time, that's dereliction of duty, so it's a criminal act. The indi-

vidual with the wires tied to their hands and standing on a box, I see
that as somebody that's being put into a stress position. I'm looking
at it and thinking, they don't look like they're real electrical wires.
Standard operating procedure—that's all it is."

Nudity, panties on the head, Palestinian hangings—these, too,
Pack regarded as standard operating procedure. "I've been in the
Army for twenty years," he said. "I've been to Desert Storm. I spent
four months at Guantánamo Bay. People that haven't been where I've
been, I can't expect them to see the pictures in the same way. All a
picture is, is frozen moments of time and of reality. You can interpret
them differently, based on your background or your knowledge. But
when it comes time where you're presenting them in court, what the
photograph depicts is what it is." And, he said, what it came down
to was: "If you were in the pictures while this stuff was going on, you
were going to be in trouble. If you make our president apologize to
the world, I would say you'd be in big trouble."

Pack was a technician. He was not concerned with motives, only
with actions. But when he looked at the pictures of what he called
"the infamous seven-man naked Iraqi stacking pyramid," he said,
"The facial expressions that you see on Graner and Harman kind of
set the tone for what they were thinking and what they were feeling
at the time. You look in their eyes, and it looks like they were having
fun, and to me this scene is what sealed their fate." Pack also said, "In
all my years as a cop, I'd say over half of all my cases were solved
because the criminal did something stupid. Taking photographs of
these things is that one something stupid."

He had spent months studying the pictures, and the soldiers who
took them and appeared in them, and he said, "I think they thought
what they were doing was acceptable. What is acceptable behavior
gets fuzzy in war." Of course, the photographs couldn't say why the
MPs on the MI block thought that, and as a prosecution witness that

didn't bother Pack. He said he had no emotional response to the pictures while he worked on them. He took pride in his clinical detachment, and what he considered to be his apolitical objectivity. Still, as a soldier, an MP no less, and as a citizen, he could not help trying to make sense of what he saw. He didn't see torture; he saw humiliation, and he saw that it cut both ways. "Absolutely," he said. "These pictures humiliated us."

THE FIRST ABU GHRAIB SOLDIER to face court-martial was Jeremy Sivits, the MP who had the least involvement in the crimes of the MI block, and who had done the most to alleviate the suffering of prisoners while he was there. As soon as the CID questioned him in January, Sivits had confessed and cooperated, and at his trial, in Baghdad, less than three weeks after the photographs got out, he pled guilty to all charges: conspiracy to maltreat prisoners, dereliction of duty, and maltreatment of prisoners. He received the maximum sentence of a year in prison, a reduction in rank, and a bad-conduct discharge.

In September, Specialist Armin Cruz, one of the MI soldiers who took part in the torment of the three alleged prison rapists, pled guilty to conspiracy and maltreatment, and was given an eight-month sentence, a reduction in rank, and a bad-conduct discharge. In October, at an Army base in Germany, Sergeant Frederick pled guilty to conspiracy, dereliction of duty, maltreatment, assault, and committing an indecent act. He was sentenced to eight years in prison, a reduction in rank to private, a forfeit of all pay and allowances, and a dishonorable discharge. Later that month, Megan Ambuhl pled guilty to dereliction of duty, and was sentenced to a reduction in rank and loss of a half month's pay. And the next year, in January, at Fort Hood, Texas, Charles Graner was found guilty of conspiracy, dereliction of duty, assault, indecent acts, and maltreatment, and sentenced to ten years in prison, a reduction in rank to private, a forfeit of all pay and allowances, and a dishonorable discharge.

That February, Javal Davis pled guilty to dereliction of duty, making false official statements, and battery, and he was given a six-month sentence, a reduction in rank, and a bad-conduct discharge. Later that month, Roman Krol, the MI soldier, was given a ten-month sentence, a reduction in rank, and a bad-conduct discharge. In May, Sabrina Harman was found guilty of conspiracy, dereliction of duty, and maltreatment, and sentenced to six months in prison, a reduction in rank, a forfeit of all pay and allowances, and a bad-conduct discharge.

Lynndie England was the last of the seven night-shift MPs to be convicted. In February 2004, shortly after the group had been moved to Camp Victory, she discovered that she was pregnant. Graner was the father, but they had broken up by then, and she was sent back to the States, to Fort Bragg. There, in October, she gave birth to a son, whom she named Carter. So he was just shy of his first birthday the next September when England was found guilty of conspiracy, maltreatment, and an indecent act, and sentenced to three years in prison, a reduction in rank, and a dishonorable discharge. By then Graner had married Ambuhl from prison.

Eventually, the dog handlers, Sergeants Cardona and Smith, were also brought to courts-martial. Cardona was convicted of dereliction of duty and aggravated assault, and sentenced to ninety days of hard labor. Smith was found guilty of conspiracy, maltreatment, simple assault, an indecent act, and dereliction of duty, and sentenced to six months in prison, a fine, a demotion to private, and a bad-conduct discharge.

The only senior officer to be court-martialed was Lieutenant Colonel Jordan. He was the last Abu Ghraib soldier to face trial, and he was not found guilty of anything. He was, however, given a reprimand for disobeying an order not to discuss an investigation into the abuse, but the reprimand was later lifted and removed from his record. Colonel Pappas, too, was given a reprimand, as well as a fine, following a noncriminal, administrative proceeding, for allowing the use of unmuzzled dogs to intimidate prisoners without getting prior authorization from General Sanchez. And there were a number of other officers who got reprimands or fines for dereliction of duty at Abu Ghraib.

But no soldier above the rank of sergeant ever served jail time. No civilian interrogators ever faced legal proceedings. Nobody was ever charged with torture, or war crimes, or any violation of the Geneva Conventions. Nobody ever faced charges for keeping prisoners naked, or shackled. Nobody ever faced charges for holding prisoners as hostages. Nobody ever faced charges for incarcerating children who were accused of no crime and posed no known security threat. Nobody ever faced charges for holding thousands of prisoners in a combat zone in constant danger of their lives. Nobody ever faced charges for arresting thousands of civilians without direct cause and holding them indefinitely, incommunicado, in concentration camp conditions. Nobody ever faced charges for shooting and killing prisoners who were confined behind concertina wire. And nobody has ever been held to account for murdering al-Jamadi in the Tier 1B shower, although Sabrina Harman initially faced several charges for having photographed him there.

"They tried to charge me with destruction of government property, which I don't understand," Harman said. "And then maltreatment for taking the photos of a dead guy. But he's dead. I don't know how that's maltreatment. And then altering evidence for removing the bandage from his eye to take a photo of it, and then I placed it back. When he died, they cleaned him all up, and then stuck the bandages on. So it's not really altering evidence. They had already done that for me. But in order to make the charges stick, they were going to have to bring in the photos, which they didn't want, because obviously they covered up a murder, and that would just make them look bad. So they dropped all the charges pertaining to the OGA guy in the shower."

That's how it worked: no photo, no crime. The ocular proof: the exposé became the cover-up.

22.

"SO A BIG CHUNK of my life is gone I can never get back," Javal Davis said. "And the privacy that I had, never going to get it back. That was stripped from me. Marriage? Destroyed. I was ostracized on national television, you know? For what? To cover up someone's lies, to cover up our tactics, procedures, that no one wants to own up to? My son still thinks that I was at work—he's still too young—I'll explain to him later on down the line, you know. My daughter, she knows. I explained it to her, and she understood. She won't be joining the military. I don't want to be a cop anymore. I'm done. I'm in sales. The career path that I have now, you know—comfortable. I deal with people on the regular basis. I'm not handling anyone's problems. I'm not dealing with anything violent. So I'm business to business, all personal, 'How you doing? I'm Javal Davis. Nice to meet you.' Everyone's happy. I like that. Sales. I'm a salesman."

"It's a hot potato, Abu Ghraib," Tim Dugan said. "I mean, what good can it come out for a politician to go in defense of somebody from Abu Ghraib? Is there any goodness that could come out of that for his political career? They're going to rip the person apart who was there. Whatever your justification, whatever you did, you're wrong. You're part of Abu Ghraib. I was really proud of everything I did at Abu Ghraib and now I'm ashamed to mention I was even there. It's a no-win scenario. If you wrote a book it would have to be fiction because nobody would believe any of this shit. I was there and I don't believe this shit. I sit here and shake about talking to you and I hyperventilate when I'm talking about it. Post-traumatic stress."

"You always feel guilty," Sabrina Harman said, "thinking you could have changed something—or, I guess, dereliction of duty for not reporting something that went on, even though people did know. I guess you could have went to somebody else. So I accept the dereliction of duty charge. Personally, I accept that one. It would be nice just to put everything behind me. It sucks, but it's a learning experience, I guess. It helps you grow, getting screwed over. I don't know. I really don't know what I want to do. I'll just get my degree in photography, and that's it for right now."

"I spent two years of my life as a soldier in Vietnam," Lane McCotter said. "And one of those years I literally lived with the Vietnamese twenty-four hours a day. Only because of politics we lost the war, because the political upper limits of our government was not willing to go forward with what we had invested in, for what, twelve, thirteen years and over fifty thousand soldiers' lives? Many of them were good friends of mine. I see some parallels, I think, to what's happening in Iraq sometimes, and it frightens me. Our interpreters, we became very good friends. A couple of them cried when I came home. 'Why are you going home? You are going to leave. Are all the Americans going to leave?' That was their biggest fear. I just hope that we don't pull out on them like we did on the Vietnamese. Americans seem to get impatient."

"How are we going to get to the truth when the truth holders are clamming up and won't talk?" Ken Davis said. "Am I un-American for saying I don't want to watch my children go to jail for following orders, when the officers are cowards and won't stand up for the orders that they gave? I told my wife, I said, 'You know, it's hard to think that out of all this, people can start to believe that the lie's the truth, and the truth is the lie.' It's like a shadow game. Me and my children, we play hide-and-seek. And I finally got my girls to play hide-and-seek in the dark. And they say, 'Daddy, why are you playing in the dark?' And I said, 'Because look, you see what's in the light, right? But, you can't see what's in the dark. And you can move around. You can hide.' The shadow game. That's what I believe these administration types and them do. They hide in the shadows. They have different people do what they want to do. And then they just disappear."

"When I got back, the first time I drove the car, I'm driving over to my brother's house," Gary Deland said. "As I'm approaching, the light turns red for me, green for the other side, and two cars are going through the intersection. And it was the perfect matchup that I would get when I was in Iraq, where you drive as hard as you can at the back end of the one car, so that without hitting them, you roll off the back bumper of both cars—if you do it right. So, instead of slowing down for the red light, I geared down on my Camaro and punched it, and I was flying into this intersection right at these two cars. And my wife screamed, and it woke me up. And I slammed on the brakes and slid sideways into the intersection. She says, 'What in the hell were you doing!' I said, 'Well, they were lined up perfect for me.' To transition home was very difficult for me. I would say, 'I'm going to lay down for a minute,' and I wake up twenty-four hours later. We went to visit some friends that we spend a week every summer with on their lake in Georgia. Got in, said, 'I'm going to lay down for a minute.' That was eleven o'clock; I woke up at eleven o'clock that night. I mean, I couldn't function. I had depression. It sounds strange, but I missed greatly being in Iraq. I really felt good about what we did over there, you know. It also bothered me greatly that we had had difficulty getting some of the Iraqis we hired to stay with us in the Corrections Academy—because we explained to them, 'You can't shake down families, you can't use brutality, you can't do this, you can't do that'—and now all of a sudden, it was Americans that were doing it! So everything we were telling these people, now they're going to say, 'Well, those hypocritical SOB Americans!' "

"My name was a good name in the military until I did what I did," Jeremy Sivits said. "My uncle died in Vietnam thirteen years to the day till I was born. My dad has two Bronze Stars for valor in Vietnam. My grandfather's got a Bronze Star from Vietnam. And then I come along and get involved in that. That just put that name in the mud. I had always wanted to make my father proud. Because the whole time I was growing up, I felt that he wasn't completely proud of me. I was pretty good on the baseball field. I was having a couple colleges, junior colleges and stuff, looking at me, and things like that. And I was really concentrating on trying to get a baseball scholarship and things. And then, when it didn't work out, I went into the military, and I seen how proud he was the night I come home with my enlistment papers. I wanted to do nothing more than be a combat veteran just like my dad and my uncle and my grandfather. I wanted to walk in their shoes, and be part of them. I wanted to be a combat veteran. And the night that I called and told my parents that I was in trouble, the only words I could say to my dad was 'Please don't disown me.' All I wanted was to get that honorable discharge, and have that combat veteran status, and to be able to say that I did my job just like my dad did, and my uncle, and my grandfather. But unfortunately, I didn't. And I think that's why I felt so embarrassed."

"Life's not fair, that's for sure," Megan Graner said. "I think I already probably knew that."

"A LOT OF PEOPLE, when they talk to me and they see what I've been through, they think that I should be this fragile little person that's about to jump at every twig that breaks," Lynndie England said. "But

I'm not like that. I don't think about it. If I think about it, it's overwhelming. It's too much to think about all the stuff that I've went through. So that's what calms me; I don't think about it. I think about something else, read a book, watch a movie, whatever.

"Sometimes I have nightmares. I don't even talk to my psychiatrist about 'em. I don't want to talk about them ever. What's it going to help to talk about it, besides reliving it? There's no point in doing that. I don't want to do that. Because, guess what—don't laugh—thoughts cause emotions. If I don't think about it, I'm not going to feel anything. If I don't think about it, then it doesn't happen. So that's what I do. I don't think about anything. I don't want to relive or feel.

"That's why I take medicine, so I don't have the nightmares. I take antidepression, anxiety pills—that, and usually my son wears me out. On the rare occasion that I forget to take my medicine, I usually have nightmares. When that guy was screaming in the shower, I hear that in the middle of the night. It'll wake me up, freak me out. It's always going to be there. The way he was screaming, it was just a death scream. He was just screaming at the top of his lungs constantly. And you're right in the next room. It's like it's vibrating your whole body, it's so loud. I don't think I'll ever get that out of my head.

"I just want to go on with life—get a job, raise my son. Now I'm going to be trying to save money for him to go to college. I don't think I have a lot of choices. It's going to be hard for me to get a job, because now I have a felony on my record. Plus, you know, people don't want the publicity. The way I feel right now in my own country, to walk down the street, I'm still scared, because there's just people that are behind me, and there's people that hate me. They feel like we shouldn't have been doing that or we were being inhumane or whatever their opinion is. I've even gotten hate mail about it.

"At least when I was in Iraq I knew who the enemy was. Here I don't. Even though I'm in my own country, I can never get away from it. I go out. I go to Wal-Mart, I go shopping, but it's like I'm always watching my back. I don't like to walk in public, I don't like to walk down the street, I don't like to walk into a room that's crowded, because it feels like everyone is staring at me. And people do. When I'm shopping for food or something, I got my son with me and I'm concentrating on him, but I know people are staring at me. They know it's me. But that's just my hometown. Some other big town, I probably wouldn't walk down the street, because I don't know what kind of people they are. I don't know if they're for me or against me. I don't want to take that risk.

"All I did was what I was told to do. I didn't make the war. I can't end the war. I mean, photographs can't just make or change a war. It just doesn't make sense. I mean, how do people see me as the villain? The government is just putting the blame on me because they can— just like a decoy. I can't get mad. I mean, I'm over it. I'm fine. I mean, I'm not fine with it, but, whatever.

"It's how the world turns, ain't it? People backstabbing other people. Unfairness. Drama. It's life. You live it. Learn from your mistakes. I learned from mine. It's like I don't need a man to survive. Forget 'em. It's like every situation that I come into now, I take a step back instead of rushing headfirst. I look at the consequences ahead of time. Before I'd just do it. It's just part of being young and naive I guess.

"I think for Sivits, there was one picture taken of him that changed his life. But for me, the moment that changed me was meeting Graner. If I wasn't involved with Graner, I wouldn't have been in that situation. Therefore I wouldn't have been in the pictures. I probably would have known it was going on, but I wouldn't have been involved and I wouldn't have therefore went to prison, or been the poster girl for this war.

"Don't cry. Hell, I ain't cried over it. Can't change anything, and if I did, then I wouldn't have Carter. I mean, I wouldn't trade him for the world. So I wouldn't want to go back and change anything. I mean, yeah, I was in pictures that showed me holding a leash around the guy's neck. But that's all I did. I was convicted of being in a picture. So if I'm a villain by standing in a picture, I mean, I've never heard of that before."

AS FOR THE GUY at the other end of the leash: from the moment Gus crawled out of the hole and the choice was his, he stopped eating, and he rejected clothes, as well. "Everything he said was, 'I refuse,' " Sergeant Hydrue Joyner said. "I was like, 'Well, son, you got to put some clothes on.' 'I refuse.' 'Son, it's going to be mighty chilly, your twig and berries are going to shrivel up. You better put something on.' 'I refuse.' 'Eat this.' 'I refuse.' 'You got to eat something.' 'I refuse.'

"Because I was the enemy. That's what he called me every day. He basically told me every day that he was going to kill me, and that his great Muslim leader Saddam Hussein would come back to kill all the Americans and the Jews. I'm like, the Jews? What'd they ever do to you? They owe you some money or something? But yeah, he was adamant about that. Gus and the Jews, he was going to kill them all. One day, trying to break the ice, so to speak, I said, 'Son, why do you hate me so?' He looked me dead in the face and said, 'Because you stole my Iraq.' I was like, 'Trust me, you can have it—all this can be yours.' So I finally asked him, 'Gus, if you could kill me right now, how would you do it?' I'm thinking the average, you know—I'd stab you or shoot you. He told me he was going to get a missile. And I'm thinking, A missile for one person? 'You really don't like me, do you?' He looked me in the face and said, 'No.' "

From the way Gus talked, the MPs assumed he was an enemy fighter or terrorist. But MI took no interest in him, and all he would say about himself was that he wanted to go to Baghdad. "Then we found out the history of his arrest," Jeffery Frost said. "It turned out he was just a normal guy who got drunk and beat someone up. He was just a regular prisoner like we'd find in one of our country jails or something. And we were like, 'Let's just release him, give him back to his family, and just have him start eating again, because we don't want the guy to die.'"

"It was getting bad," Tony Diaz said. "He was losing weight. We would say, 'Gus, get up, get up.' He wouldn't move at all. Then one day they told him, 'All right, we're going to send you to Baghdad, but you got to eat when you get there—you got to promise.' He said OK. So they put him in an ambulance and rode around the compound for thirty minutes. Of course, he couldn't see where he was going. So they just took him to that little hospital right there in that compound." Gus had ended up about a hundred feet from the hard site. But he thought he was in Baghdad, and he accepted a meal.

There weren't a lot of opportunities at Abu Ghraib to give a prisoner much comfort, so the MPs felt pretty good about Gus, at least for the few hours, until they saw him again. One of the officers who ran the clinic had found out why Gus was there. "He didn't really like the idea," Diaz said. "He said, 'No, you can't do that to the prisoners—you cannot trick them into doing things.' So they told him he was still in Abu Ghraib. They brought him back to the cell. After that he kind of lost all trust. After that, he didn't want to eat no more."

Day after day, the MPs' logbook again recorded Gus's rejection of food and all things "American." Sometimes, to get a rise out of him, the MPs would draw a star of David on his intravenous feeding bag. "The only time he was really an issue for us was when we were trying to stick him with the IV," Frost said. "That's when he would do his little fight and struggle, and say we're all going to die. Other than that, you really didn't hear a word out of him."

Is it outlandish to suggest that Gus was the conscience of Abu Ghraib? Others—captors and captives alike—made their accommodations. We all did. He preferred to belong to oblivion. So he registered his protest. When he said "I refuse" he was the closest thing there was at Abu Ghraib to a free man.

August 2006–February 2008

NOTES AND ACKNOWLEDGMENTS

PHOTOGRAPHS PLAY AN IMPORTANT PART in the story this book tells, and it may be that without photographs we still would not know the story. But the decision not to present photographs in the book was made even before the writing began. The photographs, which have so dominated and, at times, distorted perceptions of the Abu Ghraib story, are widely available in print and online; and in attempting here to see the story afresh it became clear that much of what matters most about Abu Ghraib was never photographed. The photographs have a place in the story, but they are not the story, and it would be untruthful here to submit once again to their frame.

The decision was also made early on not to identify Abu Ghraib prisoners by their proper names. This book seeks to describe the experience of the American soldiers at the prison, so we stuck to the names those Americans invented for the prisoners. Since the U.S. military ultimately found that at least three out of four of the inmates held at Abu Ghraib were not guilty of any crime, there seemed to be no value to us in naming them, whereas there could be some potential harm to them. As it is, the story of Abu Ghraib presents the investigator and the writer with a Russian novel problem—there are simply too many people who were involved at too many levels to make a comprehensive account comprehensible. Our focus has been on those

who had the greatest agency in the events of the MI block in the fall
of 2003, and we regret it if in the name of clarity we appear to ignore
anyone who should not be left off the hook.

OUR THANKS GO FIRST to those who were interviewed for *Standard
Operating Procedure* between October 2005 and November 2007: Joe
Darby, Javal Davis, Ken Davis, Gary Deland, Tony Diaz, David
DiNenna, Tim Dugan, Jeffery Frost, Megan Graner, Sabrina Harman,
Vic Harris, Steven Jordan, Hydrue Joyner, Janis Karpinski, Roman
Krol, Mary Mapes, Lane McCotter, Brent Pack, Jeremy Sivits, and
Andrew Stoltzman.

In addition, Douglas Barrett, Paul Bergrin, Torin Nelson, Sam
Provance, Richard Russell, and Holly Sivits were interviewed. For
reasons of structure, they did not appear in the narrative, but their
testimonies and insights contributed to our underlying understanding of the Abu Ghraib story.

The peculiar demands of filmmaking require not only journalistic
thoroughness from interviews, but also a great deal of repetition, and
the complete transcripts of Morris's interviews for *Standard Operating
Procedure* run to some two and a half million words—more than
twenty-five times the length of this book. In distilling this material,
compressing it, giving it shape, and seeking to serve it most effectively, every effort has been made to corroborate individual accounts
against one another and against external documents, and this book
represents the authors' determination to represent the story of Abu
Ghraib as truthfully as possible.

In quoting directly from speech, we have privileged fidelity to the
substance, the meaning, and the intelligence of the statement rather
than the cruel exactitude of transcription. Particularly when, as a
result of repetition, the same speaker told the same incident or made
the same point in multiple iterations, we have occasionally transposed
sentences and condensed monologues, in order best to serve the speak-

er's unmistakable intention. In doing so, our aim has been only to extend to those who devoted great time and effort to telling their stories the same editorial regard that we would automatically extend to ourselves in translating speech into text.

OUR THANKS GO ALSO to all those who have shared documents from official investigations with journalists and other investigators to help shed light on the darker recesses of the Abu Ghraib story. We are particularly indebted to the groundbreaking investigative reporting of Seymour Hersh, Jane Mayer, and Mark Danner. In the aftermath of the initial revelations of crimes against prisoners, a flood of previously secret policy papers, memoranda, interrogation rules, military correspondence, investigative findings, and sworn statements began to be made publicly available—and our thanks go to the leakers. They are often the greatest guardians of the public interest in an open society, and it has been a particularly dismal aspect of the war on terror that our highest officials have generally been readier to investigate and punish leaks than the crimes that the leaks reveal.

We are grateful to have had access to transcripts of lengthy interviews conducted by agents of the Army's Criminal Investigative Division with Charles Graner and Ivan "Chip" Frederick. All direct quotations from Graner and Frederick in this book are taken from those interviews, which were conducted following their convictions, under court orders, and with a guarantee of immunity from prosecution for further self-incrimination. Both men remained incarcerated during the reporting for *Standard Operating Procedure,* and were unavailable to be interviewed directly.

We are grateful also for the troves of sworn deposition statements that have come to light from the CID's investigation of Abu Ghraib. All direct quotations of Colonel Marc Warren, Captain Carolyn Wood, and Specialist Matthew Wisdom in this book come from their sworn statements to the CID.

———

THANKS TO AMANDA BRANSON-GILL, for her indefatigable dedication to gathering and managing the information from which *Standard Operating Procedure* has been composed. And thanks to her sister Rosie Branson-Gill for her great help in the same vein.

Thanks to Jeff Skoll, Diane Weyermann, Martin Levin, Robert Fernandez, Michael Vachon, and Michael and Jamie Lynton for their support.

Thanks also for the organizational and research work and support of Ann Petrone, John Purcell, Dan Polsby, and Hannah Mintz.

Thanks to Thomas Ricks and Glyn Vincent, fellow writers, for their collegiality.

Thanks to Dylan Byers and Anne Hudson-Price for research assistance. Thanks to Petrina Crockford for proofreading.

THANKS TO OUR EDITOR, Ann Godoff. Thanks also to Laura Stickney and Tracy Locke at The Penguin Press, and to Scott Moyers, who was our editor at the outset.

Thanks to Sarah Chalfant and Andrew Wylie and the team at the Wylie Agency.

THANKS TO THE CORPORATION OF YADDO, and to the Isle of Jura residency of the Scottish Book Trust, where portions of this book were written.

Thanks to the board and staff of the *Paris Review* for their support and patience.

THANKS TO VIJAY BALAKRISHNAN, Jeffrey Frank, Gilles Peress, and Charles Silver—good friends and counselors.

Thanks to Larissa MacFarquhar and Julia Sheehan, our wives, to whom this book is dedicated.